Cycling the Trails of San Diego

Cycling the Trails of San Diego

A Mountain Biker's Guide to the County

By Nelson Copp

CARTOGRAPHER
Margaret Gooding

Sunbelt Publications
San Diego, California

Cycling the Trails of San Diego
Sunbelt Publications, Inc
 First edition, 2011

Cartography by Margaret Gooding
Editing by Lowell Lindsay
Book design by Kelly Johnson
Cover design by Kathleen Wise
Project management by Jennifer Redmond
Printed in the United States of America

 Please direct comments and inquiries to:

Sunbelt Publications, Inc.
P.O. Box 191126
San Diego, CA 92159-1126
(619) 258-4911, fax: (619) 258-4916
www.sunbeltbooks.com

Library of Congress Cataloging-in-Publication Data

Copp, Nelson.
Cycling the trails of San Diego / by Nelson Copp ; cartographer, Margaret Gooding.
p. cm.
Includes bibliographical references and index.
ISBN 978-0-932653-96-3
1. Bicycle touring--California--San Diego County--Guidebooks. 2. Bicycle trails--California--San Diego County--Guidebooks. 3. San Diego County (Calif.)--Guidebooks. I. Title.
GV1045.5.C22S257 2010
796.6'409794985--dc22
2010032189

All photos by the author, except page 123 photo, by Debra Copp.

CONTENTS

INTRODUCTION

DESCRIPTION AND HISTORY

San Diego is a region of surprising diversity in both climate and topography from the blue ocean waters and bays, to the fertile inland valleys and foothills to the mountains and desert. San Diego County covers over 4200 square miles that includes a number of state parks, national forests, preserves, and local parks open to recreational use including equestrian, hiking, and mountain biking.

As San Diego County's population tops 3 million, it becomes increasingly difficult to find natural places to explore. A number of the rides in this book, no more than one or two hours away, take you to tranquil places in the countryside, mountains, and desert where you can explore California as it was before traffic and urban sprawl encroached on plant and wildlife habitat. Many of the rides are in protected areas where coastal sage uplands, native grasslands, oak woodlands, conifer forests, and wildflower-dotted desert washes still remain natural.

The Kumeyaay Indians inhabited the San Diego area for some 12,000 years before the coming of the Europeans. The Kumeyaay were seasonal hunters and gatherers who occupied a wide area including southern San Diego County, parts of Imperial County, and south into the upper regions of Baja California. As hunter-gatherers they travelled frequently, searching out certain plants and wildlife. Most of the movement was from the mountains and foothills to the desert following the ripening of various key plants including agave, acorns, pinyon nuts, cactus fruit, and other seeds. The ideal climate was instrumental in providing for crops and game they needed to sustain life. (The Blair/Little Blair Valley ride provides an opportunity to visit the location of a Kumeyaay village and take an optional hike to a Native American rock art site.)

The Portuguese explorer Juan Rodriguez Cabrillo was the first European to visit the area, sailing into what is now San Diego Bay in 1542. Don Sebastian Vizcaino arrived in 1602 and named the area for the Catholic Saint Didacus also known as San Diego. Gaspar de Portola and a group of Spanish settlers founded a military outpost on what is now Presidio Hill in 1769 and the Franciscan friars founded the Mission San Diego de Alcala, the first of 21 missions in California. San Diego and much of California were part of Mexico at this time and most people lived in what is now called Old Town at the base of Presidio Hill.

In the 1820s and 1830s San Diego swelled to more than 600 residents, and in 1823 the 8486-acre Los Peñasquitos Rancho was granted by the Mexican government to Captain Francisco María Ruíz. (The Los Peñasquitos Canyon Preserve ride travels through this rancho.)

In 1845 California Governor Pio Pico gave Rancho Cuyamaca, a 35,501 acre Mexican land grant, to Agustin Olvera. It extended south of present day Julian and included Cuyamaca Rancho State Park, Lake Cuyamaca, and Cuyamaca Peak.

In 1846 the United States declared war against Mexico, starting the Mexican American War. The Battle of San Pasqual was fought in the San Pasqual Valley in 1846. The United States won the war and the Treaty of Guadalupe Hidalgo in 1848 settled the location of the border between California and Mexico. (A number of interpretive signs on the Mule Hill/San Pasqual Valley ride explain the details of the battle in the area.) Immigrants and the military expanded into Kumeyaay territory and the number of Kumeyaay continued to decrease. With the gold rush in northern California in 1848, a large number of Americans settled in California helping push the admission of California into the United States in 1850.

In 1850 San Diego County became one of California's 27 original counties extending from the Pacific Ocean to the Colorado River and included much of today's Imperial, San Bernardino, and Riverside counties. In 1854 Warner's Pass (San Pasqual Road) was declared a public road providing the main access between San Diego and the Colorado River. (The Mule Hill and San Pasqual Valley ride is in this area.) Soon the road through the pass at Jacumba provided a shorter route.

In 1870 San Diego set aside 1,440 acres of land for City Park, now called Balboa Park, the first city west of the Mississippi to do so. (The Balboa Park-Florida Canyon ride explores the eastern side of the park.) In 1888 the Sweetwater Dam was completed as a way to lure land buyers to the area providing much-needed water and more recently, recreational areas. (The Sweetwater Reservoir ride traverses some of this scenic area along the reservoir and the Sweetwater River.)

In 1908 construction started on the San Diego and Arizona Railway, dubbed the "Impossible Railroad." The dream was for a direct rail line from San Diego to the east and construction started in 1908 and the line eventually opened in 1919 after many setbacks. (The Dos Cabezas Road ride parallels the railroad tracks to the remnants of the Dos Cabezas Station and water tower.)

In 1926 three large tracts of federal land in California were set aside for the Mt. Shasta, San Gorgonio, and Laguna Mountains Recreation Areas. The Laguna Mountains Recreation Area in the Cleveland National Forest includes 11,495 acres of conifer mountain land overlooking the desert. (The Big Laguna Trail and Noble Canyon rides explore this beautiful area.)

In 1932 several important San Diegans donated land and money to facilitate the creation of the Anza-Borrego State Park and it took 16 more years to reach its current size. In 1941 it was dedicated to the memory of Juan Bautista de Anza and other explorers. (Several of the Desert region rides showcase the great views and spring wildflowers in the park.)

Cuyamaca Rancho was established as a state park in 1933 and encompasses more than 25,000 acres with over half designated as state wilderness that now includes more than 100 miles of trails. (The three Cuyamaca Rancho State Park rides take you on a number of these trails through the conifers.)

In 1934 construction of the world's largest 200-inch telescope mirror began and in 1948, the Palomar Observatory opened on 5,600 foot Palomar Mountain, owned and operated by California Institute of Technology. (The Nate Harrison Grade and East Palomar Mountain rides explore the west and east sides of the mountain.)

In 1937 Leo Carrillo, a highly successful entertainer in stage plays and many motion pictures including Pancho, the sidekick to Cisco Kid (Duncan Renaldo), purchased Rancho de Los Kiotes in what is now southeast Carlsbad and created Rancho Carrillo on 2,538 acres. (The Rancho Carrillo ride circles the historic rancho.)

In 1974 Mission Trails Regional Park became one of the largest urban parks in the United States with more than 40 miles of multi-use trails preserving nearly 5,800 acres of open space. (The North Fortuna Peak, Suycott Wash, and Cowles Mountain rides provide three challenging routes through the park.)

In 1978 the City of San Diego dedicated land it acquired in Tecolote Canyon as Tecolote Canyon Natural Park. (The Tecolote Canyon Natural Park ride explores the Canyon and several of its tributaries.)

In 1989 the San Dieguito River Park Joint Power Authority was created by the County of San Diego and the Cities of Del Mar, Escondido, Poway, San Diego, and Solana Beach. Its responsibility was to acquire land and raise funds to provide for a 55-mile corridor along the San Dieguito River from its headwaters in the forests of Volcan Mountain in eastern San Diego County to the San Dieguito Lagoon. (The San Dieguito River Park rides cover a number of the current trails several of which are connected.)

The City of Escondido acquired Daley Ranch, a 3,058 acre conservation area in 1996 preserving the biologically diverse area and creating a beautiful recreational and historical area. (The Daley Ranch ride gives suggestions for rides from easy to Difficult in this scenic area.)

This is just a brief accounting of the history and development of the San Diego region and provides examples of the many rides in this book that travel through the various areas showcasing the majestic vistas of San Diego County and the perfect weather—both ideal for bicycling.

CLIMATE

San Diego's climate ranges from Mediterranean in the north to semi-arid to the south and east and is often described as perfect, with mild and sunny weather much of the year. The varied San Diego topography creates pockets of climatic differences called microclimates. Temperatures rarely stray outside the comfortable range of 50 to 77 degrees along the coast with rainfall averages around 10 inches. May through July, however, can be cloudy along the coast but beautiful inland (affectionately called "May Gray" and "June Gloom"). Inland areas can experience wider temperature variations with summer temperatures often exceeding 90 degrees. The mountains experience cool nights and warm days with 11–13 inches of rain a year and winter can bring some snow accumulation. The Cuyamaca and Laguna Mountains block eastern-bound moisture creating a rain-shadow effect that limits rainfall to less than 6 inches in the Anza-Borrego Desert. Winter temperatures there are a comfortable 70s by day and 40s at night making it a great place for late fall, winter and spring bike rides. When the summer desert temperatures climb above 100 degrees, the nearby mountains are 25–30 degrees cooler and the perfect place to ride.

San Diego receives about 10 inches of annual rainfall, most of it concentrated between November and March. High pressure to the east can cause hot, dry "Santa Ana" winds on occasion. As you plan your bike rides around the county, it's best to prepare based on the microclimate found in the area of the ride.

TOPOGRAPHY

San Diego topography is as varied as the climate with low-lying coastal areas and adjacent mesas to inland canyons and hills. Further inland are the Palomar Mountains, Cuyamaca Mountains, and Laguna Mountains and the Anza-Borrego Desert beyond. To understand the varied San Diego region one must look at the larger geologic forces that have dictated the topography.

The topography of the southwest is characterized by subsurface geologic plates that move relative to each other. About 1.8 billion years ago the western region was an ocean basin accumulating deep layers of sedimentary rock. Around 240 million years ago plates began to dive under the western edge of North America forming volcanoes and mountain ranges, such as the Sierra Nevada and Peninsular Ranges. The area began to rise, and continued rising until about 85 million years ago. The area is basically a large block tilted westward. Heading east from San Diego you slowly climb until you reach the Volcan Mountain area where the topography immediately drops to the Salton Sea trough below. (The Santa Ysabel and Volcan Preserve rides are along this eastern edge of this block.)

About 25 million years ago the Pacific Plate, underlying most of the Pacific Ocean, began moving northwest relative to the North American Plate. As the plates slid past each other, the stress and movement caused a number of faults in the region, the main one being the San Andreas Fault. The San Andreas Fault Zone begins in the Gulf of California, passes by the Salton Sea and runs northward through the Coachella Valley along the base of the San Bernardino Mountains and for 600 miles to northwest California. The fault zone is a two- to eight-mile-wide band of intensely twisted and folded landscape. The sputtering movement north of the Pacific Plate, about 2 inches per year, causes earthquakes and volcanic activity. Hot springs such as Warner's and Agua Caliente are an indication of this activity. Other faults of a similar nature parallel to the San Andreas Fault are the Elsinore and San Jacinto faults. The Elsinore Fault runs along the south side of Mount Palomar (the Nate Harrison Grade ride crosses the fault twice), near the south side of Lake Henshaw, and down Banner Grade heading southeast along Highway S2. You can see the trace of the fault low on the north side of Banner Canyon. (The Chariot/Oriflamme/Rodriguez Canyon ride starts in this area and heads in the same direction as the fault zone.)

Combined with the near ideal weather, the variety of topography in the region provides a number of excellent places to ride from the gentle coastal plain, through the beautiful foothills and mountains to the scenic desert beyond.

FLORA AND FAUNA

San Diego County has an amazing diversity of plant and animal life from the coast to the inland valleys, foothills, mountains, and desert. As you ride through the various areas of San Diego County you will encounter a number of plant communities, sometimes several on one ride. Heading from the coast inland, the coastal region is characterized by coastal-sage-scrub that includes common plants like the aromatic California sagebrush and white and black sages, California buckwheat, lemonade berry, laurel sumac, manzanita, chamise, and monkey flower to name a few. This plant community is often called soft chaparral because of its reliance on summer fog for moisture. Watch out for the ever present poison oak that is typically found along creeks and intermittent drainages. Animals you might encounter in these areas include sparrows, hummingbirds, quail, cottontail rabbits, mule deer, coyote, raccoon, and skunk.

Moving inland you'll encounter the chaparral community that is found on higher slopes and western foothills. It is hard brush that is not reliant on summer fog and is better adapted to heat and drier areas. Toyon, black sage, chamise, yucca, Manzanita, ribbonwood, coyote bush, and ceanothus are common plants you will find and are sometimes referred to as elfin-forest. (The Elfin Forest ride is named for this plant community.) Animals similar to the ones found in the coastal-sage-scrub region may be seen in this area as well.

Southern oak woodland is found from the foothills to the lower mountains. Engelmann oak, coast live oak, black oak, and California walnut make up the core of this plant community but you'll also find the small evergreen madrone tree with its red berries, manzanita, ceanothus, lemonade berry, and other types of chaparral. Common animals are the scrub jay, western bluebird, coyote, mule deer, raccoon, skunk, rabbit, and mountain lion. Mountain lions are shy and elusive and chances are you won't see one, but if you do, make lots of noise, do not run, and it's always best to ride with friends.

At elevations above 3,500 feet you will find coniferous forests. Palomar, Volcan, Cuyamaca, and Laguna Mountains are prime examples and cover about 80,000 acres. The primary trees in this region are the Jeffrey with vanilla scented bark, ponderosa, sugar, and Coulter pines, incense cedar, and Douglas-fir. In transition zones between the southern oak woodland and coniferous forest is the coniferous-oak forest mainly comprised of incense cedar, white fir, California black oak, canyon live oak, and coast live oak. Common birds you will may see are the Stellar's jay, American robin, western bluebird, and flycatchers. Mule deer, bobcat, snakes of various kinds, and bats frequent this habitat.

Once you leave the mountains and begin descending to the desert you will pass through the pinyon-juniper woodland where the California juniper, desert agave, and the Mojave yucca thrive. The desert floor is comprised of the creosote–bush scrub plant community, fully adapted to drought conditions. The Anza-Borrego Desert is within the Colorado Desert, a western extension of the Sonoran Desert. Vegetation you might find on your desert rides is creosote bush, various cacti, ocotillo, smoketree, palo verde, pinyon pine and California juniper. A large percentage of the plant species are annual spring grasses and wildflowers brought on by the winter rains. In the spring, wildflowers blossom and examples of the sunflower, evening primrose, and four o'clock families provide beautiful carpets of color. Much of the wildlife in the region is focused around runoff from seasonal rains and springs. If you're lucky you might encounter mule deer, jackrabbits, and Gambel's quail. The endangered Peninsular bighorn sheep frequents the hillsides in the region but is difficult to spot and should be avoided if seen.

ACKNOWLEDGEMENT

I would like to recognize the great work that Daniel Greenstadt, author of *San Diego Mountain Bike Guide*, has done for over 10 years—his guide has been enjoyed by many a cyclist in San Diego County.

USING THIS BOOK

Each of the trips in this book follow a consistent format and are arranged by region.

Coastal Region rides are along or near the coast and can be ridden year-round. Foothills rides are inland in areas like Escondido and Poway and can be hot in summer months. Mountains include rides around Palomar, Alpine, Cuyamaca and the Laguna Mountains and can be very pleasant in summer but dangerous in winter. Desert includes the transitional areas like the In-Ko-Pah and Jacumba Mountains and Anza-Borrego Desert. The true desert rides should be avoided in the hot summer months May through October. The San Dieguito River Park set of rides are separate since they span from the coast to the mountains and eventually will be a complete trail system. These rides are pleasant most times of the year. San Bernardino Mountains includes the Santa Ana River Trail bonus ride since it is such a fun trail and will acquaint you with the beauty of that area.

Use the area map of the San Diego on the inside front cover to find the general location where you are interested in riding. Select several ride choices and then use the detailed map and description of each ride to narrow down the location and gather detailed information about the rides. Appendix 1 lists the rides by difficulty.

The beginning of each ride includes a summary of information to help you select rides and to plan for them. The end of each ride describes additional useful information about each ride, including how to get to the starting point, any amenities nearby (including food and water). Links to useful web sites and nearby bike shops can be found in the San Diego Cyclist's Directory in Appendix 3.

Starting Point: Specific location and city of the starting point of the ride.

Distance: Length of the entire ride in miles as described in the text and plotted on the accompanying trip map and elevation profile. Distance does not include any optional routes unless otherwise indicated. Most rides are round-trip unless noted as out and back indicating the return route is the same as the initial route.

A few rides are indicated as one-way indicating they are usually ridden only in one direction and may require a car shuttle. Cumulative mileages are described in the text of many rides so it is useful to have a bike computer to keep track of where you are in relationship to the write-up; however, mileages may vary from computer to computer. Mountain bike rides that combine both paved and dirt roads will indicate the distance of each.

Elevation Gain/Loss: Total vertical elevation gain and loss (sum) for the whole route unless indicated as one way in which case just reverse the numbers for the return route. Steeper rides generally include an average percent grade to help you understand the trail or road steepness as it rises and falls along its route. Percent grade is calculated as the height increase divided by the horizontal distance. A 4% to 5% grade could be considered moderate while 6% to 8% more strenuous and 9%+ difficult. If the grade is steep only in a few spots those can be easily walked. Elevation contour maps are provided for trips with significant elevation change.

Riding Time: An estimate based on roughly 4 MPH average speed. Keep in mind that these are only estimates. Fast riders may be able to complete the trip in half the time while leisurely riders may take more time than stated.

Difficulty: Rating of how hard the ride is with consideration for elevation gain, trip distance, and condition of the route and is based on what a reasonably fit rider is capable of doing. Both a difficulty level and a technical rating are provided. The difficulty ratings are *easy*, *moderate*, *difficult* and *strenuous* with difficult and strenuous based on longer distance or higher elevation gain. The technical ratings are *not technical*, *technical in spots*, and *technical* indicating how hard the route is to negotiate with narrow single track, rocky sections, or precipitous exposure the primary reason for more technical ratings. Note that trail conditions can change and it is a good idea to check with bike shops or local web sites regarding the latest trail conditions.

Road Conditions: The type of surface you will ride on. The conditions are *dirt roads* and *trails* and rides that combine both paved and dirt roads that will indicate the distance of each.

Season: The best time of the year to ride a route. Desert temperatures can change dramatically so it is a good idea to start early during the warmer months to avoid afternoon high temperatures. Rides in the mountains can be warm in the summer but you may also encounter snow in the winter months. It is always a good idea to check local weather sites to prepare for your rides.

Equipment: The type of bicycle needed for the ride. A hybrid bike (if well maintained) can be used for the occasional back-country dirt road or well-graded trail while mountain bikes are required for most of the rides.

Optional Topo Map: Each ride has an accompanying detailed bike map. A summary of symbols and features used in those maps is provided in the GPS and Maps section. In addition to the detailed maps you may also want to consider taking along a topographic map with more detailed topography information. The name of the USGS topographic map(s) for the ride is listed here.

GPS AND MAPS

The mountain bike routes on the maps in this book were created by riding the trails using a handheld Global Positioning System (GPS) receiver. The starting point of each ride and a few other key points on the detailed maps are shown with the Universal Transverse Mercator (UTM) coordinate of that position. You can enter this in your GPS to help find the point or in case you get turned around, to find your way back to the starting point. If you carry a GPS, which is highly recommended for all mountain bike rides, you should always save the ride starting point as a safety precaution.

To set up your GPS to match the maps and UTM locations the datum, which is a reference surface for the map, should be set to UTM NAD 83. The units should be set to UTM/UPS (not longitude and latitude). The maps are in the UTM Zone 11, NAD 83 Coordinate System. (Note – older printed USGS topo maps use the NAD 27 datum.)

Master Legend

Bike Trail/Route
Kiosk
Bridge
Restrooms
Waterfall
Trail/Road Junction
Mortero
Mine/Quarry
Indian Hill/Rock Art
Ruins
OHV Area
Fire Tower
Ranch
Mile Marker
Campground
Gate
Not Authorized
Park
Parking
Spring
Start
Visitor Center
Restaurant
Road Ends
Tower/Windmill
Cave
View Point
Water Tank
Wash/Creek
Roadway
Stream
Indian Reservation
Earthquake Faults
Lakes
National Parks and Monuments

MAP SYMBOLS AND FEATURES

SOURCES FOR MAPS

- DEM/Hillshades: National Elevation Data (USGS)
- Streams and Lakes: National Hydrography Dataset (USGS, EPA, US Forest Service)
- Faults: California Geological Survey (2005)
- Roads, Cities, Parks/Preserves and Indian Reservations: County of San Diego (2010) SanGIS and SanDAG
- Major roads (inset map): BLM
- Lakes (inset map): State of California

SPECIAL OFF-ROAD PREPARATION

A big part of the enjoyment of mountain biking is exploring new areas and experiencing the beauty of the outdoors and whether you're riding on trails near town or in the backcountry, a few precautions should be taken to ensure your safety and the integrity of your equipment. Mountain bike riding can be a dangerous sport for both you and your equipment and now and then you will fall off your bike or will have equipment failures. You can increase your enjoyment and safety by always carrying plenty of food, water, a knife, and a first aid kit with basic items to help with scrapes and cuts. A comb or tweezers is useful for extracting cholla balls or other cactus spines. A map and compass are advised for routes where the city will not always be in sight and a light for longer or late afternoon rides. Sunglasses and sunscreen are especially important during warmer months and remember that higher elevations provide more exposure to the sun's harmful rays. Sun protective clothing is the best choice to prevent over-exposure to the sun.

Always ride with several friends and try to stay together. If someone gets hurt or has a major equipment failure, one or more people can stay behind and others can go for help. Cell phones work in some places but do not rely solely on them. Also, do not rely on your friends to carry your extra equipment, food, or water. Carry more than what you think you'll need in case you get separated or your friend is relying on you. Tell someone at home where you will be riding and when you will return, in case you do not return when expected.

Before you leave home always check your tires, chain (make sure it is lubed), brakes, and shifting mechanism to make sure they are in good working order. A tune-up at a bike shop is recommended if you have not ridden your bicycle in awhile. You should carry at least the following equipment with you:

- 1–2 spare inner tubes (more for rides with lots of cacti or use a slime product in your tubes)
- Patch kit (make sure the glue is still good)

- Tire pump (test it beforehand)
- Tire levers
- Allen wrenches of varying sizes to fit your bike
- Multipurpose or all-in-one type tool
- Spoke wrench that fits your spokes
- Chain tool (some all-in-one tools include this)
- First aid kit
- Map and compass
- GPS and extra batteries (not a substitute for a compass and map)
- Knife
- Extra food
- Water—several liters, more for long rides
- Comb or tweezers for cactus
- Light with fresh batteries
- Sunscreen
- Sunglasses, helmet, bicycle gloves
- Windbreaker for longer or afternoon rides

RESPONSIBLE RIDING

Many health-conscious people are enjoying bicycle riding as a popular way to exercise and to enjoy the outdoors. As energy costs soar people are also looking for alternative means of transportation, like bicycling. As a result, more people are bicycling on and off the road and it becomes more important for everyone to follow basic guidelines to increase safety and enjoyment and to prevent trails from becoming off limits to bicycles. A balance must be maintained between enjoying our natural surroundings and preserving them for current and future generations. Unlimited use of outdoor areas is just not feasible any more. In order to continue using the trails we must all abide by these guidelines.

As a bicyclist you must follow traffic laws, including stopping at stop signs and red lights and riding in the same direction as traffic when on the road. Always position yourself where motorists can see you. Many bicycle accidents occur when riders do things motorists are not expecting. Always signal your intentions and you will have a more enjoyable and safe ride.

The San Diego region has a number of wonderful trails and when riding off-road there is a certain level of responsibility you must assume as a trail user. You will share most trails with hikers and equestrians and in both cases you must yield the right of way. The International Mountain Bicycling Association (IMBA) has a set of Rules of the Trail that should be followed to ensure safe and enjoyable use of the trails. If you are already following these rules you are going a long way towards safe and courteous riding on shared-use trails.

INTERNATIONAL MOUNTAIN BICYCLING ASSOCIATION (IMBA) RULES OF THE TRAIL

These guidelines for trail behavior are recognized around the world. IMBA developed the "Rules of the Trail" to promote responsible and courteous conduct on shared-use trails. Keep in mind that conventions for yielding and passing may vary, depending on traffic conditions and the intended use of the trail.

1. RIDE ON OPEN TRAILS ONLY

Respect trail and road closures—ask a land manager for clarification if you are uncertain about the status of a trail. Do not trespass on private land. Obtain permits or other authorization as may be required. Be aware that bicycles are not permitted in areas protected as state or federal Wilderness.

2. LEAVE NO TRACE

Be sensitive to the dirt beneath you. Wet and muddy trails are more vulnerable to damage than dry ones. When the trail is soft, consider other riding options. This also means staying on existing trails and not creating new ones. Don't cut switchbacks. Be sure to pack out at least as much as you pack in.

3. CONTROL YOUR BICYCLE

Inattention for even a moment could put yourself and others at risk. Obey all bicycle speed regulations and recommendations, and ride within your limits.

4. YIELD TO OTHERS

Do your utmost to let your fellow trail users know you're coming—a friendly greeting or bell ring are good methods. Try to anticipate other trail users as you ride around corners. Bicyclists should yield to all other trail users, unless the trail is clearly signed for bike-only travel. Bicyclists traveling downhill should yield to ones headed uphill, unless the trail is clearly signed for one-way or downhill-only traffic. Strive to make each pass a safe and courteous one.

5. NEVER SCARE ANIMALS

Animals are easily startled by an unannounced approach, a sudden movement or a loud noise. Give animals enough room and time to adjust to you. When passing horses, use special care and follow directions from the horseback riders (ask if uncertain). Running cattle and disturbing wildlife are serious offenses.

6. PLAN AHEAD

Know your equipment, your ability and the area in which you are riding—and prepare accordingly. Strive to be self-sufficient: keep your equipment in good repair and carry necessary supplies for changes in weather or other conditions. Always wear a helmet and appropriate safety gear.

http://www.imba.com/

Trip C1 – Guajome Park

Starting Point	North Santa Fe Drive, Oceanside
Distance	2.7 miles
Elevation Gain/Loss	15'/15'
Riding Time	0.5–1 hour
Difficulty	Easy, not technical
Road Conditions	Dirt trails and roads
Season	Year-round
Equipment	Hybrid or mountain bike
Optional Topo Map	San Luis Rey, CA

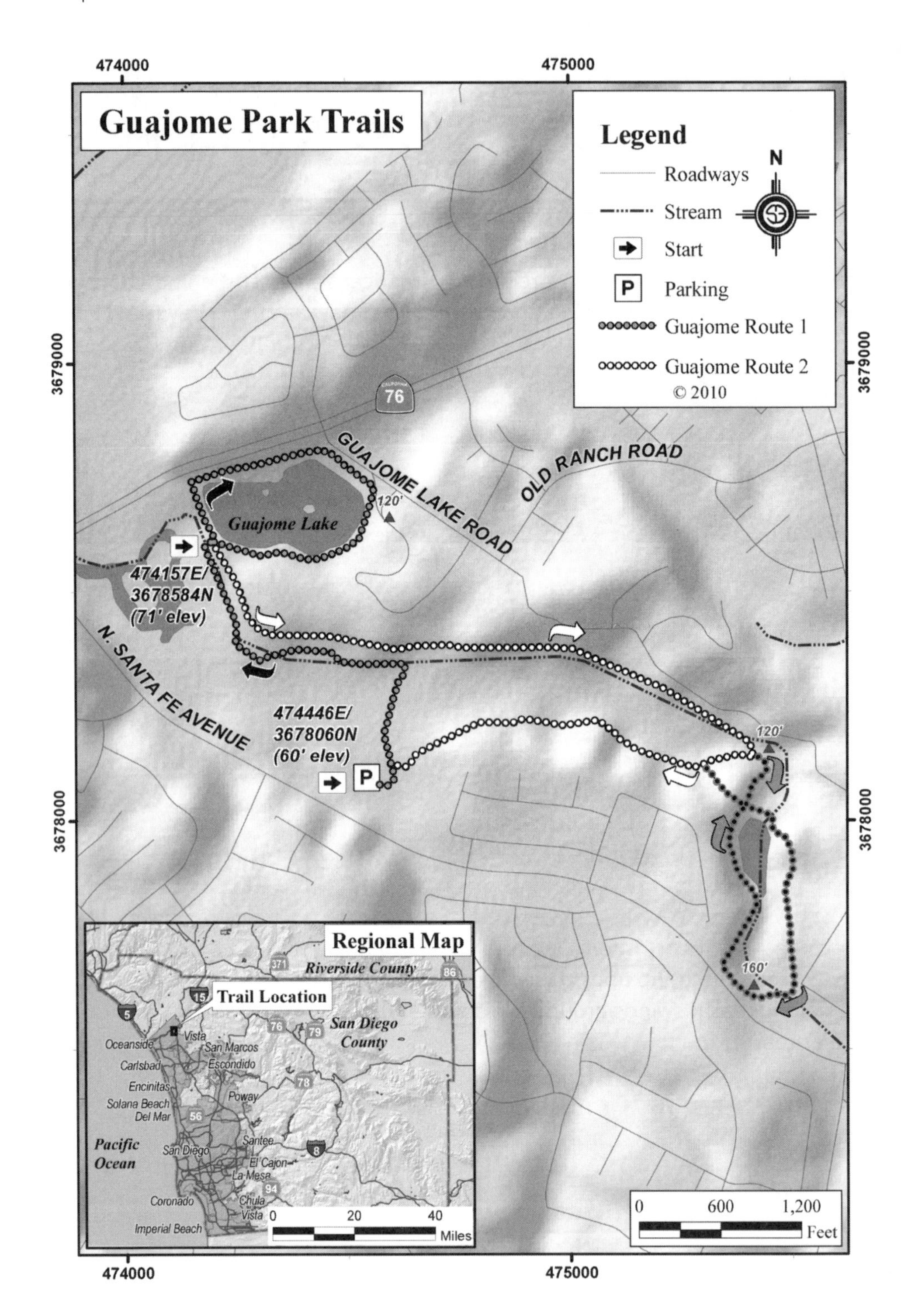

Guajome Park Trails
Legend
Roadways
Stream
Start
Parking
Guajome Route 1
Guajome Route 2
© 2010
N
474000
475000
3679000
3678000
76
Guajome Lake
GUAJOME LAKE ROAD
OLD RANCH ROAD
N. SANTA FE AVENUE
120'
160'
474157E/
3678584N
(71' elev)
474446E/
3678060N
(60' elev)
P
Regional Map
Trail Location
Riverside County
San Diego County
Pacific Ocean
Oceanside
Carlsbad
Encinitas
Solana Beach
Del Mar
San Diego
Coronado
Imperial Beach
Vista
San Marcos
Escondido
Poway
Santee
El Cajon
La Mesa
Chula Vista
0 20 40
Miles
0 600 1,200
Feet

Guajome Park is located in the coastal community of Oceanside and offers hiking, fishing, camping, and many other activities. It is a riparian area with spring-fed lakes, marshland, grasslands, and is home to a large diversity of plant and animal life including many migratory birds that stop here. The park also contains the historic Rancho Guajome adobe, built in the 1850s by Cave Johnson Couts that is designated as both a State and a National Historic Landmark.

Early inhabitants of the area were Native Americans who left behind not much more than rock art. In the 1950s and 1960s it was known as the Buteyn Bird Farm with exotic birds and a small zoo. In the 1970s, the County of San Diego purchased the land to create the park. There are 4.5 miles of multi-use trails and this ride will take you on a couple of loops, one around the wetlands and lake and another around the grasslands and marsh where you can enjoy the scenery. Keep your pace slow and respect other trail users.

To follow the lake loop ride, head north on the trail from the south picnic area and turn left at the nature trail. It follows the south side of a small creek through a wonderful wetlands area with numerous cattails and reeds. Follow the trail as it swings north, and then turn left at the small wooden bridge. Continue around the north end of the lake and keep your eyes open for the many ducks and birds that frequent the area.

Soon you'll pass by the main park entrance on your left, but stay right and complete the loop around the lake through a nice picnic and playground area. Migratory birds stop here and provide a lot of color. Turn left when you come to a T in the trail, and follow it along the north side of the same creek and alongside the campground.

To continue on to the grasslands loop, follow the trail straight through the grasslands area and bear right past the small wooden bridge and creek (straight ahead takes you to the upper pond, see Options). To complete the loop, follow the trail right as it swings around the south end of the marsh and returns to the picnic area.

GETTING THERE

From I-5, take Highway 76 east 7.5 miles to North Santa Fe Drive. Turn right and drive a short distance to the picnic area entrance on your left. An alternate starting point is the main entrance on Highway 76 at Guajome Lake Road. Turn right there and proceed to the park main entrance. A small day use fee is collected at either entrance.

From I-15, take Highway 76 west for 10 miles to North Santa Fe Drive. Turn left and drive a short distance to the picnic area entrance on your left. An alternate starting point is the main entrance on Highway 76 at Guajome Lake Road. Turn left there and proceed to the park main entrance. A small day use fee is collected at either entrance.

OPTIONS

There are several other trails you can explore including the upper pond at the south end of the park. In the grasslands area described above, stay straight and ascend to the upper pond where you can do a 0.8 mile loop and return to complete the ride above. Take your time and explore the area. There are a number of places to stop and have a snack and enjoy the scenery.

AMENITIES

There are a few stores and restaurants in the area west of the park near Highway 76 and College Boulevard. Restrooms and water are available in several places in the park, including the picnic area where the ride starts. Camping is available in the park.

Trip C2 – Calavera Lake

Starting Point	Oak Riparian Park, Carlsbad
Distance	1.6-mile lake loop and many other choices
Elevation Gain/Loss	50' to 350' depending on route
Riding Time	1–2 hours depending on route
Difficulty	Easy to difficult, technical in spots
Road Conditions	Dirt trails and graded roads
Season	Year-round
Equipment	Mountain bike
Optional Topo Map	San Luis Rey, CA

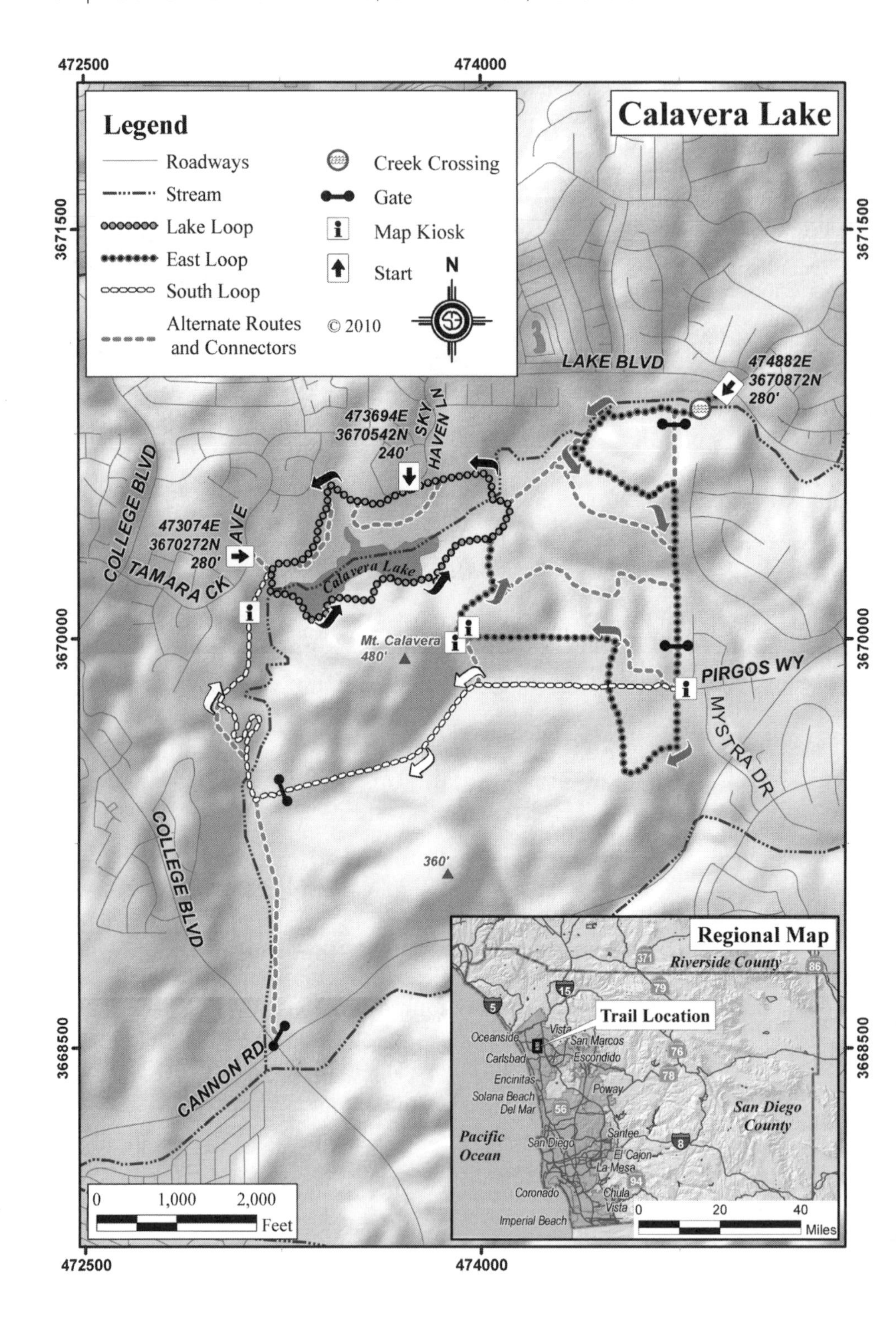

Calavera Lake
Legend
Roadways
Stream
Lake Loop
East Loop
South Loop
Alternate Routes and Connectors
Creek Crossing
Gate
Map Kiosk
Start
© 2010
N
472500
474000
3671500
3670000
3668500
LAKE BLVD
474882E
3670872N
280'
473694E
3670542N
240'
SKY HAVEN LN
473074E
3670272N
280'
COLLEGE BLVD
TAMARA CK
AVE
Calavera Lake
Mt. Calavera
480'
PIRGOS WY
MYSTRA DR
360'
COLLEGE BLVD
CANNON RD
0
1,000
2,000
Feet
Regional Map
Riverside County
Trail Location
Oceanside
Vista
San Marcos
Carlsbad
Escondido
Encinitas
Poway
Solana Beach
Del Mar
San Diego County
Pacific Ocean
San Diego
Santee
El Cajon
La Mesa
Coronado
Chula Vista
Imperial Beach
0
20
40
Miles

Calavera is a natural open space located in Carlsbad. Calavera means skull, which may be attributed to the interesting shape of 480-foot Mount Calavera in the center of the area. It is a 22 million-year-old volcanic plug that was once a volcano that solidified its central core. What's left is the vertical plug that is slowly eroding. Gravel mining in the 1900s also contributed to the demise of its west face. Lake Calavera is a water reservoir owned by the Carlsbad Municipal Water District, and is home to many plants, birds, and mammals including several endangered species.

Calavera Lake is also a fun place to ride on many varied trails. You can choose an easy ride around the lake or step it up a level or two and try some of the steeper, rocky technical trails. The map shows a number of possible routes, only a couple of them will be described here. You can design a different ride every time you ride here. Even though there are many small unmarked trails, it is best to stay on the trails designated for bicycle use.

From Oak Riparian Park, start the ride by heading south across the creek on a small wooden bridge. If it's been raining recently, and the creek is high or the trail is muddy, do not take this route since there is sensitive habitat farther downstream. Instead, ride west along Lake Boulevard to where you can drop onto the start of the dirt trails near the lake.

After a short distance, you'll come to a gated fire road on your left that climbs sharply to the top of a small hill. You can ride around the left side of the gate. This is a good place to start if you want to explore some of the trails to the south, or take the loop ride around Mount Calavera. You can also continue straight but will have to cross a series of small bridges (watch for the poison oak in spots). Soon after that, a left leads you up a steep rocky slope to the top of the same hill.

To explore the easier lake loop and the nearby trails, continue straight ignoring any left turns. When you reach the lake, the 1.6-mile loop can be done in either direction, but the recommended route is counter clockwise.

Access to the lake route is easiest from the Skyhaven Lane starting point at the north side of the lake. From there drop down to the trails and ride either way around the lake.

GETTING THERE

From Highway 78 exit College Boulevard and head south. Turn left on Lake Boulevard, and drive about 2 miles to Ridge Road on your left and turn right into Oak

Riparian Park. An alternate starting point is Skyhaven Lane. Drive 1 mile on Lake Boulevard and turn right on Skyhaven Lane. Continue 0.3 mile and park when you see the lake.

OPTIONS

Calavera Lake has many interconnecting trails so you can pick the difficulty and length of your ride and rarely do the same route twice. One fairly easy loop around the lake is fun to do as well as a little more difficult loop around Mount Calavera, both described above. Feel free to create your own ride linking together various trails.

AMENITIES

Stores and restaurants including a couple of bike shops are located nearby on Plaza Drive.

Trip C3 – Rancho Carrillo

Starting Point	Poinsettia Lane, Carlsbad
Distance	3 miles
Elevation Gain/Loss	180'/180'
Riding Time	30 minutes
Difficulty	Easy, not technical
Road Conditions	Well graded trails, 0.5 mile paved
Season	Year-round
Equipment	Hybrid or mountain bike
Optional Topo Maps	Rancho Santa Fe, San Marcos, CA

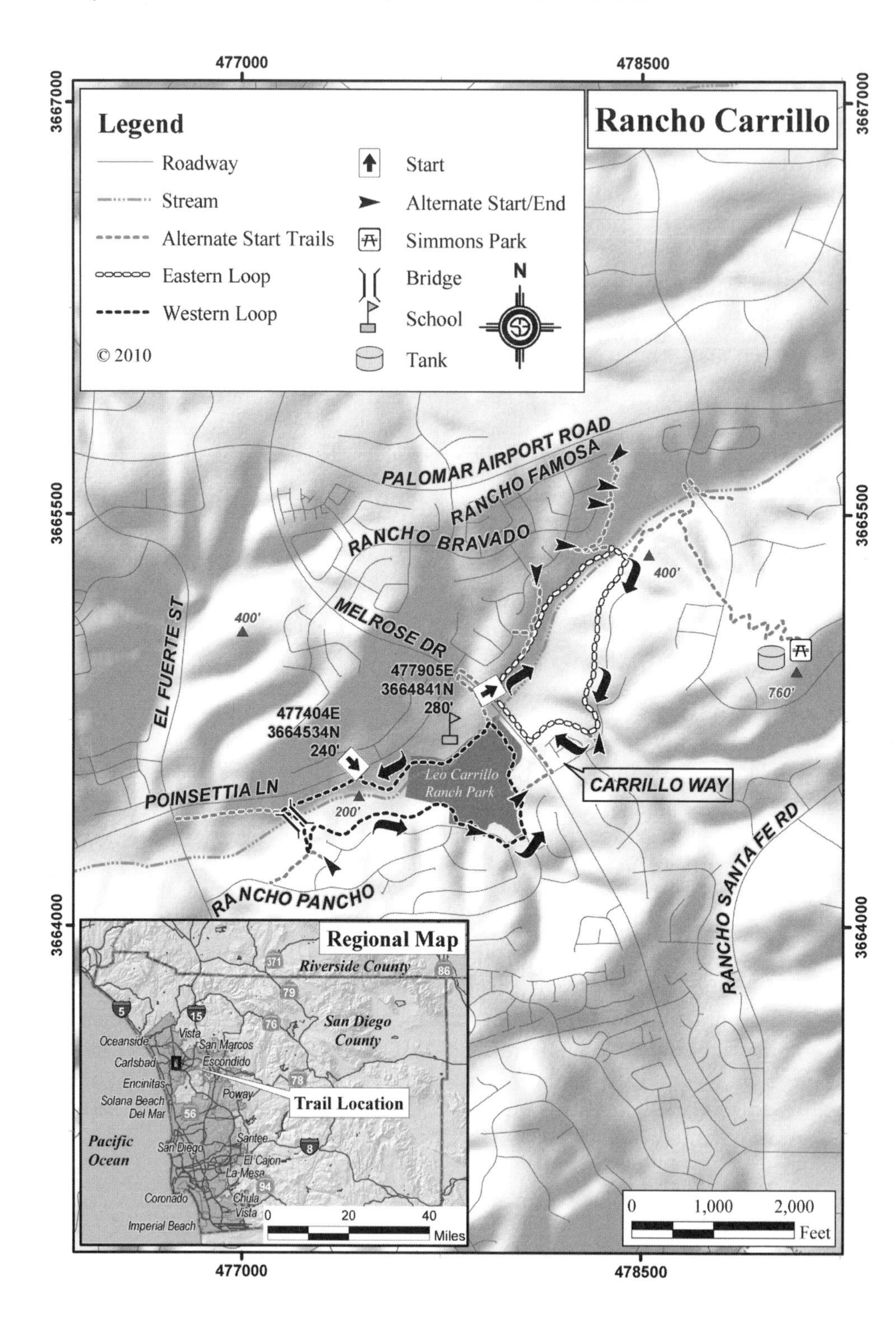
Rancho Carrillo
Legend
Roadway
Stream
Alternate Start Trails
Eastern Loop
Western Loop
© 2010
Start
Alternate Start/End
Simmons Park
Bridge
School
Tank
N
477000
478500
3667000
3665500
3664000
PALOMAR AIRPORT ROAD
RANCHO FAMOSA
RANCHO BRAVADO
MELROSE DR
EL FUERTE ST
POINSETTIA LN
RANCHO PANCHO
CARRILLO WAY
RANCHO SANTA FE RD
Leo Carrillo Ranch Park
477905E
3664841N
280'
477404E
3664534N
240'
400'
200'
760'
Regional Map
Riverside County
San Diego County
Oceanside
Vista
San Marcos
Carlsbad
Escondido
Encinitas
Solana Beach
Del Mar
Poway
Santee
Pacific Ocean
San Diego
El Cajon
La Mesa
Coronado
Chula Vista
Imperial Beach
Trail Location
0
20
40
Miles
0
1,000
2,000
Feet

Near busy Palomar Airport Road in Carlsbad, is a tranquil 27-acre canyon and former working ranchero, once owned by actor Leo Carrillo. Carrillo, a highly successful entertainer in stage plays and many motion pictures including Pancho, the sidekick to Cisco Kid (Duncan Renaldo) purchased Rancho de Los Kiotes in what is now southeast Carlsbad and created Rancho Carrillo. In this secluded canyon the Leo Carrillo Ranch, a designated Historic National Landmark was opened to the public in 2003. The park contains adobe buildings, antique windmills, and other historic structures that harken back to a quieter time in California before the busy roads and sea of houses encroached upon the area. The canyon open space includes riparian woodland, freshwater marsh, scrub, and non-native grasslands along a seasonal creek. This easy ride circumnavigates the ranchero on the Rancho Carrillo trail that connects to the Carlsbad and San Marcos trail systems.

From the parking lot starting point, follow the paved trail west as it descends toward the seasonal creek area. During wetter times, you may hear a small waterfall below. Stay left at the first junction (right here is not an official trail yet, but will connect to the Bressi Ranch trails) and follow the large bridge across the creek. This is a great place to view the freshwater marsh area, and perhaps glimpse a California gnatcatcher.

Follow the trail right, as it ascends to a junction of three trails. Turn sharply left and follow the wide gravel trail past well-groomed ceanothus and large pepper trees. The flat trail contours above the creek below, and soon turns to pavement and begins ascending. At Via Conquistador, turn left, and then left again on Rancho Caballo and quickly left onto Carrillo Way. To continue the west loop, turn left at Flying CC Lane and stay right onto a small sidewalk that descends quickly on the east side of the park. At the bottom of the hill turn left and follow the trail back to the starting point.

To connect to the east loop instead, stay straight on Carrillo Way, cross Melrose Drive and continue straight for a short distance until you see a trail entrance on your left, just before the private traffic gate. Once on the trail turn right at the next junction (left goes directly to Melrose Drive) and follow the trail as it curves around the head of a small canyon, and contours its way around the small, dry valley below. At the paved road, turn left then left again to stay on the trail (straight across here connects you to trails heading into the San Marcos trail system).

Follow the continuation of the east loop as it descends to Melrose Drive. Turn right and ride to Poinsettia Lane, and then left across Melrose Drive. Turn left onto the sidewalk along Melrose Drive, and follow it a short distance and pick up the descending trail on the right. At the bottom turn right, and then jog left and right past the wooden gate entrance to Leo Carrillo Ranch. Follow the west loop trail back to the starting point.

GETTING THERE

Take I-5 to Palomar Airport Road exit, and drive east 4.7 miles to Melrose Drive. Turn right (south) on Melrose Drive and go 0.8 mile to Poinsettia Lane. Turn right on Poinsettia Lane and continue west to the light at Paseo Escuela. Turn into the Carrillo Elementary School parking lot and stay right into the trail parking area.

OPTIONS

There are several entrances to the trail system indicated on the map. There are two loop routes, one on each side of Melrose Drive. You can park near any of those trailheads and start the ride. The 1.25-mile east loop connects to the city of San Marcos trail system. The 1.6-mile west loop connects to future trails of Bressi Ranch, Villages of La Costa, and Alga Norte Park.

AMENITIES

The nearest stores and restaurants are on Palomar Airport Road. Water and restrooms should be available in those areas.

Trip C4 – Rancho La Costa

Starting Point	Rancho Santa Fe Road, Carlsbad
Distance	4–6 miles depending on route
Elevation Gain/Loss	550'/550', 4.5% – 16% grade
Riding Time	2–3 hours depending on route
Difficulty	Difficult, technical in spots
Road Conditions	Rough trails and graded roads
Season	Fall, Winter, and Spring
Equipment	Mountain bike
Optional Topo Map	Rancho Santa Fe, CA

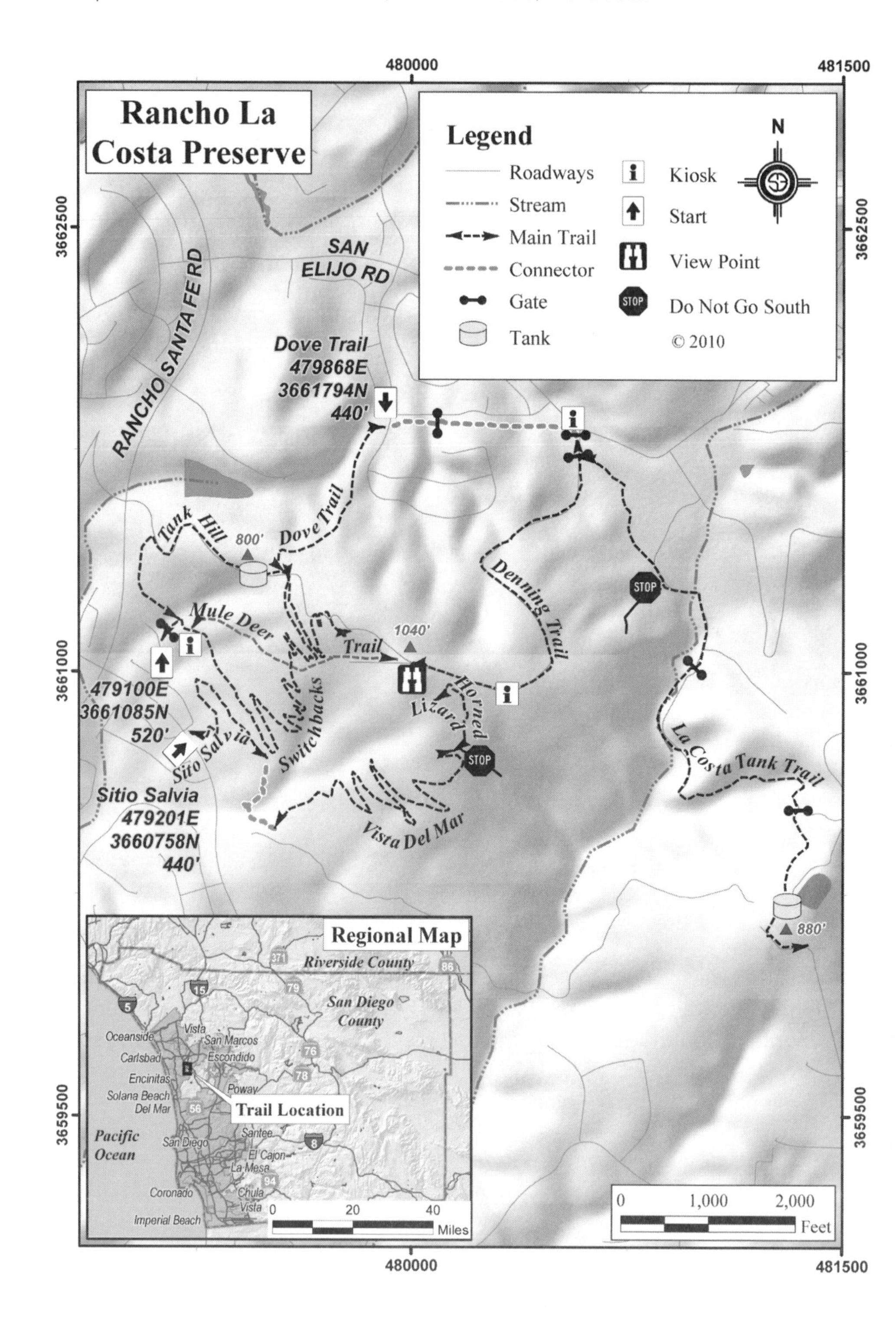
Rancho La Costa Preserve
Legend
Roadways
Stream
Main Trail
Connector
Gate
Tank
Kiosk
Start
View Point
Do Not Go South
© 2010
N
480000
481500
3662500
3661000
3659500
SAN ELIJO RD
RANCHO SANTA FE RD
Dove Trail
479868E
3661794N
440'
Tank Hill
800'
Dove Trail
Mule Deer Trail
1040'
Denning Trail
STOP
479100E
3661085N
520'
Sito Salvia
Switchbacks
Horned Lizard
Sitio Salvia
479201E
3660758N
440'
Vista Del Mar
La Costa Tank Trail
880'
Regional Map
Riverside County
San Diego County
Oceanside
Vista
San Marcos
Carlsbad
Escondido
Encinitas
Solana Beach
Del Mar
Poway
Trail Location
Pacific Ocean
San Diego
Santee
El Cajon
La Mesa
Coronado
Chula Vista
Imperial Beach
0 20 40 Miles
0 1,000 2,000 Feet

On a clear day, Denk Tank Mountain, the highest point in Carlsbad, offers a spectacular panoramic view of much of coastal San Diego, from Camp Pendleton to La Jolla and east to the hills bordering San Marcos. In springtime, colorful native flower blooms coat the green hillsides. In summer, the coastal sage of the hillsides offers little relief from the hot sun. This ride takes you on a number of the rugged trails in the Rancho La Costa Preserve, which is managed by the Center for Natural Lands Management.

From your parking spot near Sitio Salvia, ride a short distance on Sitio Salvia to the gravel road heading east past a gate. Left at the next junction takes you on the paved, but steep Tank Hill Trail (0.6 mile, 255' elevation gain, 8% grade to the tank). It is the quickest way to the top, but steep. Right takes you to the base of the steep Mule Deer Trail (0.5 mile, 440' elevation gain, 16% grade in places), or the easier Switchbacks Trail (1.9 mile, 450' elevation gain, 4.5% average grade).

The recommended route is right onto the Switchbacks Trail. Follow the trail a short distance, and stay left at the next junction. The trail bends this way and that as it switchbacks its way up the western flank of Denk Tank Mountain. The flat sections allow you to catch your breath, and enjoy the great views to the west. At 1 mile you'll reach the Mule Deer Trail junction. Stay straight and continue on to a very long north switchback that heads toward the water tank. Stay right and negotiate some rocky sections, and then follow the trail toward the top of the mountain.

Near the top of the mountain the steep Mule Deer Trail heads downhill sharply right, left is Denning Road, and straight takes you to the viewing area. Covered benches at the summit provide great 360 degree views and a respite from the heat on a warm day.

The most fun way down is the Horned Lizard Trail. Head south from the summit and follow the trail as it winds its way south and then west along the flank of the mountain. Continue following the trail southwest, as it switchbacks and soon turns into the Vista Del Mar Trail. Eventually you descend to Corte Romero near where you parked. Some riders begin their ride from this point.

GETTING THERE

From I-5, take La Costa Avenue or Leucadia Boulevard east to South Rancho Santa Fe Road. Turn right on Camino Junipero then left on Corte Romero, and park by the side of the road near Sitio Salvia. From I-78 take South Rancho Santa Fe Road south, and turn left on Camino Junipero after San Elijo Road.

An alternate starting point is Dove Tail Drive south of San Elijo Road. From there you can take the extremely steep trail up the north side of the mountain (not recommended), or more easily reach the Denning Trail and La Costa Tank Trail.

OPTIONS

There are several starting points and options for the Rancho La Costa Preserve trail system indicated on the map. The most popular ones are near Sitio Salvia that provides access to the Tank Trail, Mule Deer Trail, and the switchbacks. The Dove Tail Drive Trailhead provides easier access to the difficult Dove Trail, Denning Trail, and La Costa Tank Trail. The Denning Trail is an alternate way to get to the top of the mountain but is fairly rutted (1 mile, 550' elevation gain, 10% grade).

A nice optional ride is the La Costa Tank Trail (1.9 miles, 460' elevation gain, 4.6% average grade). It's a moderate climb to the top of the hill, but affords great views of the valleys below. From the Dove Tail Road parking area, follow the gravel trail east. After it intersects San Elijo Road, turn right onto a dirt road past a locked gate. Take the first left (straight is Denning Road) and then turn right. Soon the trail follows along the eastern foot of Denk Tank Mountain a short distance, and then swings east toward the closed San Marcos recycling station (don't be tempted to take the right that appears to climb the mountain—that area is off limits). Once near the station, turn right on the gravel road and follow it past a gate. The road follows a rocky stream bed alongside a seasonal creek, and soon, a small sign marks the trail heading left on a graded dirt road. The road steadily ascends east alongside a small canyon. As you cross the head of the canyon the road swings south past a gate, and ascends sharply in several places and thankfully, soon reaches the tank. Roads lead in several directions; some gated and signed No Trespassing. The best alternative is to return the way you came. This trail may connect to the Elfin Forest trail system at some point.

AMENITIES

The nearest stores and restaurants are on east on San Elijo Road or south on South Rancho Santa Fe Road. Water and restrooms should be available in those areas.

Trip C5 – Los Peñasquitos Canyon Preserve

Starting Point	Rancho Peñasquitos or Carmel Valley
Distance	12 miles out and back
Elevation Gain/Loss	325'/325' depending on route
Riding Time	2–3 hours depending on route
Difficulty	Easy to Moderate, north side technical in spots
Road Conditions	Rough trails and graded roads
Season	Year-round
Equipment	Mountain bike
Optional Topo Maps	Del Mar, Poway, CA

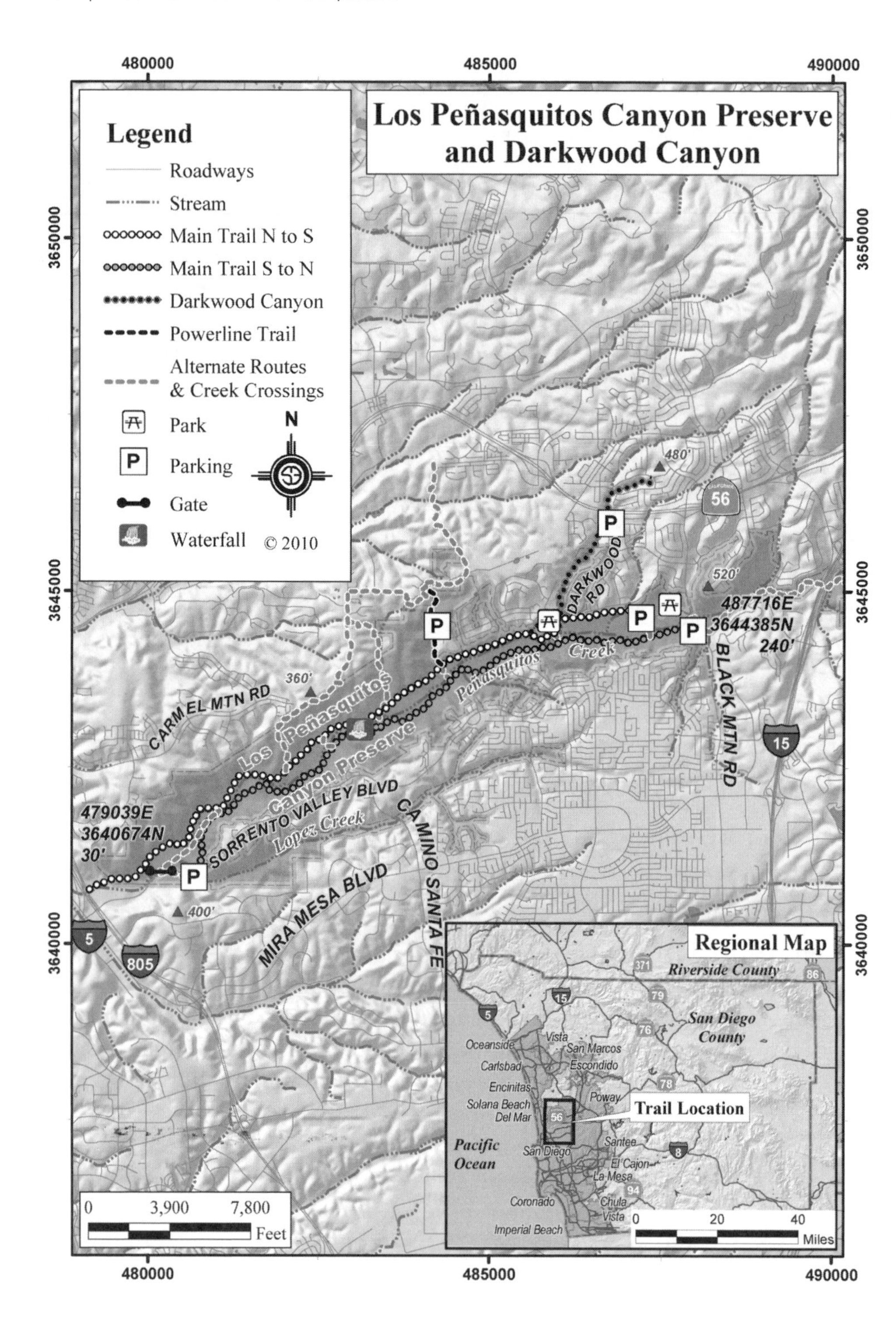

Los Peñasquitos Canyon Preserve and Darkwood Canyon
Legend
Roadways
Stream
Main Trail N to S
Main Trail S to N
Darkwood Canyon
Powerline Trail
Alternate Routes & Creek Crossings
Park
Parking
Gate
Waterfall
N
© 2010
480000
485000
490000
3650000
3645000
3640000
480'
56
DARKWOOD RD
520'
487716E
3644385N
240'
BLACK MTN RD
15
360'
CARMEL MTN RD
Los Peñasquitos Canyon Preserve
Peñasquitos Creek
SORRENTO VALLEY BLVD
Lopez Creek
CAMINO SANTA FE
479039E
3640674N
30'
400'
MIRA MESA BLVD
5
805
0 3,900 7,800 Feet
Regional Map
Riverside County
San Diego County
Oceanside
Vista
San Marcos
Carlsbad
Escondido
Encinitas
Poway
Solana Beach
Del Mar
Trail Location
Pacific Ocean
San Diego
Santee
El Cajon
La Mesa
Coronado
Chula Vista
Imperial Beach
0 20 40 Miles

The Los Peñasquitos Canyon Preserve, between Mira Mesa and Rancho Peñasquitos, is 6 miles long and encompasses some 4000 acres of land. The main canyon and its tributary, Lopez Canyon, contain a surprising variety of plants and animals. On any given day you might see birds of all kinds, coyote, and mule deer. Native Americans used the canyon as far back as 7,000 years, and later the area was the first Mexican land grant in California, Rancho del los Peñasquitos. The ruins of an old adobe from the 1840s are found near the west end of the canyon, and the Johnson-Taylor adobe, built in 1860, near the east end. The County of San Diego acquired the land for park and open space use.

At first blush, the main trail appears to be an easy, 12-mile out and back ride with a few small hills in the middle—perfect for a weekend afternoon. But further exploration of the north side of the canyon, reveals a number of steep ascents, descents, and mesa trails that will challenge even the best of riders. The main canyon ride is described below, with several other trails listed in the Options section.

From the eastern staging area, follow the trail west along the south side of Peñasquitos Creek. Soon you'll pass the Ranch House Crossing that provides access to Rancho de los Peñasquitos and the Canyonside Community Park area. It's also a way to access the north side of the canyon. Continuing on the south side, the trail enters the riparian woodland along the creek, with large California live oaks and beautiful sycamore trees. The trail meanders through the trees, and soon you'll pass the 5-mile marker (measured from the west end of the canyon) and the Peñasquitos Creek Park Crossing at 1.1 miles. The trail begins to enter more open grassland areas, and passes Carson's Crossing at about 2.3 miles. This is a great place to cross the creek, and access the power line road and others farther west that ascend to the mesa.

Continuing west the trail ascends a small rise at 3 miles, and the viewing area for the waterfall. You can leave your bike in the rack, and walk a short distance to see the creek, and a small waterfall cascading over volcanic rock. From here the trail descends sharply, swings west and then south again, ascending a moderate hill. A nice downhill ride takes you past the Sycamore Crossing at 3.7 miles. You'll pass more oaks and sycamores in an area frequented by deer, and then ascend a small ridge that begins the final stretch of trail heading to the west staging area, passing the Wagon Wheel Crossing around 5 miles. Straight at the next junction, leads to the El Cuervo Adobe Ruin and Sorrento Valley Boulevard (you can carefully cross the road and follow it left to the staging area). Left ascends a short, steep hill and curves under Sorrento Valley Boulevard, briefly into Lopez Canyon, and then right across Lopez Creek ending at the staging area. You can reverse your route to return, or cross Peñasquitos Creek at the Wagon Wheel Crossing and enjoy the north side of the canyon on your way back.

GETTING THERE

There are two primary entrances to the Preserve. The east entrance staging area is located at the intersection of Black Mountain and Mercy Roads. From I-56, head south on Black Mountain Road, or west on Mercy Road from I-15. You can also park a little farther north on Black Mountain Road at the Canyonside Community Park. The north side of the canyon is easiest to access from there.

The west entrance staging area is on the south side of Sorrento Valley Boulevard, about 1 mile east of Vista Sorrento Parkway. From I-805, exit Mira Mesa Boulevard and head straight onto Vista Sorrento Parkway. Turn right on Sorrento Valley Road, and drive 1 mile east to the staging area on your right. From I-5, exit Carmel Creek Road. Head north and turn right on Vista Sorrento Parkway. Turn left on Sorrento Valley Road and drive 1 mile east to the staging area on your right.

OPTIONS

There are many trails in Los Peñasquitos Canyon, with unlimited ways to link them together into unique rides for any ability level. The main north to south route is described above and suitable for all levels, but it's also the most crowded on weekends. Some alternate, less crowded choices include riding the moderate north side of the creek, with some fun single track over rolling terrain, as it hugs the north side of the canyon. From that trail, there are several steep, narrow trails that ascend the north side of the canyon and follow the ridge route along the mesa. Several ridge trails are now rerouted due to construction leaving a less than natural environment, but still interesting to ride.

Another short, easy trail on the mesa is accessed from Rancho Toyon Place. From I-56 take Carmel Country Road south and turn left on Del Mar Mesa Road. At the T intersection of Del Vino Court turn left, and quickly right past Hooterville Estates onto Rancho Toyon Place. Park anywhere in this area, and ride east as the road changes to The Preserve Way. Follow a maintained trail on the right, as it descends below the houses. It contours the hillside with great views into the canyon below. When you reach the end of the maintained trail, the mesa trails are straight ahead with access almost to I-56 (there are lots of steep sections once you leave the mesa, and not for beginners). A steep, rutted descent right, leads to the power line road, passing an exit to Park Village Road, and eventually Carson's Crossing and is also not a beginner trail.

A relatively unused trail, that is part of the Trans-County Trail reaching from Torrey Pines State Reserve to Anza-Borrego Desert, continues east from Peñasquitos Canyon along Peñasquitos Creek and under I-15. From the east staging area, stay to the left and follow the trail under Black Mountain Road (if wet, use the small trail on the right by the rocks). Curve right, and continue straight across the entrance road to the horse park, staying between the fences. Turn left at the Trans Country Trail sign and follow the trail as it easily ascends past the equestrian area, and descends paralleling Mercy Road. The canyon soon begins to narrow, leaving the sounds of traffic behind, and crosses the creek several times through willows and sycamores. At 1.3 miles, you'll pass under the huge I-15 overpasses and the smaller bridge that once served traffic, and now only bicycles. At the paved road, turn left and you'll come to a small area with benches and planted trees. It's a memorial to Cara Knott, and in memory of Sam Knott, the founder of San Diego Crime Victims. This is a good place to turn around and return to the staging area. The trail does continue east, around the pumping station, and ascends a rough, rutted section, and then contours its way toward Sabre Springs Parkway and beyond.

AMENITIES

The nearest stores and restaurants on the east side are located north or south on Black Mountain Road. On the western side, the Plaza Carmel Shopping Center is located near I-56 and Valley Centre Drive. Water is not available at either trailhead.

Trip C6 – Darkwood Canyon

Starting Point	Darkwood Road, Rancho Peñasquitos
Distance	3 miles out and back
Elevation Gain/Loss	150'/150'
Riding Time	30 minutes
Difficulty	Easy, not technical
Road Conditions	Smooth trails
Season	Year-round
Equipment	Hybrid or mountain bike
Optional Topo Map	Del Mar, CA

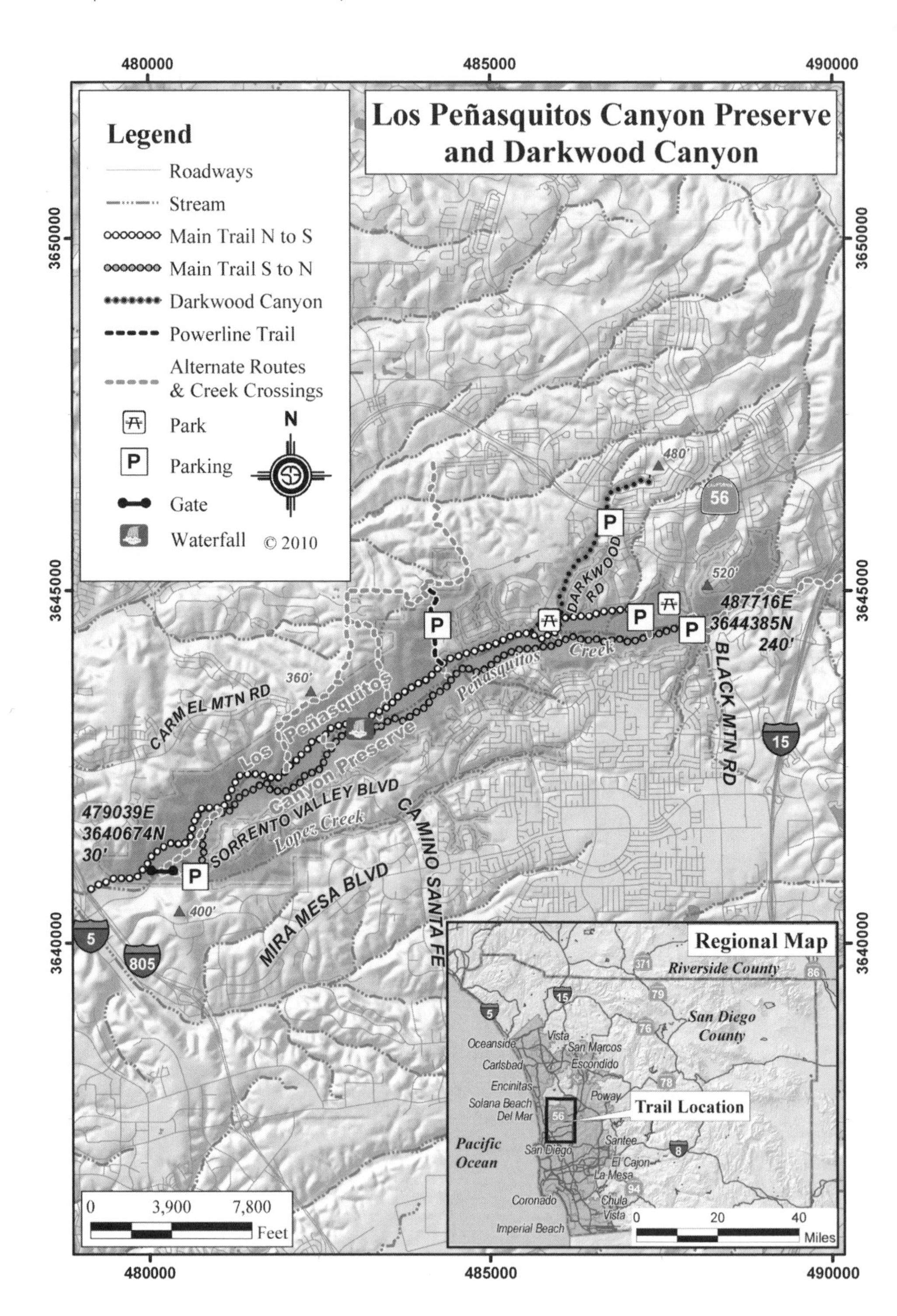

Los Peñasquitos Canyon Preserve and Darkwood Canyon
Legend
Roadways
Stream
Main Trail N to S
Main Trail S to N
Darkwood Canyon
Powerline Trail
Alternate Routes & Creek Crossings
Park
Parking
Gate
Waterfall
N
© 2010
480000
485000
490000
3650000
3645000
3640000
480'
520'
360'
400'
487716E
3644385N
240'
479039E
3640674N
30'
DARKWOOD RD
BLACK MTN RD
CARMEL MTN RD
SORRENTO VALLEY BLVD
CAMINO SANTA FE
MIRA MESA BLVD
Los Peñasquitos Canyon Preserve
Peñasquitos Creek
Lopez Creek
56
15
5
805
0
3,900
7,800
Feet
Regional Map
Riverside County
San Diego County
Oceanside
Vista
San Marcos
Carlsbad
Escondido
Encinitas
Solana Beach
Del Mar
Poway
Trail Location
Pacific Ocean
San Diego
Santee
El Cajon
La Mesa
Coronado
Chula Vista
Imperial Beach
20
40
Miles

The Los Peñasquitos Canyon Preserve, between Mira Mesa and Rancho Peñasquitos, is 6 miles long and encompasses some 4000 acres of land. A number of highly used trails run the length of the canyon, and some ascend the north side and follow the mesa. Several tributaries, including Lopez Canyon on the west end of the preserve also contain trails and are much less traveled. Another tributary on the east end of the canyon, below Darkwood Road, offers a short but enjoyable ride and connects to Los Peñasquitos Canyon if you want to extend the ride a bit.

From the street entrance, follow the concrete path as it descends between two houses to the canyon floor near an overpass on I-56. Turn left, and follow the smooth trail south. Prickly pear cactus, black sage, and the invasive pampas grass line the trail below houses on both rims of the canyon. It's very quiet here, with only the sounds of birds and your tires on the dirt. At about 1 mile as the canyon begins to widen, the Park Village Elementary School appears on the right. All too soon you reach a gate and Park Village Road, the silence broken by passing cars. To explore the north side of Los Peñasquitos Canyon, turn right on Park Village Road and then left at the light on Camino Del Sur. The signed trail is on the right, farther down the parking lot. Turn around to retrace your route to the starting point.

GETTING THERE

From I-56, head south on Black Mountain Road and turn right on Park Village Road at the light. At the 4th street turn right on Rumex Lane and then right again on Darkwood Road. Just before Darkwood Road curves right, the trail entrance is on your left between two houses. Park on the side of the road.

From I-15, take Mercy Road west to Black Mountain Road and then right to Park Village Road. Turn left at the light and follow the directions above.

OPTIONS

Once you follow the concrete entry trail to the canyon bottom, the trail also goes north under I-56. It's not quite as easy as the south section of trail, but it's interesting to explore. Follow the trail right along the small creek, avoiding the mud as you pass under I-56. At 0.3 mile, the trail steeply ascends a small hill to Sundance Road. You can turn around here, or cross the road and continue. The trail passes a gate, and descends into the northeast continuation of the canyon. The trail follows the small creek below houses on both rims of the canyon. At 0.75

mile the canyon ends with houses encircling the top. You can return the way you came, or explore a small wooden board crossing the creek, and a narrow access trail between two houses that exits on Twin Trails Drive.

AMENITIES

The nearest stores and restaurants on the east side of Los Peñasquitos Canyon are located north or south on Black Mountain Road.

Trip C7 – Lusardi Creek Loop

Starting Point	San Dieguito Road, Rancho Santa Fe
Distance	9.5 miles
Elevation Gain/Loss	1030'/1030'
Riding Time	2 hours
Difficulty	Moderate, not technical
Road Conditions	Dirt trails, dirt roads
Season	Year-round, can be warm in summer
Equipment	Mountain bike
Optional Topo Maps	Del Mar, Rancho Santa Fe, CA

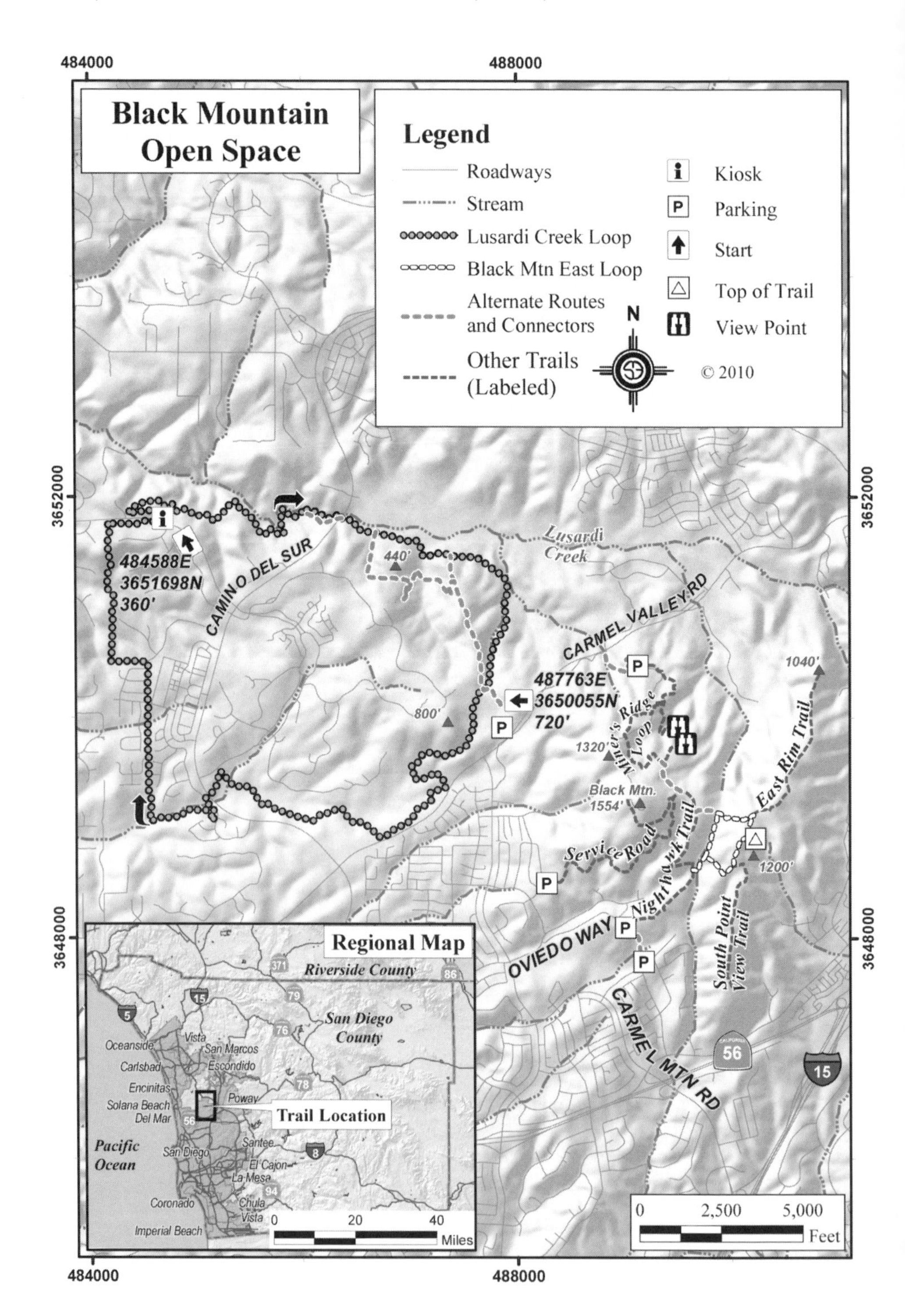

Black Mountain Open Space
Legend
Roadways
Stream
Lusardi Creek Loop
Black Mtn East Loop
Alternate Routes and Connectors
Other Trails (Labeled)
Kiosk
Parking
Start
Top of Trail
View Point
N
© 2010
484000
488000
3652000
3648000
484588E
3651698N
360'
487763E
3650055N
720'
CAMINO DEL SUR
Lusardi Creek
CARMEL VALLEY RD
440'
800'
1320'
1040'
1200'
Black Mtn. 1554'
Miner's Ridge Loop
Service Road
Nighthawk Trail
East Rim Trail
South Point View Trail
OVIEDO WAY
CARMEL MTN RD
56
15
Regional Map
Riverside County
San Diego County
Oceanside
Vista
San Marcos
Carlsbad
Escondido
Encinitas
Solana Beach
Del Mar
Poway
Trail Location
Pacific Ocean
San Diego
Santee
El Cajon
La Mesa
Coronado
Chula Vista
Imperial Beach
0 20 40 Miles
0 2,500 5,000 Feet

The Lusardi Creek Preserve is part of the Black Mountain Open Space Park. It includes 10 miles of multi-use trails comprised mainly of rough-graded utility roads. The trails range from easy to moderate through valleys, grasslands, chaparral and sage covered hills, and along a beautiful riparian habitat. Many species of birds, mammals, amphibians, and reptiles are found here and the area gives you an idea of what coastal southern California was like before urban development.

From the San Dieguito Road staging area, follow the trail west as it ascends a small ridge with great views north and east. The trail quickly descends and curves north, and then east passing a small "Trail" sign for the San Dieguito River Park Coast-to-Crest Trail (the trail west from here is sketchy and not rideable at this time).

The road continues east through a beautiful valley along Lusardi Creek, named for Peter Lusardi, an Italian immigrant who owned a ranch nearby and settled in the area in 1872. Douglas Fairbanks, Sr., purchased the ranch and named it "Rancho Zorro" after the popular movie Zorro.

At 1 mile, there is a great view east of Woodson Mountain above the Camino Del Sur bridge. The trail begins to ascend and then descend, passing several informative signs with details about the riparian habitat and native plants found along the trail. Soon the trail follows along gurgling Lusardi Creek and at 1.6 miles reaches the creek. Cross the small wooden bridge to the left and follow the trail along the north side of the creek, as it passes under the bridge on Camino Del Sur.

Cross the creek on the concrete ford, and continue following the nearly flat road as it begins to head east through a large valley. At 2.1 miles, an optional signed trail leads right (south) up a moderately steep hill. That route also heads east along a small plateau and eventually descends into a finger valley and then ascends moderately up to a power line access road. The suggested route continues straight at this point.

The road ascends and descends easily as it continues east, with views of the Carmel Valley Road bridge and Black Mountain in the distance. At 2.7 miles, you'll pass the junction of the power line road descending steeply from the right. This is one exit from the optional trail. Stay straight, and then at 3 miles, veer right at the Y junction onto a double track trail. The trail ascends alongside a small seasonal creek and by fields of thistles. The ascent steepens, and soon you'll curve right and join the power line road at a triangle junction with a kiosk.

Left takes you to Black Mountain Ranch Community Park, an alternate start/exit. Follow the trail southwest as it ascends a small hill and passes near the ball fields and joins with a dirt service road. Stay to the left, and at 3.9 miles look for a small trail sign on the right just past two round sewer vents leading to a hard-to-spot single track trail in the chaparral. The trail passes a small pond and then bends this way and that as it ascends slightly, and then descends into a scenic valley through thick aromatic California sage and black sage. Follow the trail across a small bridge and turn left where the trail then ascends to the head of a small drainage and then parallels Carmel Valley Road for awhile.

When you reach a small paved access road, jog left then right to stay on the trail. The trail then descends quickly through the valley, curves right, then left and ascends to Lazanje Pass Road at 6.4 miles (see Options for an alternate paved exit, if you want to avoid the very steep ascents and descents on the power line road ahead). Turn left and follow the dirt shoulder under Camino Del Sur. At the T intersection, cross the road and follow the sidewalk left a short distance, where the trail descends a concrete road on the right. The route turns to a rutted dirt road and heads west into a canyon. At the concrete ford, turn right and ascend past Eucalyptus trees to Camino Del La Luna. Follow the dirt shoulder to Camino Del La Rosa (you can also exit here and follow the surface streets to Camino Del Sur and turn left).

Cross Camino Del La Rosa and follow the continuance of the trail across the road. Turn left at the next road, and follow it to the power lines. Turn right and continue north on a series of steep ascents and descents that lead to San Dieguito Road. Stay right on the trail, and ascend to San Dieguito Road and jog left to the parking area.

GETTING THERE

There are two starting points for this ride. To reach the western staging area from I-15 or I-5, take Highway 56 to Camino Del Sur and head north. Turn left on San Dieguito road and drive 0.6 mile west to a small parking area and kiosk on the right (north) side of the road.

The alternate starting point is from Black Mountain Ranch Community Park on Carmel Valley Road, just north of Black Mountain Road. From I-15 or I-5, take Highway 56 to Black Mountain Road and head north. Turn right on Carmel Valley Road and take the first left at the stoplight into the community park. Park there, and head around the ball fields to a gate and kiosk on the north end of the parking area.

OPTIONS

The beautiful, 9.5-mile Lusardi Creek Loop is a moderate ride with no technical sections but has a few steep hills along the power line road near the end of the ride. These can be avoided by exiting onto the pavement at Lazanja Pass Road, and taking the small dirt trail just across the road and following it to the left of the traffic gate and guard shack to Camino Del Sur. Turn right, and then left on San Dieguito Road and back to the start. A dirt trail on the south side of San Dieguito Road starts just past the bridge and is a more enjoyable return route than the pavement.

AMENITIES

The nearest shopping center is south on Camino Del Sur near I-56. A small store is located at the corner of San Dieguito Road and El Apajo in Fairbanks Ranch.

Trip C8 – Black Mountain

Starting Point	Rancho Peñasquitos
Distance	2–10 miles with various options
Elevation Gain/Loss	475'/475' Miners Loop, other trails vary
Riding Time	1–3 hours depending on route
Difficulty	Moderate to Difficult, technical in spots
Road Conditions	Rough dirt trails and roads
Season	Year-round, can be warm in summer
Equipment	Mountain bike
Optional Topo Maps	Del Mar, Poway, CA

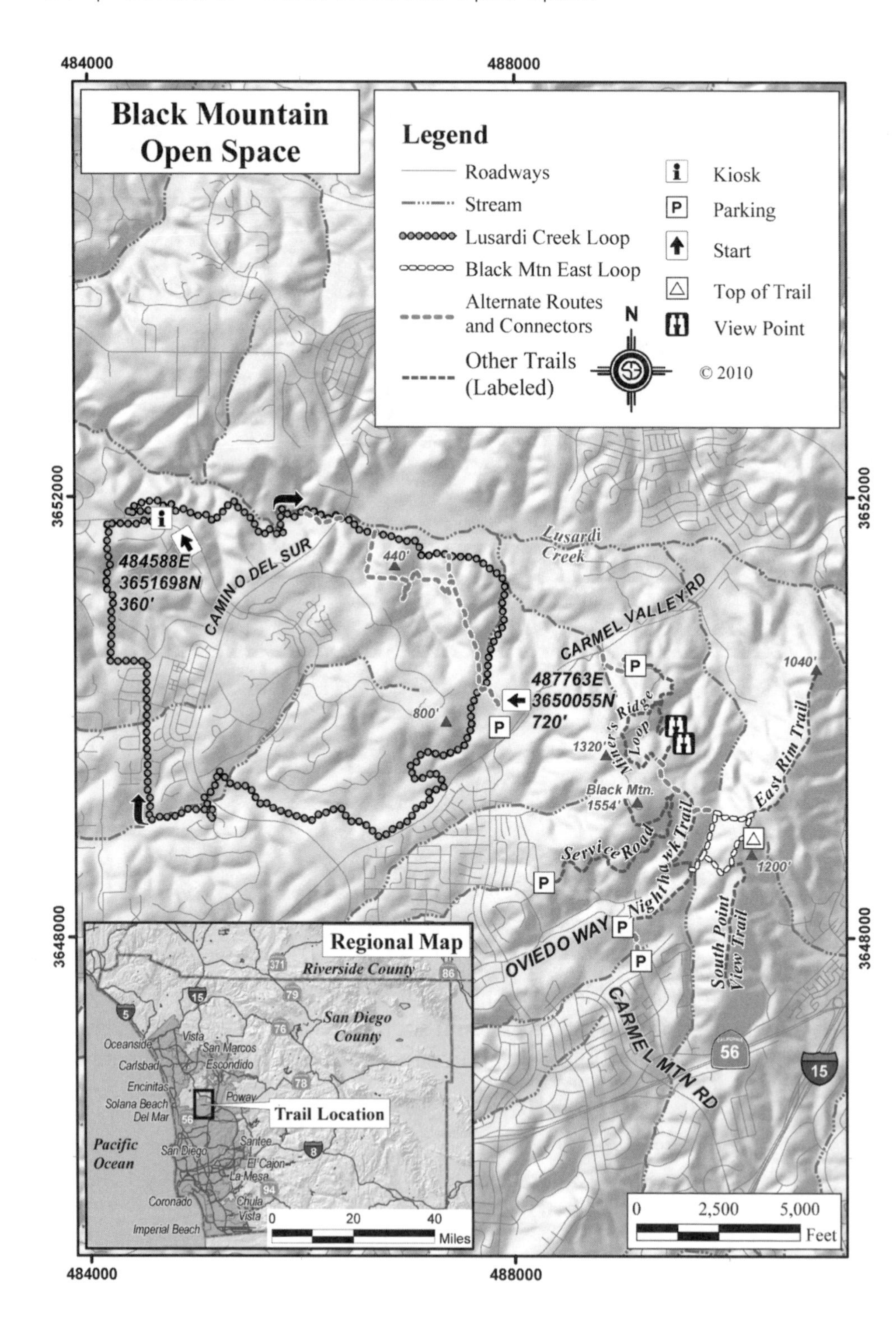

Black Mountain Open Space
Legend
Roadways
Stream
Lusardi Creek Loop
Black Mtn East Loop
Alternate Routes and Connectors
Other Trails (Labeled)
Kiosk
Parking
Start
Top of Trail
View Point
N
© 2010
484000
488000
3652000
3648000
484588E
3651698N
360'
CAMINO DEL SUR
440'
800'
Lusardi Creek
CARMEL VALLEY RD
487763E
3650055N
720'
1040'
Miner's Ridge Loop
East Rim Trail
1320'
Black Mtn.
1554'
Service Road
Nighthawk Trail
1200'
South Point View Trail
OVIEDO WAY
CARMEL MTN RD
56
15
Regional Map
Riverside County
San Diego County
Oceanside
Vista
San Marcos
Carlsbad
Escondido
Encinitas
Poway
Solana Beach
Del Mar
Trail Location
Pacific Ocean
San Diego
Santee
El Cajon
La Mesa
Coronado
Chula Vista
Imperial Beach
0
20
40
Miles
0
2,500
5,000
Feet

Black Mountain Open Space Park is owned and managed by the City of San Diego, and consists of a series of chaparral and sage covered hills, ridges, and canyons. Located north of San Diego at 1554 feet in elevation, Black Mountain and its microwave antennas dominate the landscape in Rancho Peñasquitos. From the summit and the hills surrounding it, you can see all the way to the ocean and the mountains to the north and east. It's a wonderful place to get away from the traffic and urban sprawl, and enjoy a quiet ride through the chaparral and sage-scrub. Every trail seems to head uphill, so be prepared for a lot of climbing and white-knuckle descents.

There are a variety of trails in the Black Mountain Open Space Park. The moderate 2.5-mile Miner's Loop Trail, explores the north slope of the mountain. The views to the north are great, and the dense chaparral is over head high in places. Lemonade berry, chamise, manzanita, and toyon are some of the plants you will see along the trail. From the Miner's Loop Trailhead, follow the trail east as it gradually curves southward, and then begins moderately ascending the hillside. At 0.3 mile, you reach a small crest with great views north and east. Stay right at 0.4 mile, as the trail ascends more sharply and carefully pick your line through some rocky sections. Soon you'll pass a trail junction on the right with the Ridge Loop Trail heading left. Follow the trail left as it begins to easily ascend and descend with a few brief steep ascents. At 1.3 miles, just before the Nighthawk Trail joins from the right, carefully negotiate a few rocky descents. You'll pass two short trails to the right that offer nice views to the north and east. The trail descends from here, and heads back to the starting point.

The Nighthawk Trail provides access to a number of fun, steep rides on the south and east slopes of the park. Flattop buckwheat, laurel sumac, and the aromatic white and black sage accent the hillsides in this area. Eighty species of birds frequent the area, as well as many animals. You might see mule deer or the more elusive bobcat. From the Hilltop Community Park Trailhead, follow the rough road near the power lines left, and then right, as it sharply ascends a ridge overlooking the park. You'll soon gain the top, where the view of the city below is wonderful. Black Mountain and its access road dominate the view to the north.

At 0.6 mile, you'll reach the junction of the Little Black Loop descending right, Blackhawk continues straight. From here you can continue on Blackhawk, which soon curves sharply west, then resumes it northerly trend on a moderate ascent. At 1 mile it crests the ridge, and rolls along easily to a junction right, that descends to the north end of the Little Black Loop with access to the East Rim

Trail. If you stay straight there, you will soon join a trail descending left from the service road, and curving north to eventually join the Miner's Ridge Trail.

To explore the Little Black Loop, East Ridge, or Southpoint View Trails, descend right at the junction at 0.6 mile, and follow the trail as it ascends to a junction. The Little Black Loop circles the hill before you, returning to this point on the trail descending from the left. Turn right, and ascend moderately southeast and then northwest where a junction right takes you along the Southpoint View Trail. Staying left here, the trail ascends very steeply to the top of a hill with an old concrete structure, at 1.1 miles. The view is spectacular from here. On a clear day the Coronado Islands are visible, the Palomar ridge, the three Cuyamaca Peaks, and much of the city below. Black Mountain blocks the view to the west.

The trail descends quickly, crossing several water bars that prevent erosion, to the junction of the Little Black Loop Trail at 1.3 miles. You can follow left (west), around the north end of the hill you just descended, and then left again to the junction mentioned earlier, and back to the start. To continue on the East Ridge Trail, keep going straight. The trail ascends sharply again to gain the top of another ridge. Ignore the left that dead ends, and follow the rolling ridge trail north, with most of the hard work behind you (until you return of course). Soon the wide trail narrows to a single track, as it descends quickly through dense chaparral with a few rocky drops here and there. One final ascent and you can enjoy the view into the valley below from the north end of the trail at 2.3 miles. The recommended route is to return the way you came, turning right on the Little Black Loop trail below the hill with the concrete structure and then left to return to the start.

The 1.7-mile Black Mountain service road, with access to the top of the mountain, starts at the east end of Laurentian Drive off of Stargaze Avenue. You won't be able to ride all the way to the top, but you will have awesome views on the ride up. Watch for service vehicles that share the road.

GETTING THERE

Black Mountain Open Space Park is accessible from several trailheads. For the Nighthawk Trailhead, from I-15 or I-5, take Highway 56 to Black Mountain Road and head north. Turn right on Oviedo Street and keep right on Oviedo Way. Proceed to the top of the hill, and park at the east side of Hilltop Community Park. The trailhead is just to the east by the kiosk.

To reach the Miner's Ridge Loop Trailhead, continue north on Black Mountain Road until you reach Carmel Valley Road. Turn Right (east) on Carmel Valley Road and continue approximately 0.75 mile to the entrance you will see on your right. The trailhead is at the end of the paved road.

The access road to Black Mountain Peak starts at the end of Laurentian Drive off of Stargaze Avenue.

OPTIONS

The Black Mountain trails are quite steep in places, and include some technical rocky sections with a few small drops, and are not for beginners. These trails range from 1.2 miles for Little Black Loop, 1 mile for East Rim Trail, 1.4 miles for Blackhawk Trail, and 2 miles for Miner's Loop. However to reach the East Rim Trail, for example, you need to start on the Nighthawk Trail, turn right onto Little Black Loop, and then continue on the East Rim Trail for a one-way distance of about 2.3 miles.

AMENITIES

Shopping centers and some restaurants are found throughout the Black Mountain area. Bathrooms and water are available at Hilltop Community Park.

Trip C9 – Rose Canyon Open Space Park

Starting Point	Regents Road, University City
Distance	7.6 miles
Elevation Gain/Loss	250'/250'
Riding Time	1–2 hours
Difficulty	Easy to Moderate, not technical
Road Conditions	Trails and graded roads
Season	Year-round
Equipment	Mountain bike
Optional Topo Map	La Jolla, CA

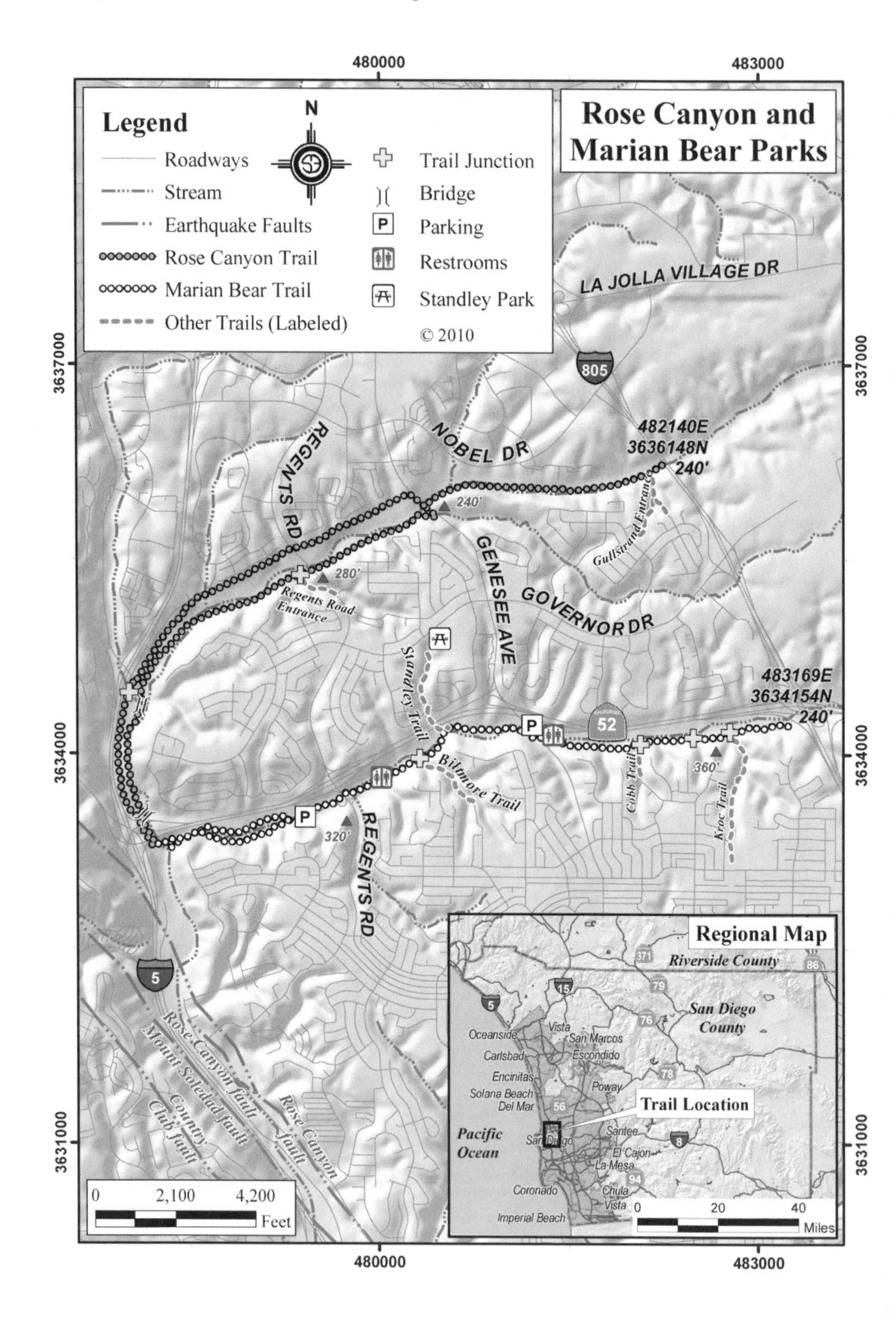

Rose Canyon and Marian Bear Parks
Legend
Roadways
Stream
Earthquake Faults
Rose Canyon Trail
Marian Bear Trail
Other Trails (Labeled)
N
Trail Junction
Bridge
Parking
Restrooms
Standley Park
© 2010
480000
483000
3637000
3634000
3631000
LA JOLLA VILLAGE DR
805
NOBEL DR
REGENTS RD
482140E
3636148N
240'
240'
Gullstrand Entrance
GENESEE AVE
GOVERNOR DR
280'
Regents Road Entrance
Standley Trail
483169E
3634154N
240'
52
Biltmore Trail
Cobb Trail
360'
Kroc Trail
320'
REGENTS RD
5
Rose Canyon fault
Mount Soledad fault
Country Club fault
Rose Canyon fault
0 2,100 4,200
Feet
Regional Map
Riverside County
San Diego County
Oceanside
Carlsbad
Encinitas
Solana Beach
Del Mar
Vista
San Marcos
Escondido
Poway
Trail Location
Pacific Ocean
San Diego
Santee
El Cajon
La Mesa
Coronado
Chula Vista
Imperial Beach
0 20 40
Miles

Rose Canyon is an open-space park managed by the City of San Diego. It's located in busy University City, near houses and noisy traffic, but you would never know it once you're riding along its quiet trails. The Kumeyaay Indians were the original inhabitants of the canyon camping near the stream, gathering acorns, and hunting small game. In 1853 Louise Rose, the canyon's namesake, purchased acreage and built a ranch here complete with a tannery and vineyard. In 1882, the California Southern Railroad laid tracks in the canyon and built a station near Gilman Drive named Elvira (you can still see the control point sign along the tracks near I-5). Other than a few trains passing through the canyon, it's a great place to enjoy a quiet morning or afternoon ride through the riparian oak woodland.

From the Regents Road entrance on the north side of the canyon, the trail heads east or west staying high on the canyon edge. Heading west, the trail soon dead ends at the power lines above the railroad tracks. Riding along the tracks is not permitted; instead head right onto the shoulder of La Jolla Colony Drive, and follow it to the junction of Gilman Drive. The Rose Canyon, Mount Soledad, and Country Club faults all parallel I-5 just to the west of here. Hopefully they will remain dormant during your ride.

Follow the bike trail south paralleling I-5 and descend carefully into the culvert, if it's dry, near the I-52 overpass. Follow the culvert north and veer right onto a trail that crosses a small bridge. Ignore the trail intersecting from the right along I-52 and continue north following the ascents and descents of a power line road. At 0.6 mile, cross the small creek and follow the single track trail as it swings northeast into Rose Canyon.

Soon you'll cross a nice bridge built by an Eagle Scout in 2006, and continue your journey through the beautiful coastal live oak trees and riparian habitat. The trail continues on, sometimes through thick vegetation and sometimes in the open, paralleling the tracks as they march eastward through the canyon. Another bridge at 1.2 miles leads you to the south side of the creek, as the trail nestles close to the hills.

At 1.8 miles, the south entrance from Regents Road branches right into a small canyon. Soon you reach a small bench, and a short hiking trail on the right. Ahead you'll ascend a small hill to reach Genesee Avenue at 2.6 miles. Jog left, cross at the light, and follow the trail to the left of the University City High School driveway. The trail descends into the canyon and crosses several rocky seasonal creeks, swings near the tracks, and then ends at the I-805 freeway at 4 miles.

The Miramar Air Station is past this point, and is off limits. Turn around here, and follow the trail back to Genesee Avenue. Cross at the light and turn right (north), and follow the sidewalk to the dirt service road on your left. Follow that road as it descends and ascends sharply several times and follows the canyon top, back to your starting point.

GETTING THERE

There are several entrances to the canyon. One is where Regents Road dead ends on the north side of the canyon, two blocks south of Governor Drive. A second entrance is where Regents Road dead ends on the south side of the canyon. You may also enter on Genesee Avenue, across from the University City High School. Parking is available there during non-school hours or along Decoro Street just north of the entrance on Genesee Avenue.

OPTIONS

The ride described above starts at the north Regents Road entrance. If you start at the south Regents Road entrance, pick up the trail description there, and head east to enjoy the ride. The trail on the north side of the tracks is moderate with a number of ascents and descents. For an easier ride, start from the south Regents Road entrance and stay on that side of the creek.

AMENITIES

The nearest stores and restaurants are in University City south of the canyon, or the UTC area north of the canyon. Restrooms and water should be available in those locations.

Trip C10 – Marian Bear Park

Starting Point	Regents Road, University City
Distance	6.5 miles out and back
Elevation Gain/Loss	150'/150'
Riding Time	1.5 hours
Difficulty	Easy, not technical
Road Conditions	Trails and graded roads
Season	Year-round
Equipment	Mountain bike
Optional Topo Map	La Jolla, CA

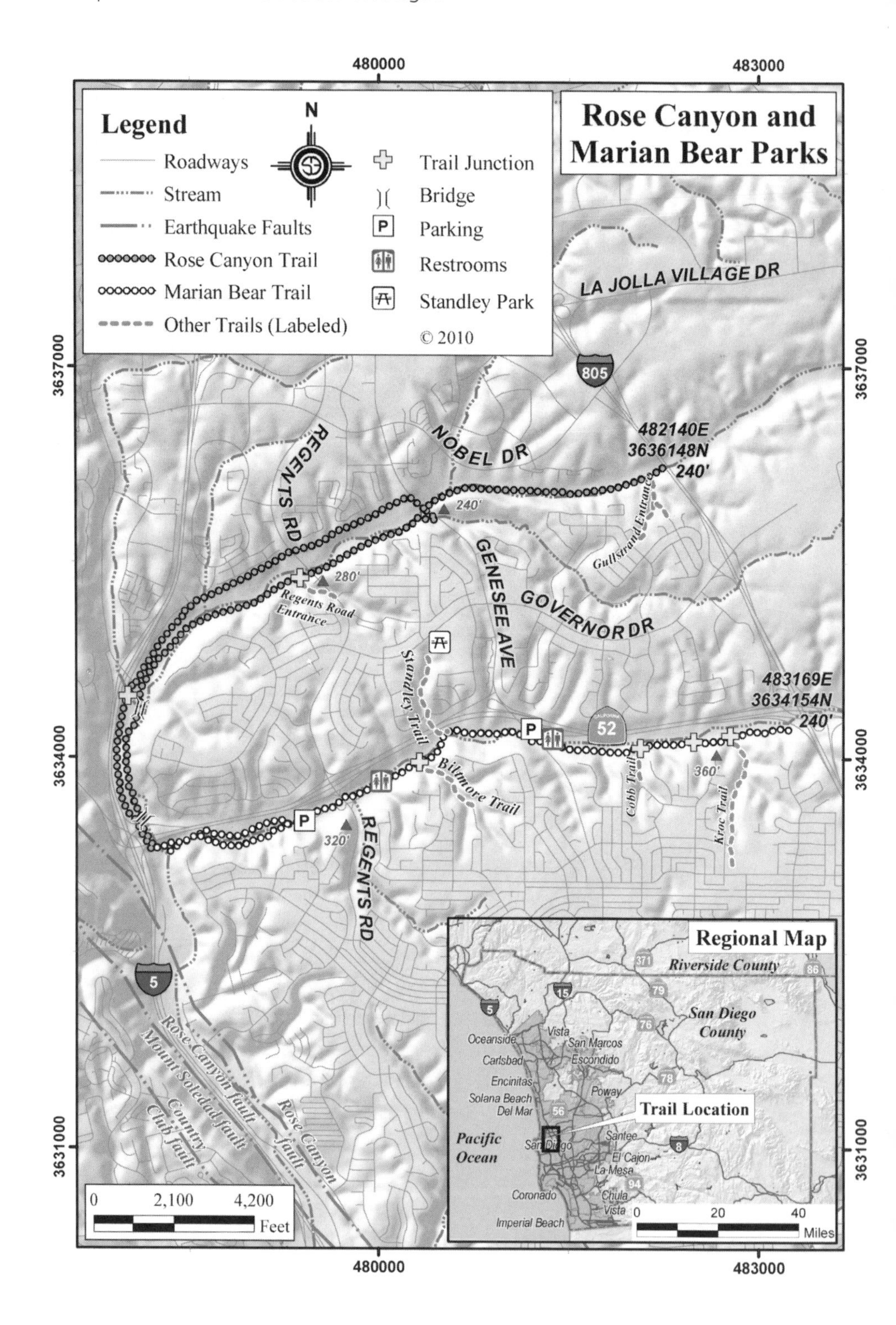

Rose Canyon and Marian Bear Parks
Legend
Roadways
Stream
Earthquake Faults
Rose Canyon Trail
Marian Bear Trail
Other Trails (Labeled)
Trail Junction
Bridge
Parking
Restrooms
Standley Park
© 2010
N
480000
483000
3637000
3634000
3631000
LA JOLLA VILLAGE DR
805
NOBEL DR
REGENTS RD
482140E
3636148N
240'
240'
GENESEE AVE
Gullstrand Entrance
280'
Regents Road Entrance
GOVERNOR DR
Standley Trail
483169E
3634154N
240'
52
Bilmore Trail
Cobb Trail
360'
Kroc Trail
320'
REGENTS RD
5
Rose Canyon fault
Mount Soledad fault
Country Club fault
Rose Canyon fault
0
2,100
4,200
Feet
Regional Map
Riverside County
San Diego County
Oceanside
Vista
San Marcos
Carlsbad
Escondido
Encinitas
Poway
Solana Beach
Del Mar
Trail Location
Pacific Ocean
San Diego
Santee
El Cajon
La Mesa
Coronado
Chula Vista
Imperial Beach
0
20
40
Miles

Marian Bear Memorial Park is located in San Clemente Canyon and stretches eastward over 467 acres from I-5 to I-805. The beautiful natural canyon contains a number of native plant communities including riparian woodland, coastal sage-scrub, and chaparral. Live oaks, sycamores, willows, and many other plants make this a unique habitat for a number of animals. You may see skunks, rabbits, and coyotes as you leisurely bike through the canyon. Marian Bear, an energetic planner, naturalist, and conservationist helped preserve the open space in its natural state. She was instrumental in the effort to realign Highway 52 from the canyon bottom to the north side of the canyon, and the canyon was rededicated in her honor in 1979.

From the Regents Road staging area you can head west or east in the canyon. Heading west, you'll cross a seasonal rocky creek among numerous oak trees. At the junction of a trail heading left, stay right. At 0.5 mile the trail crosses the creek again and ascends the bank to a bench. Stay right, and follow the trail as it crosses a moderate hill. Stay right, and you'll end up near the culvert that leads to Rose Canyon (see the Rose Canyon ride). Return the same way to the staging area. Note that there are many trails that crisscross in the canyon, heading in many directions. It's best to remain on the main east-west trails throughout the canyon.

Heading east from the staging area, follow the trail on the north side of the parking area. It briefly follows the pavement under Regents Road, and then resumes on the left following the creek. Picnic benches, restrooms, and water are available as you pass the east end of the staging area. Stay right there and follow the trail eastward through the canyon. Except for the din of freeway traffic, you can almost imagine the Native Americans that inhabited the riparian woodland area for thousands of years—hunting game and harvesting food. You can still see lots of wildlife including raccoons, skunks, rabbits, and coyotes.

The Biltmore Trail intersects from the right at 0.6 mile and the Standley Trail from the left at 0.8 mile (see Options for the additional trails). When you reach Genesee Avenue, follow the trail under the overpass and stay right. Then curve left, to join the descending trail from the Genesee staging area at 1.4 miles (bathrooms and water are available here). Stay to the right to continue the ride east passing the Cobb Trail at 1.8 miles. Soon you'll cross a small hill and pass the Kroc Trail at 2.3 miles. The trail ends at the massive overpass of I-805 at 2.6 miles. Return to the trailhead the way you came.

GETTING THERE

There are several neighborhood trails descending into the canyon (see Options) and two trailhead staging areas in the canyon itself. The first trailhead, and where this ride description starts, is on Regents Road just south of Highway 52, on the west side of the road. The other popular trailhead is on Genesee Avenue, also just south of Highway 52 on the east side of the road.

OPTIONS

There are several neighborhood trails that provide access to the canyon, albeit more difficult in some cases. Note that all of these side canyons have poison oak, so be careful. The 0.3 mile Biltmore Trail on the south side of the canyon starts from the end of Biltmore Street in Clairemont. It descends sharply on a loose dirt slope, angles around a large tree, and crosses a small creek several times that could be impassible during wetter times. You'll pass through a wonderful oak forest, cross a bridge over a small chasm, and then join the main canyon trail. This is not an easy trail to negotiate near the top.

The 0.5-mile Standley Trail, descends from the Standley Community Park area north of the canyon in University City. You can actually ride from the park to the canyon, but it's not recommended. The trail just below the park is not easily ride-able, as it zigzags moderately down through eucalyptus trees and across wood-en erosion barriers. You then negotiate a very narrow, rutted trail through dense chaparral. Soon you'll cross Syracuse Avenue, which is a better place to start rather than Standley Park. From here, the trail descends easily passing under Highway 52, and then swings east to join the main canyon trail.

The next trail you'll encounter on the south side of the canyon heading west to east, is the Cobb Trail. It's a short, 0.17-mile gentle ascent through oak trees, with a small drainage on the right. All too soon, it dead ends at a steep slope, acces-sible only by a large number of steps. It's fun to explore from the canyon bottom, but it's not an entrance or exit for a bicycle.

The last optional entrance is the 0.7-mile moderate Kroc Trail, on the south side of the canyon. The fun, narrow trail ascends and descends, and zigzags follow-ing a small creek bed on the left. At 0.3 mile, it ascends to join a power line maintenance road heading north-south. Turn left, and follow the road past an exit to Lehrer Drive on the right, and on to Conrad Avenue near a school and across from a church.

There is a signed entrance from the end of Limerick Avenue at the very east end of the canyon, but it is very steep and heavily eroded—almost impossible to hike, let alone bike.

AMENITIES

The nearest stores and restaurants are in University City north of the canyon, or the Clairemont area south of the canyon. Restrooms and water are available at both trailheads.

Trip C11 – Tecolote Canyon Natural Park

Starting Point	Tecolote Road, San Diego
Distance	6.2 miles out and back, main canyon
Elevation Gain/Loss	300'/300' main canyon
Riding Time	1.5 hours
Difficulty	Easy to Moderate, not technical
Road Conditions	Rough Trails and graded roads
Season	Year-round
Equipment	Mountain bike
Optional Topo Map	La Jolla, CA

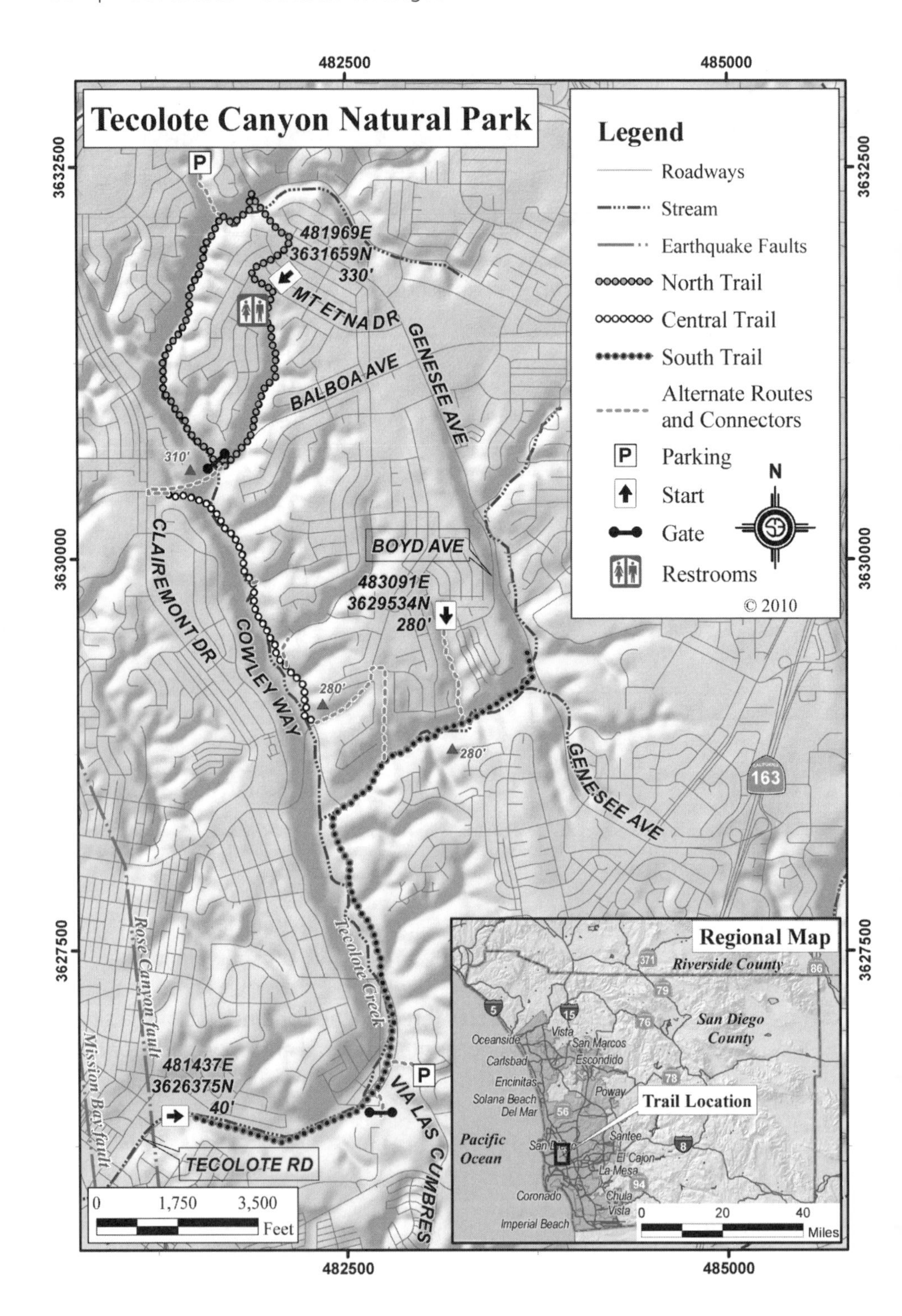

Tecolote Canyon Natural Park
482500
485000
3632500
3630000
3627500
Legend
Roadways
Stream
Earthquake Faults
North Trail
Central Trail
South Trail
Alternate Routes and Connectors
Parking
Start
Gate
Restrooms
N
© 2010
481969E
3631659N
330'
MT ETNA DR
GENESEE AVE
BALBOA AVE
310'
CLAIREMONT DR
COWLEY WAY
BOYD AVE
483091E
3629534N
280'
280'
280'
GENESEE AVE
163
Rose Canyon fault
Mission Bay fault
Tecolote Creek
481437E
3626375N
40'
TECOLOTE RD
VIA LAS CUMBRES
0
1,750
3,500
Feet
Regional Map
Riverside County
San Diego County
Oceanside
Vista
San Marcos
Escondido
Carlsbad
Encinitas
Solana Beach
Del Mar
Poway
Trail Location
Pacific Ocean
Santee
El Cajon
La Mesa
Coronado
Chula Vista
Imperial Beach
0
20
40
Miles

Tecolote Canyon, a natural park right in the middle of the communities of Clairemont and Linda Vista, is a wonderful open space that provides 6 miles of hiking and mountain biking trails. Although the generally north-south trending canyon is surrounded by development, it's a great, relatively quiet place to get away from the busy traffic nearby. Early settlers farmed and grazed cattle here until the early 50s. After the City of San Diego acquired the land in 1978, it was officially named Tecolote Canyon Natural Park (Tecolote is Spanish for owl, a few of the nighttime residents that frequent the canyon). There are several trails throughout the park, and this ride will direct you along some of the best routes.

The main north-south trail begins at the south end of Tecolote Canyon, next to the nature center. The center, closed on Mondays, has a variety of exhibits on the animal and plant life in the canyon. You can also obtain a trail map at the kiosk in front of the center. The Rose Canyon Fault crosses Tecolote Road just a little west of the ride start and parallels I-5. Start by riding the wide trail east, and soon you can spot on the canyon rim to the southeast, the Spanish Renaissance architecture of the Immaculata Parish Church and other buildings on the University of San Diego campus. At 0.8 mile a paved road joins from the right that ascends a steep hill to Cunningham Stadium, home of the University of San Diego Toreros baseball team.

The canyon bends to the north here, and the trail passes another junction on the right at 0.9 mile that ascends sharply to Via Las Cumbres, an optional entrance. The trail follows the power lines north, passing under a beautiful large oak tree and soon reaches the southern end of the Tecolote Canyon Golf Course. The moderate trail from here ascends and descends sharply as it parallels the power lines. This is a good place to turnaround for a round-trip distance of 2.6 miles, if you'd rather keep the ride on the easy side.

To get more of a workout, stay left on the single track trail that hugs the golf course fence. It ascends steeply, and briefly joins the power line road as it then quickly descends. On the next ascent, stay left onto the continuation of the single track. This aerobic pattern of alternating single track trail and power line road will continue a few more times. The trail will ascend a final time where the canyon begins to swing east, and then descend quickly to a very oak-shaded spot alongside a creek at 2 miles. The Tecolote Canyon Golf Course driving range is just north of here. This is a nice spot to take a break, but watch out for poison oak.

The trail winds this way and that through the trees, and then crosses our old friend, the power line road, at 2.3 miles. Cattails and willows guard the creek along this stretch of trail. At 2.4 miles, the trail crosses the creek, which could be impassible in wetter times. Just beyond the crossing the trail splits. Stay right, and ride through a rocky section of the creek a short distance. The trail again zigzags through the small trees and poison oak, staying above the creek. You'll cross the creek several more times, once on a small concrete dam. As you near the eastern end of the canyon, the vegetation turns to sage-scrub and the trail curves north (left), crossing a small drainage and ascends to Genesee Avenue at 3.1 miles. Retrace your route to return to the start.

GETTING THERE

There are several entrances to the canyon. The main entrance is on the south end of Tecolote Canyon, next to the nature center. Exit I-5 at Sea World Drive/Tecolote Road, and turn left on Tecolote Road. Drive east to the entrance of Tecolote Canyon Natural Park, and continue to the end of the parking area at the nature center. For other entrances, see Options.

OPTIONS

There are a number of finger canyons in the area that have short, but fun moderate trails you can ride. On warm afternoons, the tree-lined canyons can be quite a bit cooler than ambient temperature. One starts from Mount Etna Park, on Mount Etna Drive off of Genesee Avenue. Ride through the parking lot, past the restrooms and between the ball fields. Curve left and follow the signed trail as it descends an easy slope through oaks and sycamores. Ignore any turns, and stay straight following the creek bed. The trail crosses three drainages, the middle one you'll have to carefully lower your bike down and then up the other side. The trail ascends a small hill, and ends at Balboa Avenue. Climb over the low railing, and ride 0.2 mile west (right) on Balboa Avenue to the next canyon on your right. Pedal past the gate, as the trail descends into the canyon. The trail crosses a small dry creek, then another on a small bridge and reaches a junction at 2 miles. Straight follows the drainage a short distance and then ascends a very steep hill you'll have to push your bike up, to North Clairemont Community Park on Bannock Avenue. Right—the easier alternative, easily ascends to Genesee Avenue. Turn right on Genesee and then right again on Mount Herbert Avenue, and left on Mount Etna Drive to return to the start, for a distance of 2.7 miles.

Another short moderate trail starts near the junction of Clairemont Drive and Balboa Avenue. Park in the small Garfield Shopping Plaza on the southeast corner of that junction, and ride on the sidewalk past the last building, to the signed trail entrance on the right. The trail descends and crosses Tecolote Creek. The trail crosses a small bridge, and passes two junctions on the left to neighborhood streets (Mount Ashmun Drive and Mount Ariane Drive). Soon you'll encounter trails crisscrossing in all directions. Stay generally straight, descend a rutted slope, and at 0.7 mile the trail ends at Mount Acadia Boulevard, across from the entrance to the Tecolote Golf Course (there is no connection to the main canyon from the golf course). Note that you can connect the optional ride above to this one, by ascending Balboa to Clairemont and entering this trail on the south side of Balboa.

AMENITIES

Restrooms and water are available in the park near the start of the ride. The nearest stores and restaurants are located south of the entrance to the park.

Trip C12 – Balboa Park/ Florida Canyon

Starting Point	Florida Canyon, San Diego
Distance	3–5 miles depending on route
Elevation Gain/Loss	50'/50' varies depending on route
Riding Time	1–2 hours, varies
Difficulty	Easy to Moderate, technical in spots
Road Conditions	Dirt trails
Season	Year-round
Equipment	Mountain bike
Optional Topo Map	Point Loma, CA

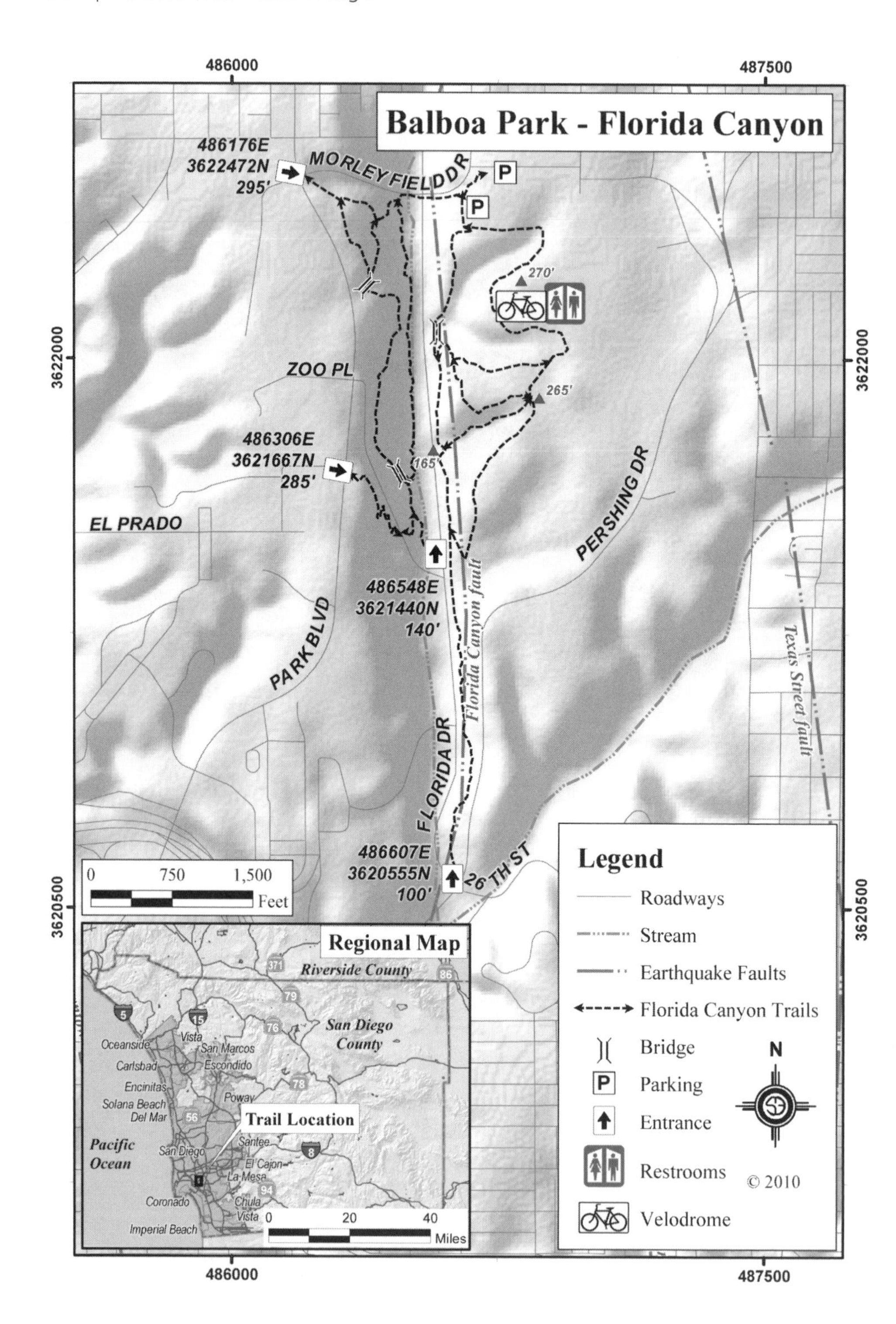

Balboa Park - Florida Canyon
486000
487500
3622000
3620500
486176E
3622472N
295'
MORLEY FIELD DR
P
270'
ZOO PL
265'
486306E
3621667N
285'
165'
EL PRADO
PERSHING DR
486548E
3621440N
140'
Florida Canyon fault
PARK BLVD
Texas Street fault
FLORIDA DR
486607E
3620555N
100'
26 TH ST
0
750
1,500
Feet
Regional Map
Riverside County
San Diego County
Oceanside
Vista
San Marcos
Carlsbad
Escondido
Encinitas
Solana Beach
Del Mar
Poway
Trail Location
Pacific Ocean
San Diego
Santee
El Cajon
La Mesa
Coronado
Chula Vista
Imperial Beach
0
20
40
Miles
Legend
Roadways
Stream
Earthquake Faults
Florida Canyon Trails
Bridge
Parking
Entrance
Restrooms
Velodrome
N
© 2010

Balboa Park has a number of nice hiking trails through lushly vegetated areas that many people have hiked at one time or another. But few people are familiar with the wilder trails found on the lesser-used eastern side of the park in Florida Canyon. This sparsely vegetated canyon has several miles of dirt trails winding up and down the canyon sides and alongside Florida Drive that can provide for several hours of fun riding.

The canyon bottom trails are relatively easy but the trails up and down the sides of the canyon are more challenging. There are many choices and loops you can fashion into a nice afternoon ride. One fun loop is to ride down the eastern trail paralleling Florida Drive all the way to Pershing Drive. The Florida Canyon Fault runs right through this canyon no doubt responsible for its linear nature and the Texas Street Fault parallels the canyon just to the east. When you reach Pershing Drive turn around, follow the trail back to Zoo Place, carefully cross Florida Drive and pick up the trail heading back up the west side. The trails dips into the creek bed and then follows above it most of the way back to Morley Field Drive.

You can also start from the dog park area and follow the east rim of the canyon south, taking your pick of several challenging routes that quickly descend to the canyon bottom. From there head left or right to find another way back up to the rim. This is a great place to piece together your own route and have some fun.

GETTING THERE

You can access the Florida Canyon trails from several locations, but the easiest place to park is near the tennis courts at the northeast end of the canyon by Morley Field Drive and Jacaranda Place. Take the Pershing Drive exit from I-5, and go 0.5 mile north on Pershing and turn left on Florida Drive. Follow Florida Drive 1.5 miles to Morley Field Drive, and turn right and park by the tennis courts or by the dog park area.

OPTIONS

There are several miles of multi-use trails in the canyon and your options are quite varied. Stay near the bottom of the canyon for easier trails or head up and down the side trails to get more of a workout.

AMENITIES

Water and restrooms are available in the park area behind the tennis courts. Stores and restaurants can be found in several nearby areas.

Trip C13 – Sweetwater Reservoir

Starting Point	Sweetwater Summit Campground, Bonita
Distance	14.5 miles out and back
Elevation Gain/Loss	800'/750' one-way
Riding Time	3–4 hours
Difficulty	Moderate, technical in spots past ramada
Road Conditions	Dirt trails and graded roads
Season	Fall, Winter, and Spring
Equipment	Mountain bike
Optional Topo Maps	Jamul Mountains, National City, CA

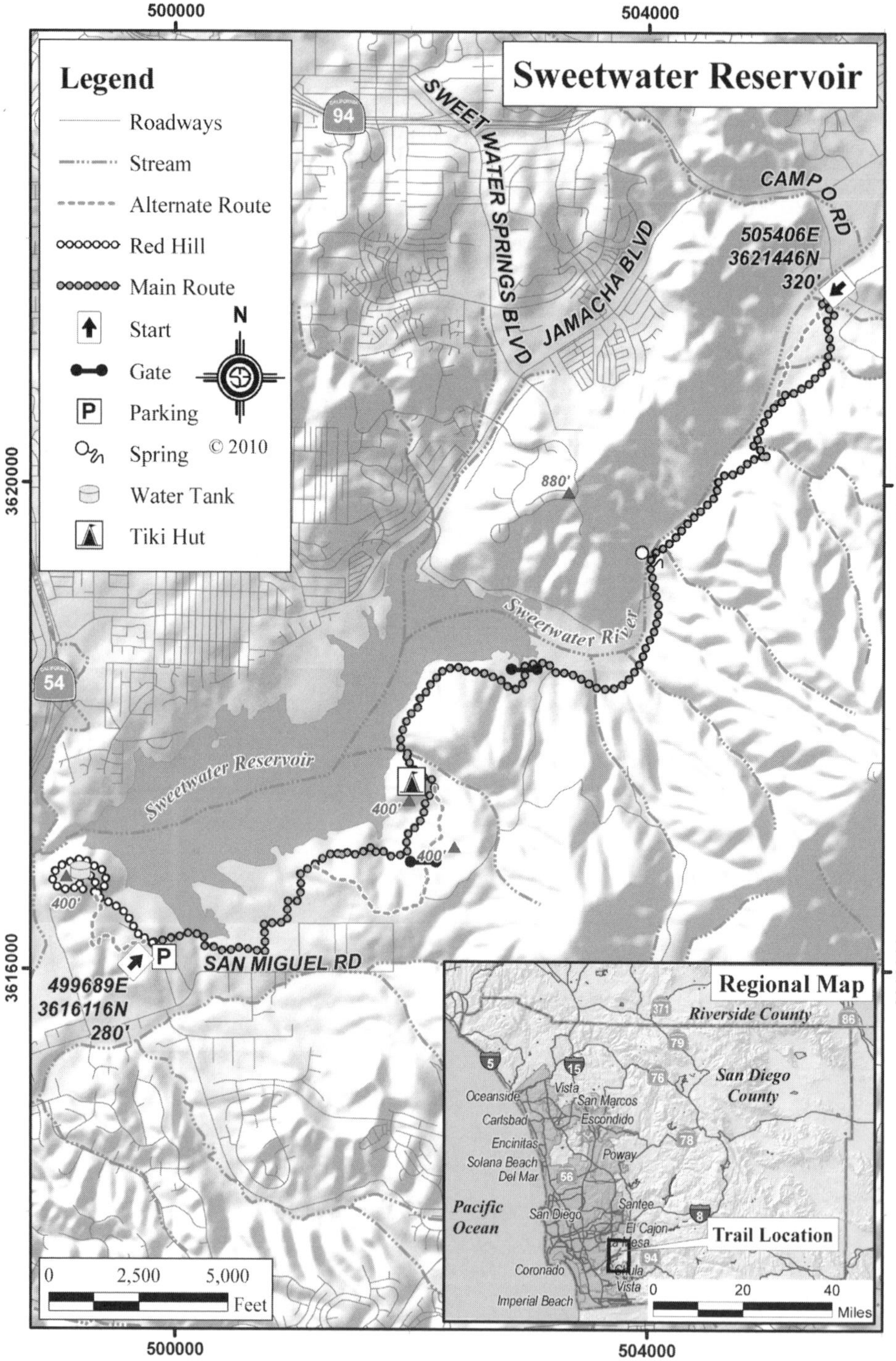

Sweetwater Reservoir

Legend
Roadways
Stream
Alternate Route
Red Hill
Main Route
Start
Gate
Parking
Spring
Water Tank
Tiki Hut

N

© 2010

500000
504000
3620000
3616000

94
54
SWEET WATER SPRINGS BLVD
JAMACHA BLVD
CAMPO RD
505406E
3621446N
320'
880'
Sweetwater River
Sweetwater Reservoir
400'
400'
400'
SAN MIGUEL RD
499689E
3616116N
280'

0 2,500 5,000
Feet

Regional Map
Riverside County
San Diego County
Oceanside
Vista
San Marcos
Carlsbad
Escondido
Encinitas
Poway
Solana Beach
Del Mar
Pacific Ocean
San Diego
Santee
El Cajon
La Mesa
Coronado
Chula Vista
Imperial Beach
Trail Location
371
86
5
15
79
76
78
56
8
94
0 20 40
Miles

If you're looking for a great place to ride in the south county area, look no further than the Sweetwater Reservoir. This challenging, but fun ride takes you on some of the trails and access roads that are near the Lindbergh Field flight path. As weary travelers are putting their seat backs and tray tables up, you are going to take off on one of the best rides in south county.

The Sweetwater Dam was completed in 1888, amid much fanfare, as a way to lure land buyers to the area. With plentiful water, prosperity in the form of agriculture and land development would surely follow. A number of cycles of drought and heavy rain taxed the dam, but construction finally ended in 1911 with its current height of 110 feet. You can now enjoy the beautiful reservoir and Sweetwater River, from the surrounding sage-dotted hills. The Sweetwater Authority manages the reservoir, and a narrow buffer zone around it. The trail and access roads can take you all the way to Highway 94. But the right-of-way for some of that extension is not completely settled.

Start by entering the road to the campground briefly, and look sharp right for the Sweetwater Trail heading east. The trail hugs the fence bordering the reservoir, and passes by a small dam. Follow the Sweetwater Trail straight past a gate, ignoring a gravel road heading left (north) to the fishing area and a right turn into an area with a few buildings.

The trail soon makes a sharp left turn and then another sharp right at 1.2 miles, and then begins a series of steep ascents and descents. Note the trail on your right, descending from a small hill at 1.3 miles. You'll be returning on that trail later. After a steep descent at 1.5 miles, you'll tackle some sharp switchbacks ascending the other side of a small drainage. The trail drops into a valley with small finger canyons running east and southeast, and then ascends a rutted slope passing through a sweet-smelling anise forest. The trail continues through grasslands dotted with oaks burned from a previous fire.

When you can see the tiki hut (shade ramada) on top of the hill to the north, the trail splits. The left branch—a more rugged alternative—ascends sharply north up a rutted trail to the top of the hill. A more pleasant alternative is the right branch that climbs easily to a small level area, and the junction of a trail heading north-south. Remember this spot, for on your return trip, the preferred route back is south (right) on this trail.

Turn left and follow the trail as it first continues north, and then swings west and ascends to the tiki hut and picnic table. This is a wonderful spot to sit and enjoy the view of the reservoir and South Bay area, and hopefully a few cool breezes. For a 5 mile round-trip ride, this is a good spot to turn around. To explore the eastern end of the reservoir and Sweetwater River, head north and follow the narrow trail down a steep, rutted hill.

The rough trail bottoms out at a small seasonal creek crossing, and then follows the fence paralleling the lake on a wonderful single track trail with a number of fun, small ascents and descents. After a short distance the trail curves eastward into a valley with the reservoir partially filling the north side. Ignore the next few lesser trails heading right, and follow the trail as it bends north. At 3.1 miles, you'll reach a pole gate and the junction of a graded road.

Turn right on this access road, and in 0.6 mile veer left ignoring several roads branching right. The road continues easily north alongside the lazy Sweetwater River, guarded by cattails, reeds, and thick vegetation. At almost 5 miles, the road curves right uphill, you stay left onto a nice single track trail. There are a few rocky spots, and a short steep ascent back to the access road. Turn left, and in a short distance stay straight onto a single track trail continuing northeast as the access road veers left across a locked pipe bridge.

The trail is steep and loose in a few spots, with a number of shorts ascents and descents. You'll then ascend to a small open area, and then quickly descend through a few switchbacks to the river and a large wooden bridge. Follow the trail right alongside the south side of the river winding this way and that through light vegetation. At the next junction stay left across a field and through some trees ending at the old Steel Canyon Bridge. The Parker Truss bridge was built in 1929, and is one of the few remaining examples of a bridge suspended from steel girders, instead of supported by plain concrete pilings.

To return, stay straight across the field, once past the small dip in the trail, and follow the trail back to the tiki hut. At the tiki hut hill, descend east the way you came and instead of dropping down into the canyon south of the hill, stay straight and follow the alternate road south toward the power lines in the distance. The road descends for a short distance and then ascends to the top of a small ridge. Bear right at the next junction before reaching a barn-like structure, and pass by a small weather station. You'll soon reach a small, flat top area with a great 360 degree view. Continue west, then northwest and descend quickly to the trail you rode earlier. Turn left and ride back to the start.

GETTING THERE

Exit I-8 at Bonita Road and head east about 4 miles. Stay straight onto San Miguel Road, where Bonita Road curves north to cross the Sweetwater River. In about 1 mile, turn left on Summit Meadow Road and follow it to the parking area outside the Sweetwater Summit Campground.

OPTIONS

There are a number of access roads that head off in many directions along this route. It's possible to create a different ride each time you ride here. From the parking area, the trail system also heads west to Red Hill. These easy to moderate trails wind around Red Hill providing great views of the reservoir and parts of South Bay.

AMENITIES

Water and restrooms are available in the campground area. Stores and restaurants can be found on Bonita Road including a bike shop.

Trip F1 – Daley Ranch

Starting Point	La Honda Drive, Escondido
Distance	3–9 miles, many route options
Elevation Gain/Loss	200' to 600' depending on route
Riding Time	1.5–3 hours depending on route
Difficulty	Moderate to Difficult, technical in spots on west side
Road Conditions	Dirt trails and rough graded roads, rough paved entrance road
Season	Fall, Winter, and Spring
Equipment	Mountain bike
Optional Topo Map	Valley Center, CA

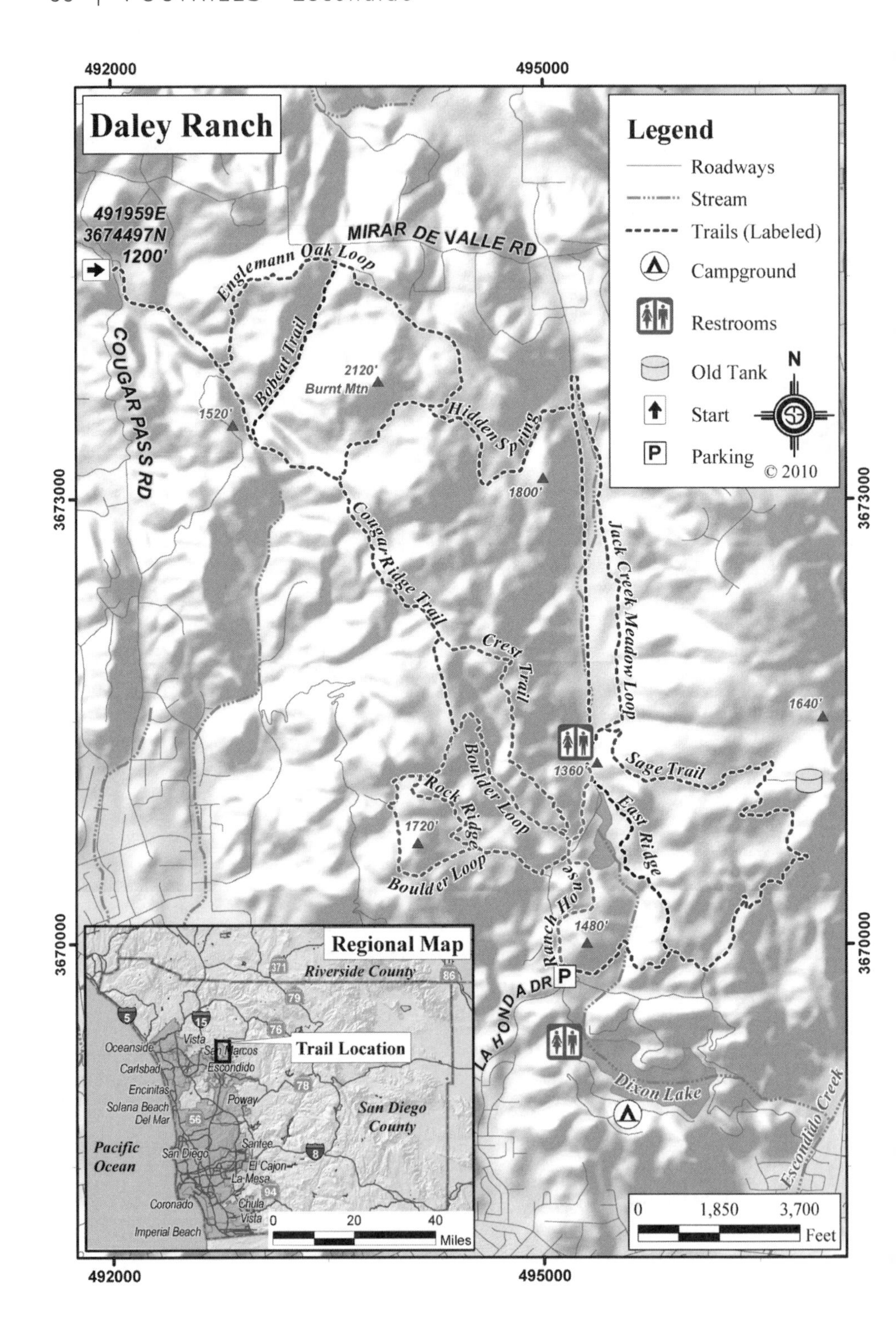

Daley Ranch
Legend
Roadways
Stream
Trails (Labeled)
Campground
Restrooms
Old Tank
Start
Parking
N
© 2010
492000
495000
3673000
3670000
491959E
3674497N
1200'
MIRAR DE VALLE RD
COUGAR PASS RD
Englemann Oak Loop
Bobcat Trail
2120'
Burnt Mtn
1520'
Hidden Spring
1800'
Cougar Ridge Trail
Jack Creek Meadow Loop
Crest Trail
1640'
Boulder Loop
Sage Trail
1360'
Rock Ridge
East Ridge
1720'
Boulder Loop
Ranch House
1480'
LA HONDA DR
Dixon Lake
Escondido Creek
0
1,850
3,700
Feet
Regional Map
Riverside County
Trail Location
Oceanside
Vista
San Marcos
Carlsbad
Escondido
Encinitas
Poway
Solana Beach
Del Mar
San Diego County
Pacific Ocean
San Diego
Santee
El Cajon
La Mesa
Coronado
Chula Vista
Imperial Beach
0
20
40
Miles

Daley Ranch is a 3,058-acre conservation area located in the northeastern portion of Escondido. The City of Escondido purchased the land in 1996, to prevent developers from turning it into a sea of houses, and to preserve it as a biologically unique and diverse area. The ranch includes oak woodlands, coastal sage-scrub, chaparral, grasslands, and riparian areas. Daley Ranch has over 20 miles of multi-use trails for hikers, mountain bikers, and equestrians.

There are many trails to choose from ranging from easy in the valley, to moderate on the east side, and moderate to difficult on the west side. Novices to experienced riders are sure to find trails that will suit them. The map shows a number of trails and loops that are described below. Feel free to explore and link together your own ride, and remember to yield the trail to hikers and equestrians so mountain bikers may continue to enjoy the area.

To explore the east loops, begin by starting up the paved road under the Daley Ranch sign. An immediate right will start you on the Creek Crossing Trail that connects to the East Ridge and Sage Trails. After 0.6 mile, the East Ridge joins from the left. It ascends two moderate hills over about 1 mile, and then descends to the Ranch House area.

To take the longer 3.5-mile Sage loop, turn right on East Ridge and then left on Sage. This is a nice loop that gradually climbs through chaparral covered hills, with great views of the mountains to the east and Escondido to the south. You'll pass the rough rutted road to the old water tank, and an optional climb to Stanley Peak, cruise west through a beautiful valley past a small pond, and then descend quickly to the valley floor. Two small single track trails, Diamond Back and Coyote Run, crisscross between East Ridge and Sage. You can shorten or lengthen your ride using these fun trails.

To ride the central valley, begin by starting up the rough paved Ranch House Road, and follow it over a nice warm-up hill. Continue straight to the ranch house area, passing the two trailheads for Boulder Loop on your left. Robert Daley, a young English immigrant, settled in this valley in 1869 and built a small log cabin. Later he built a small pine house that is still standing on a small hill across from the current Daley ranch house that was built in 1928.

Continuing north, the road turns to dirt and the trail splits just past the last of the buildings. Follow the right Jack Creek Meadow Loop trail 1.75 miles over rolling terrain, past a number of large Engelmann oak trees. In the spring, wildflowers pave some of the areas alongside the trail. At the end of the valley, swing left and follow the trail 1.4 miles back through tall grasses, to the ranch house area. Several small hills make this side of the trail more interesting.

To explore the more difficult loops on the west ridge, you've got some climbing ahead of you. However, from the top of Cougar Ridge you can see the Palomar range, the Cuyamaca peaks, and Mount Woodson, so it is well worth the effort. You can reach the western side from the main Ranch House Road (or from Cougar Pass Road, see Getting There below). From the main parking area, follow paved Ranch House Road north, and take the second Boulder Loop left (the first Boulder Loop road is much steeper, and more fun to come down at the end of your ride). The Crest Trail exits immediately on your right. Continue straight ahead, and follow the trail as it climbs alongside a small valley to the junction of Cougar Ridge and Boulder Loop. Left here completes the 2.4-mile Boulder Loop, with a white-knuckle final downhill (stay left toward the bottom).

To continue to the Engelmann Oak Loop, turn right at the junction instead, and follow undulating Cougar Ridge road. You can continue 1.3 miles to Engelmann Oak Trail, or exit to the right in 0.4 mile on the Crest Trail. The Crest Trail follows the spine of the ridge south between the valley and Cougar Ridge with a final, slalom-like downhill, back to the bottom of Boulder Loop.

If you've chosen to continue, follow Cougar Ridge 1.3 miles to the junction of the Engelmann Oak Loop. The loop circumnavigates boulder-covered Burnt Mountain, and returns to this junction in 3.3 miles, with 540' of elevation gain and loss. The recommended route is counter-clockwise, with a long thigh burner climb back up the trail on your left.

Stay right on the Engelmann Oak Trail, as it heads eastward through chaparral and coast live oaks, and then begins to descend as it curves west around Burnt Mountain. The trail passes through a beautiful valley with Engelmann oaks dotting the landscape. A shortcut on Bobcat Trail heads left though a beautiful 1 mile chaparral and live oak covered ravine, which is highly recommended. You'll then steeply ascend rutted Cougar Ridge Trail. Bear right at the top to continue on Cougar Ridge, to the exhilarating downhill eastern end of Boulder Loop Trail.

GETTING THERE

Daley Ranch is located in the northeastern portion of the City of Escondido, north of Dixon Lake and west of Valley Center Road. From I-15, take El Norte Parkway 3.3 miles east, turn left on La Honda Drive and drive 1.1 miles to the parking area by the entrance to Dixon Lake.

The Cougar Pass Road entrance is on North Broadway. This is a rough dirt road, not recommended for low clearance vehicles. This entrance takes you to the difficult west side and is not for beginners.

OPTIONS

Many ride options are available. The description above lists several of the more popular loops, but many more routes of various lengths and difficulties are easy to link together.

AMENITIES

Restrooms and water are available at Dixon Lake, however, a day use fee may apply if you drive in. Portable toilets are available just north of the ranch house, but no water. Stores and restaurants are located on El Norte Parkway near I-15. Dixon Lake provides camping spots for tents and RVs.

Trip F2 – Elfin Forest

Starting Point	Elfin Forest, Escondido
Distance	3–10 miles depending on route
Elevation Gain/Loss	715'/715', 10% grade "Way Up" trail, others vary
Riding Time	2–4 hours, varies
Difficulty	Moderate to Difficult, technical in spots
Road Conditions	Rough, rutted dirt trails and rough graded dirt roads
Season	Fall, Winter, and Spring
Equipment	Mountain bike
Optional Topo Map	Rancho Santa Fe, CA

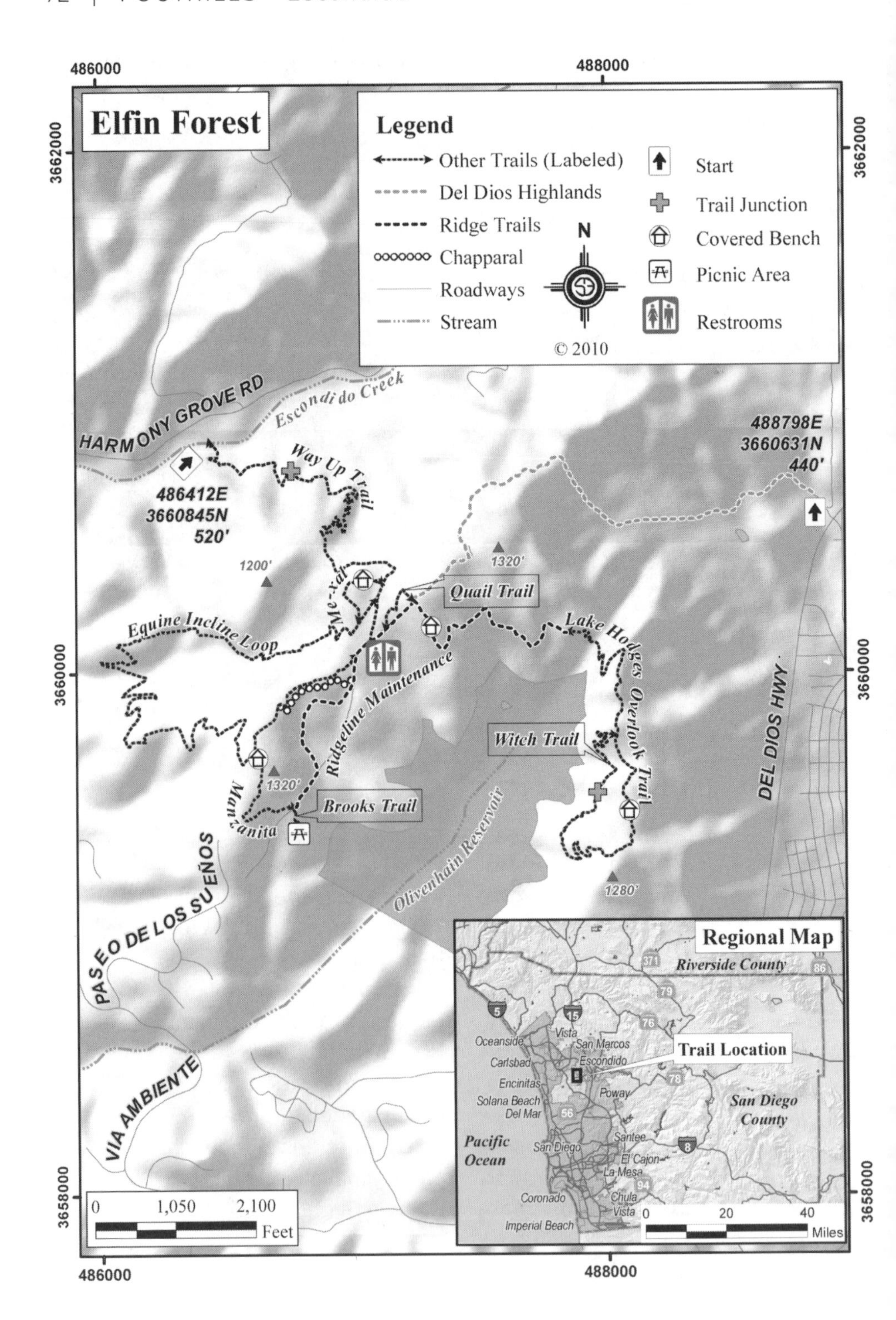
Elfin Forest
Legend
Other Trails (Labeled)
Del Dios Highlands
Ridge Trails
Chapparal
Roadways
Stream
Start
Trail Junction
Covered Bench
Picnic Area
Restrooms
N
© 2010
HARMONY GROVE RD
Escondido Creek
Way Up Trail
486412E
3660845N
520'
488798E
3660631N
440'
1200'
1320'
Quail Trail
Me-xal
Equine Incline Loop
Lake Hodges Overlook Trail
Ridgeline Maintenance
Witch Trail
Brooks Trail
Manzanita
1320'
1280'
Olivenhain Reservoir
DEL DIOS HWY
PASEO DE LOS SUEÑOS
VIA AMBIENTE
0 1,050 2,100 Feet
Regional Map
Riverside County
Trail Location
Oceanside
Vista
San Marcos
Carlsbad
Escondido
Encinitas
Poway
Solana Beach
Del Mar
San Diego County
Pacific Ocean
San Diego
Santee
El Cajon
La Mesa
Coronado
Chula Vista
Imperial Beach
0 20 40 Miles
486000
488000
3662000
3660000
3658000

Elfin Forest conjures up images of elves dancing among multi-colored, lichen covered trees. However, Elfin Forest actually refers to the term naturalists use to describe the vegetation that used to cover most of southern California. It is sometimes called chaparral, coastal scrub, and elfin-wood, and provides refuge for many plants and animals including a number of endangered species.

The Elfin Forest Recreational Reserve provides 11 miles of hiking, mountain biking, and equestrian trails with many scenic overlooks and picnic areas. The Reserve includes native plant communities such as oak woodland, oak riparian, coastal sage scrub and chaparral. Remember to watch your speed and always yield to hikers and equestrians so bicyclists may continue to use the trails.

Start from the staging area, and follow the trail across the bridge over delightful Escondido Creek. The creek forms a wildlife corridor from Harmony Grove to Carlsbad. Dawdle while you can, because the trail quickly begins climbing. Switchbacks and rock water bars make the climb challenging, and all but the most experienced riders will put a foot or two down now and then, before reaching the summit.

At 1 mile, you can catch your breath and enjoy the valley below at the Harmony Grove Overlook. Thankfully, at 1.3 miles you reach the top and can coast straight ahead to the Ridge Top picnic area, where you can find water, portable toilets, and picnic tables with a nice view of the reservoir.

The 2.6-mile Equine Incline Trail is a great loop that includes a few fun downhill sections and some good climbs as well (520' elevation gain and loss) with some rocks here and there to challenge you. From the Ridge Top picnic area, head north the way you came in and turn left at the signed Equine Incline Trail. The recommended route is counter clock-wise, which loops to the west and eventually takes you to the Elfin Forest Overlook. It's a great place to have a snack and enjoy the view to the west. From there you can take several trails back to the ridge top area.

Another nice route is the Ridgeline Maintenance Road to the Lake Hodges Overlook Trail. It circles the eastern end of the reservoir, and climbs the eastern ridge between the reservoir and Lake Hodges, far below. From the Ridge Top picnic area, head north and take the first right on the maintenance road east up the hill. Immediately on your left, follow the Quail Trail 0.16 mile to the top, which is a fun alternative to the rutted maintenance road. Continue south past the Escondido Overlook (just past the Quail Trail is a graded road joining from the left that steeply descends to the Del Dios Highlands staging area on Del Dios Highway). Follow the well graded road to the east end of the reservoir. The road narrows to a single track, and descends a few steep switchbacks to the reservoir. Follow it up a few switchbacks to the ridge, and then it's a quick ride to the Lake Hodges Overlook. Enjoy the view, you've earned it.

From there, follow the Lake Hodges Overlook Loop as it bends this way and that, descending toward the reservoir. At the bottom of the trail, stay left onto the new Witch Trail that takes you through a habitat restoration project area, burned by the October 2007 Witch Creek Fire. The charred remnants of Laurel sumac, lemonade berry, chamise, and many other plants are staging a comeback. Stay on the trail to promote re-growth of the plants. After a few rocky sections and sharp turns, you'll gain the ridge again, and can retrace your route back to the main area.

There are many more trails to ride of various lengths and difficulties. When you've had enough, follow the "Way-Up" trail back to the staging area. Watch your downhill speed and yield to other trail users. If you have some time, the Interpretive Center is very interesting and informative.

GETTING THERE

The Reserve is located between mile markers 6 and 6.5 on Harmony Grove Road. Parking is limited, and fills quickly on weekends with overflow parking just east of the main driveway. None of the rides are for beginners, since the "Way Up" trail is a moderate to difficult climb with some technical sections thrown in.

From San Marcos/Escondido, take I-78 to the Nordahl Road exit and turn south. After the Mission Road intersection Nordahl becomes Citracado Parkway. Turn right on Country Club Lane, and proceed to Harmony Grove Road and then drive 1.5 miles to the entrance on your left.

From I-15, exit Auto Parkway and turn left on 9th Avenue. After you cross Valley Parkway, the road bends sharply to the left and becomes Hale. Follow it to Harmony Grove Road and turn right. Take the first two lefts to stay on Harmony Grove Road, and drive 3 miles to the entrance on your left.

From I-5, work your way to Rancho Santa Fe Road on Leucadia Boulevard or La Costa Avenue, and turn east on San Elijo Road. Turn right on Elfin Forest Road, and follow it 9.6 miles as it becomes Harmony Grove Road, to the entrance on your right.

OPTIONS

There are 11 miles of trails in the Reserve so it's possible to link together rides of various lengths and difficulties. The description above mentions a couple of the more popular routes. Feel free to come up with your own variations. None of the rides are for beginners since the "Way Up" trail is a moderate to difficult climb in places.

An optional starting point at the Del Dios Highlands Trailhead is on Del Dios Highway a short distance south of Via Rancho Parkway. It is a wide graded road that is extremely steep in places (1.3 miles, 13% grade) and only recommended for those in great shape. This area is not as crowded as the Harmony Grove Road entrance for obvious reasons. No facilities are available at this trailhead.

AMENITIES

Water and portable toilets are available at the Reserve staging area. The nearest stores are in San Elijo Hills (corner of San Elijo Road and Elfin Forest Road) or in Escondido near West Valley Parkway and I-15.

Trip F3 – Sycamore Canyon and Goodan Ranch

Starting Point	Sycamore Canyon Road, Poway
Distance	4–6 miles, depending on route
Elevation Gain/Loss	400' to 600', depending on route
Riding Time	1–2 hours, depending on route
Difficulty	Easy to Difficult, upper Martha's Grove technical
Road Conditions	Graded roads, some difficult single track
Season	Fall, Winter, and Spring
Equipment	Mountain bike
Optional Topo Map	San Vicente Reservoir, CA

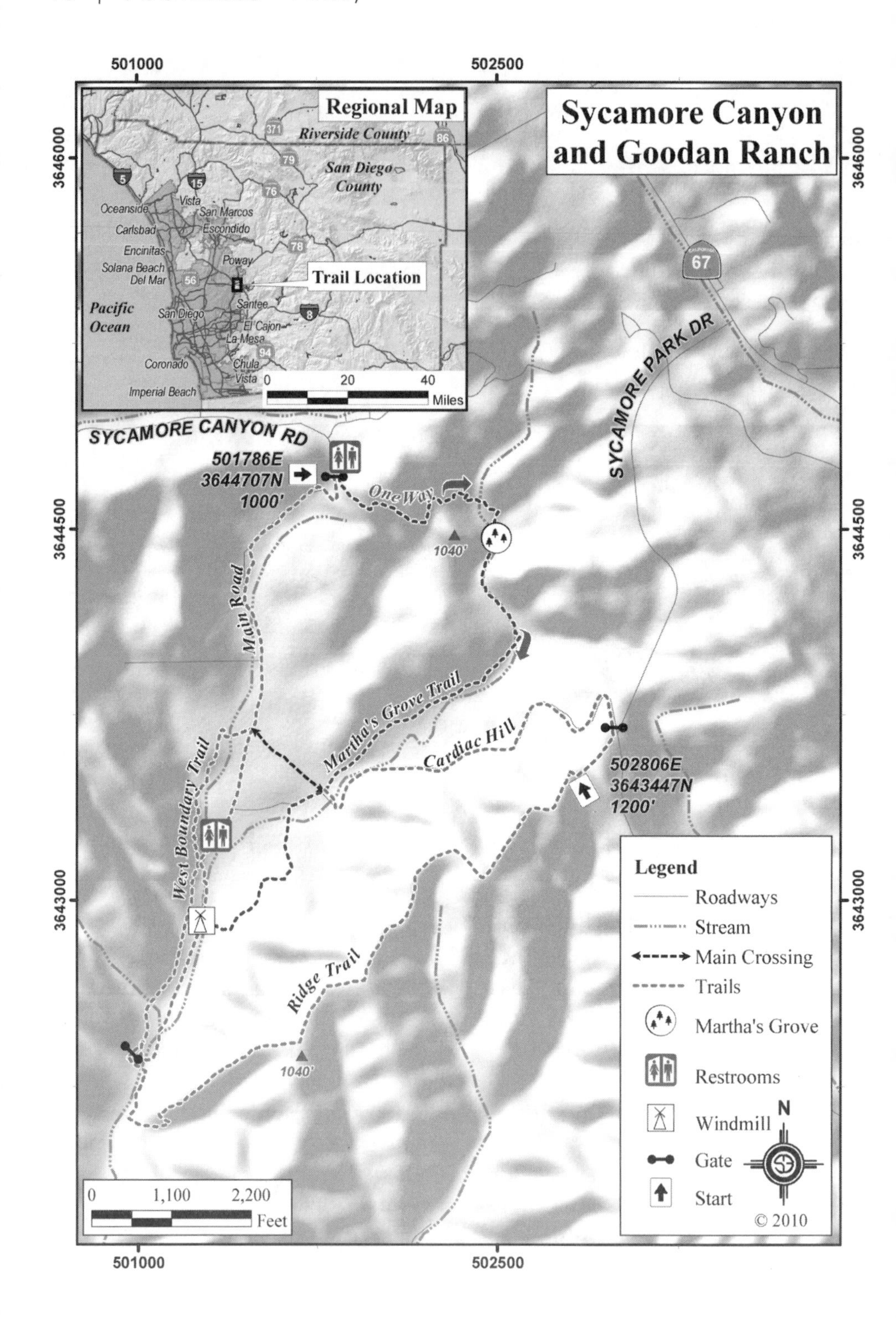

Sycamore Canyon and Goodan Ranch
Regional Map
Riverside County
San Diego County
Oceanside
Vista
San Marcos
Carlsbad
Escondido
Encinitas
Poway
Solana Beach
Del Mar
Trail Location
Pacific Ocean
San Diego
Santee
El Cajon
La Mesa
Coronado
Chula Vista
Imperial Beach
0 20 40 Miles
SYCAMORE CANYON RD
SYCAMORE PARK DR
501786E
3644707N
1000'
One Way
1040'
Main Road
Martha's Grove Trail
Cardiac Hill
West Boundary Trail
502806E
3643447N
1200'
Ridge Trail
1040'
0 1,100 2,200 Feet
Legend
Roadways
Stream
Main Crossing
Trails
Martha's Grove
Restrooms
Windmill
Gate
Start
N
© 2010
501000
502500
3646000
3644500
3643000

You would never know driving through busy, noisy Poway that a few miles south is a quiet canyon that was once a ranch in the late 1930s. The 325-acre Goodan Ranch, along with the 1700 acre Sycamore Canyon Open Space Preserve that borders the ranch, provides a valuable resource to protect the abundant plant and animal life in the canyon. Coast live oaks and olive trees along with scrub-covered hills once provided a scenic landscape for equestrians, hikers, and bicyclists. The 2003 Cedar Fire destroyed the entire preserve, including the early 1900s barn and the original ranch house. The new Goodan Ranch Center was opened in 2007, and designed to have limited impact on the environment. There are plans to eventually connect Goodan Ranch to Mission Trails Regional Park.

There are several trails to choose from in the preserve, ranging from relatively easy in the canyon bottom, to the moderate Ridge Trail, to the difficult and somewhat technical upper Martha's Grove Trail. Novices to experienced riders are sure to find trails that will suit them. The map shows a number of trails and loops that are described below. Feel free to explore and link together your own ride, and remember to yield the trail to hikers and equestrians, so mountain bikers may continue to enjoy the area. Note that some trails may be closed after recent rains.

The easiest route follows the main road south from the staging area, to the Goodan Ranch Center. It starts with a fun descent, and then levels out to reach the Center in 1.2 miles. Continue south past the windmill, to the lower gate. Retrace your route for a total distance of about 3.6 miles. Another fun option is to turn left on the mid junction road at 0.8 mile, and then right on Lower Martha's Grove, and follow it to the lower gate, returning north on the main road, for a total of about 4 miles.

The difficult upper Martha's Grove Trail is one-way, starting at the main Goodan Ranch staging area. Start by the bathrooms, and follow the trail as it sharply ascends a small ridge, and crests with a great view into the valley below. The trail curves north, and then east as it descends quickly, zigzagging through some rocky sections with small drop-offs. You'll reach what's left of Martha's Grove at 0.75 mile. The 2003 wildfires burned all of the beautiful trees that once shaded this area, but the vegetation is staging a comeback. From here, the fun trail ascends and descends, and reaches the junction of Cardiac Hill at 1.7 miles. Left here ascends the moderate 1.1 mile graded road to the upper staging area. The trail is completely exposed and not much fun on a warm day, but leads to the moderate Ridge Trail.

Continue straight on Martha's Grove Trail as it descends along the eastern side of the valley, and ends at the windmill by the main road. The Ranch Center and restrooms are a short 0.17 mile to the right. To continue the loop, turn left and descend 0.4 mile to the lower gate. Turn right and follow either the West Boundary Trail or the main road north. From the Ranch Center, it's 1.2 miles, with a moderate last ascent to the staging area for a loop distance of about 4.3 miles.

The moderate Ridge Trail starts from the upper Highway 67 staging area. The trail follows the east ridge above the valley, as it moderately ascends and descends a number of small hills. Soon the trail starts shedding elevation quickly on a rutted trail, and swings north to intersect the canyon bottom. Turn right to reach the lower gate, and continue north on either the West Boundary Trail or the main road. If you parked at the Highway 67 staging area, you'll need to cross over to the Cardiac Hill Trail, and commence the moderate ascent to the trailhead.

GETTING THERE

To reach the main Goodan Ranch staging area, exit I-15 at Poway Road going east. Stay right onto Garden Road at 5 miles when Poway Road curves north. In 1 mile, turn right on Sycamore Canyon Road and follow it to the staging area. There is no access to Sycamore Canyon Road from Scripps Poway Parkway. From Highway 67 drive to Poway Road and turn left on Garden Road. In 1 mile, turn right on Sycamore Canyon Road and follow it to the staging area.

The Highway 67 entrance is just south of Scripps Poway Parkway on the west side of the road. It's 1.4 miles to the staging area. This trailhead is only open on weekends, and provides access to the Ridge Trail and Cardiac Hill to Martha's Grove Trail.

OPTIONS

Many ride options are available. The description above lists several of the more popular loops, but many more routes of various lengths and difficulties are easy to link together.

AMENITIES

Portable toilets are available at the Goodan Ranch staging area. Restrooms and water are available at the Goodan Ranch Center in the preserve. Restaurants and stores are available on Poway Road.

Trip F4 – Lake Poway and Twin Peaks

Starting Point	Lake Poway
Distance	11 miles
Elevation Gain/Loss	550'/550'
Riding Time	3 hours
Difficulty	Moderate, technical in spots on Del Poniente Trail
Road Conditions	Dirt trails and roads, 2.6 miles paved
Season	Year-round, but can be warm in summer
Equipment	Mountain bike
Optional Topo Maps	Escondido, Poway, CA

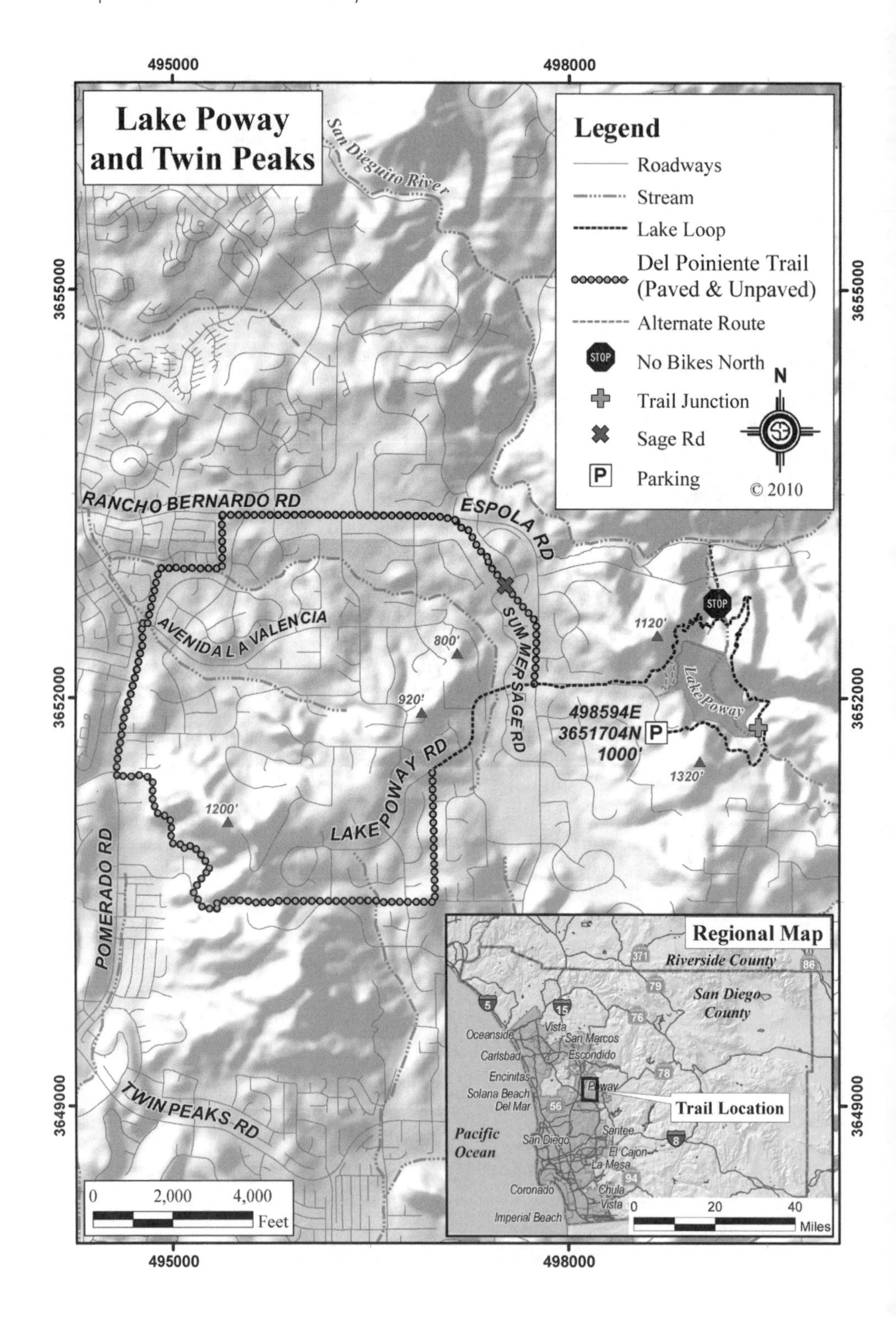

Lake Poway and Twin Peaks
Legend
Roadways
Stream
Lake Loop
Del Poiniente Trail (Paved & Unpaved)
Alternate Route
No Bikes North
Trail Junction
Sage Rd
Parking
N
© 2010
495000
498000
3655000
3652000
3649000
San Dieguito River
RANCHO BERNARDO RD
ESPOLA RD
AVENIDA LA VALENCIA
SUMMER SAGE RD
LAKE POWAY RD
POMERADO RD
TWIN PEAKS RD
Lake Poway
498594E
3651704N
1000'
1120'
800'
920'
1320'
1200'
STOP
0 2,000 4,000 Feet
Regional Map
Riverside County
San Diego County
Oceanside
Vista
San Marcos
Carlsbad
Escondido
Encinitas
Solana Beach
Del Mar
Poway
Trail Location
Pacific Ocean
San Diego
Santee
El Cajon
La Mesa
Coronado
Chula Vista
Imperial Beach
0 20 40 Miles

Poway describes itself as *The City in the Country,* and it's easy to see why. The City of Poway is serious about providing trails and recreational areas for its residents, with over 80 miles of city-maintained hiking, biking, and equestrian trails. The Poway trail system will eventually connect San Diego River Park's 55-mile Coast to Crest Trail corridor in the north, to the approximately 110-mile Trans-County Trail in the south. The northern link from Poway's Old Coach Trail to San Diego River Park's Mule Hill Trail is expected to be completed soon. The time for the completion of the planned southern link from Espola Trail to South Poway (Trans-County) Trail is unknown.

Currently all trails in Poway may be used for hiking, biking or horseback riding except for the Blue Sky Trail on which biking is prohibited. To help ensure the remaining trails stay open to bicyclists, make sure you yield the right-of-way to hikers and horseback riders and watch your speed.

This ride takes you around Lake Poway, with beautiful views of the lake and surrounding countryside, with an optional ride by Twin Peaks on the Del Poniente Trail. The Lake Poway Recreation Area is surrounded by the 400-acre Clyde E. Rexrode Wilderness Area. Named for Poway's first Mayor, the area has many miles of trails.

Begin the Lake Poway loop from the staging area, and head east past the kiosk onto the Lake Poway Trail. The road climbs a bit, and at 0.3 mile it rises rather sharply with great views of the lake. Soon the road tops out, and begins to circle around the head of the canyon above Boulder Bay and past the Sumac Trail.

At 0.75 mile, the Mount Woodson Trail joins from the right. The Fry/Kaegel Trail is 1.6 miles farther on this route, and Mount Woodson summit, a steep 2.9 miles and ascent of 1800 feet. You need to be in great shape and carry plenty of water to explore that trail.

Stay straight, and soon the trail passes a bench and nice lake viewing spot near Hidden Bay. The trail starts to climb again, and at 1.25 miles crests with a great view of Lake Ramona Dam to the northeast and the Blue Sky Ecological Reserve in the valley below. The trail swoops downhill, and passes the hiking-only Blue Sky trail junction at 1.82 miles. Stay left, and begin the steep zigzag climb where you'll gain the slope above the dam.

At the top, several trails head left toward the parking area. To continue on to Twin Peaks and the Del Poniente Trail, follow the trail straight past the maintenance buildings, and begin the descent alongside Lake Poway Road. Stay on the dirt shoulder and cross Espola road at the light. Continue on a steady climb 0.7 mile to the signed Del Poniente Trail on your left at about 3.8 miles.

The Del Poniente Trail is more difficult, and follows a narrow corridor between houses. Turn right and cross Midland Road, and then jog right and left to continue on the trail. The trail begins climbing, and then ascends sharply as you near the crest at about 5 miles. Catch your breath with great views east of Mount Woodson and Iron Mountain behind you.

The trail then begins a fun descent toward Pomerado Road, with some rocky and loose dirt sections. When you reach the bottom and a T in the trail behind Seacrest Village retirement home, turn right and follow the trail through a sharp dip and a quick ascent and then descend to the driveway behind the Gateway retirement home. Turn right, and follow the dirt shoulder to the continuation of the trail on your right, between two split rail fences and on to Pomerado Road.

Turn right on Pomerado Road and follow it 0.75 mile to Avenida Valencia. Turn right, and follow the trail immediately on your left between the houses. It soon curves right and narrows, following a small creek upstream. Follow it left to Espola Road. Turn right onto the pavement, and ride 1 mile east to the continuation of the trail on your right, in an open grassy area.

The trail ascends a narrow path between houses and scattered eucalyptus trees. You jog right and then left, and soon cross Sage Road with a nice view of the hills north of Lake Poway. Follow it straight to Espola Road, turn right, and ride on the dirt shoulder back to Lake Poway Road. Turn left to return to the start.

OPTIONS

The Del Poniente Trail can be ridden as an 8.5 mile loop by itself. Instead of turning east (left) from Espola Road onto Lake Poway Road, turn west instead and drive 0.7 mile to the signed Del Poniente Trail on your left. Park on the road there, and follow the directions above for the Del Poniente part of the ride.

GETTING THERE

From I-15 take Rancho Bernardo Road east and continue as it becomes Espola Road. After about 4 miles, turn left on Lake Poway Road. Bear right after the entrance station, and continue to the staging area on the east side of the park.

There is a nominal fee of $5 for non-residents on weekends and holidays, well worth it to help support Poway and its strong support of trails.

AMENITIES

Stores and restaurants are located on Pomerado Road. Portable toilets are located in several locations around the lake. Water and bathrooms are located in the park by the lake.

Trip F5 – North Fortuna Peak

Starting Point	Mission Trails Regional Park Visitor Center
Distance	8.5 miles
Elevation Gain/Loss	1530'/1530', 16% grade Oak Canyon to peak
Riding Time	2.5–3 hours
Difficulty	Strenuous, technical
Road Conditions	Rough dirt roads and trails, 2 miles paved
Season	Fall, Winter, and Spring
Equipment	Mountain bike
Optional Topo Map	La Mesa, CA

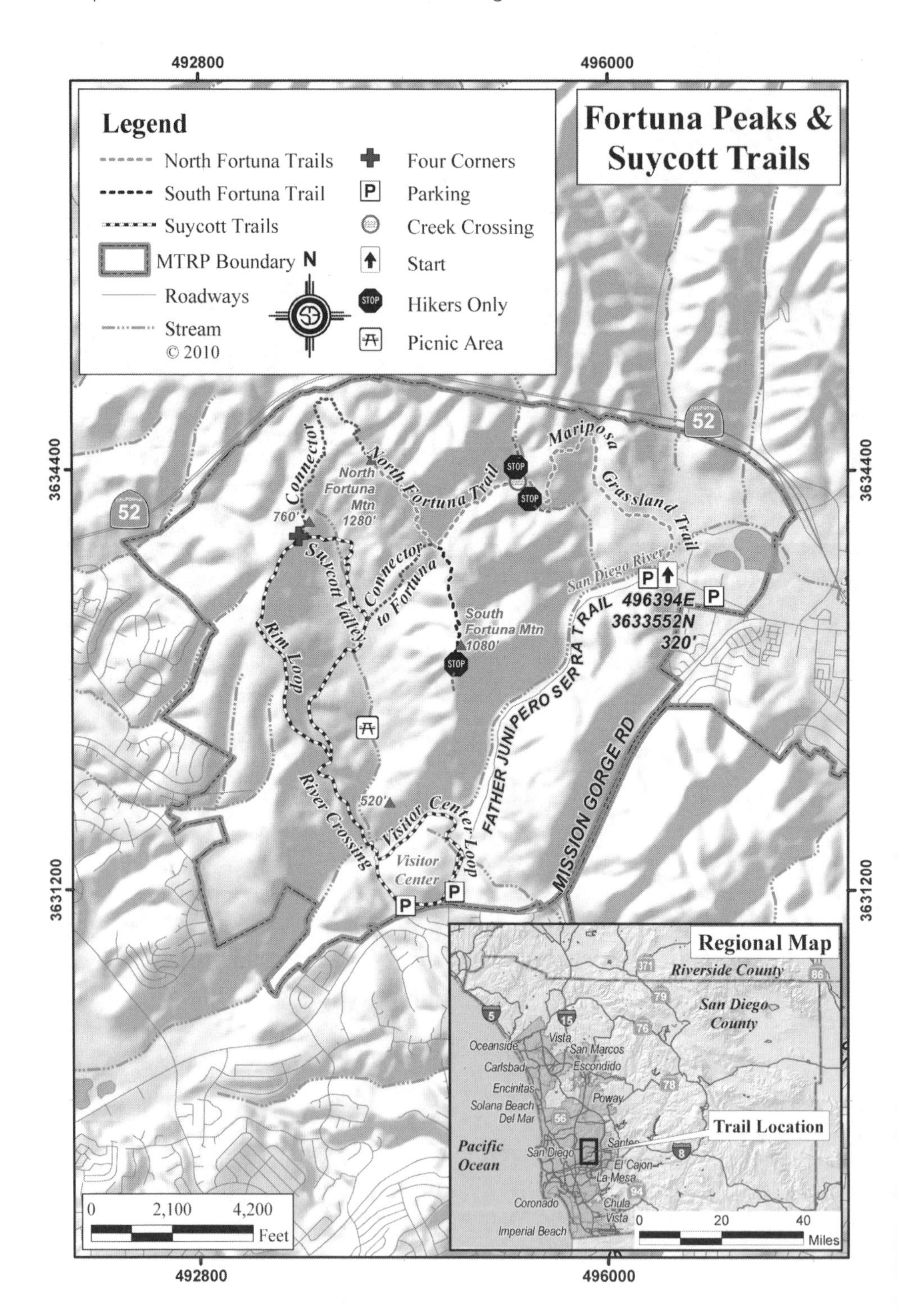

Fortuna Peaks & Suycott Trails
Legend
North Fortuna Trails
South Fortuna Trail
Suycott Trails
MTRP Boundary
Roadways
Stream
© 2010
Four Corners
Parking
Creek Crossing
Start
Hikers Only
Picnic Area
N
492800
496000
3634400
3631200
52
Connector
North Fortuna Mtn 1280'
760'
North Fortuna Trail
Mariposa
Grassland Trail
Suycott Valley
Connector to Fortuna
South Fortuna Mtn 1080'
Rim Loop
San Diego River
496394E
3633552N
320'
FATHER JUNIPERO SERRA TRAIL
MISSION GORGE RD
520'
River Crossing
Visitor Center Loop
Visitor Center
0
2,100
4,200
Feet
Regional Map
Riverside County
San Diego County
Oceanside
Vista
San Marcos
Carlsbad
Escondido
Encinitas
Poway
Solana Beach
Del Mar
Pacific Ocean
San Diego
Trail Location
El Cajon
La Mesa
Coronado
Chula Vista
Imperial Beach
0
20
40
Miles

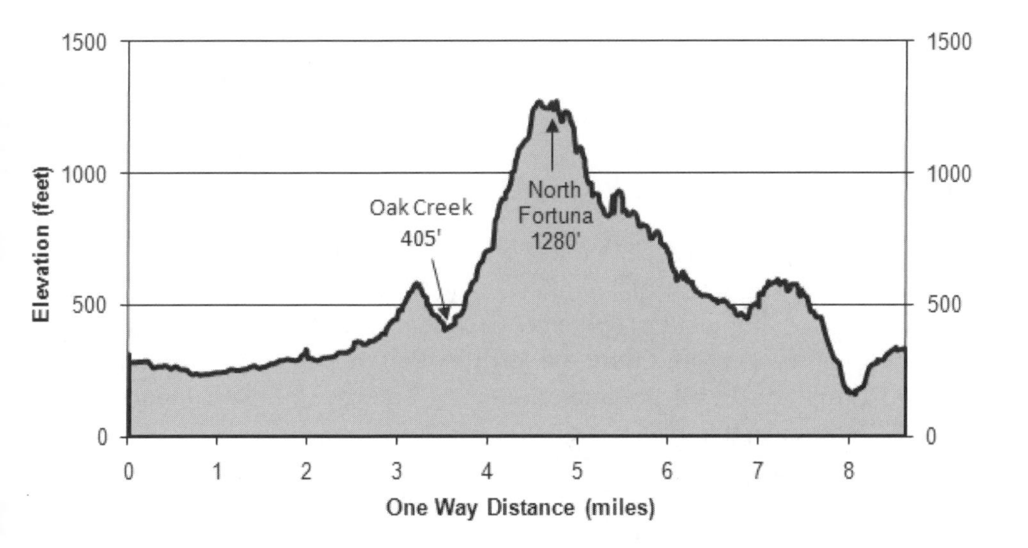

Mission Trails Regional Park, with 5,800 acres of natural and developed land and 40 miles of trails, is one of the largest urban parks in the country. Comprised of rugged hills, valleys, and open areas it is a reminder of what southern California was like before the large influx of people. Just eight miles northeast of San Diego, Mission Trails Regional Park is an ideal place to spend a few hours riding trails away from the nearby noisy, crowded urban areas.

This ride starts near the informative visitor center, and will take you past the site of the Old Mission Dam, built to store water for the Mission San Diego de Alcala, and through areas once frequented by the Kumeyaay people.

From the visitor center, head northeast on Father Junipero Serra Trail and follow it through Mission Gorge. South Fortuna Peak rises above you on the left as you cruise toward the Old Mission Dam. Pass through the gate, and in a short distance turn left onto the paved trail heading across a bridge to the Grasslands Crossing. Continue straight a short distance, and veer left at the Grasslands Loop Trail/Fortuna Peak sign and ride toward the power lines.

Continue following the signs toward Fortuna Mountain. Soon the trail heads north toward I-52 and the cruising ends as the trail swings left and starts climbing. At 3.4 miles, you'll reach a junction to Shepard Canyon and hiking-only Oak Canyon on the right and North Fortuna Mountain to the left. Stay left and quickly descend south, and then north to Oak Canyon with colorful oak and sycamore trees. Ride through the rocky creek and follow the wide, rough-graded road as it climbs steeply and then almost vertically it seems, the last few hundred feet on what some people call "Blood Hill." If you've made it this far, you're at the saddle between South Fortuna Peak to your left and North Fortuna Peak to your right. The ride continues right to Fortuna Peak, but see options below if you would rather skip the steep rocky climb and descent.

The trail to the peak is rideable in a few spots, and others are impossibly rocky. Once at the 1280 foot peak at 4.6 miles, put your name in the register and spend a few minutes scouting out the horizon. On a clear day you can see the Coronado Islands, Catalina and San Clemente Islands, Palomar Mountain, Mount Baldy through a small dip in the Palomar range, Hot Springs Mountain, Mount Woodson, Iron Mountain, the Cuyamaca peaks and so on.

The trail continues north across several small hills and a few rough switchbacks and descends sharply toward I-52. Turn left and follow the single-track trail slightly up and left as it heads toward the Suycott Trail. Continue straight toward the four corners junction and turn left onto the Suycott Wash Trail just before the junction. This fun trail dips and climbs through several small drainages, and joins the graded road from the left, descending from the Fortuna Saddle. Stay right, and follow the road as it heads southwest and then south, and ascends to meet the bottom of the rim trail.

The road then sharply descends toward the seasonal San Diego River crossing. If the water is deep, stay slightly to the right and walk your bike across a concrete slab. Once across, head up the road to the right and follow the Visitor Center Loop Trail past the Jackson Drive Trailhead on your right and north around the hill to the visitor center.

GETTING THERE

This ride starts at Mission Trails Regional Park Visitor Center, just north of Mission Gorge Road and east of Jackson Drive. From I-8, take the Mission Gorge/Fairmount Avenue exit. Head east 4.2 miles on Mission Gorge Road, and look for the large wooden Mission Trails Regional Park sign on the left. From I-52, take the Mast Boulevard exit east to West Hills Parkway, and right on Mission Gorge Road. Proceed south 2.4 miles, and look for the large wooden Mission Trails Regional Park sign on the right. Park on Father Junipero Serra Trail before the gate, or in the visitor center parking lot.

OPTIONS

You can skip the steep rocky climb to the peak by staying straight after reaching the saddle between South and North Fortuna Peaks, and descending to the Suycott Wash Trail. This will cut about 2 miles off the ride. Another option is to turn left at the saddle, and climb South Fortuna Peak instead which is a gain of about 180 feet versus 345, and not as rocky as North Fortuna Peak.

Another option is to park near the Old Mission Dam, and do an out and back to either North or South Fortuna Peak. It's a steep climb to the peaks, but a quick, exhilarating downhill return.

AMENITIES

Restrooms and water are available at the Mission Trails Regional Park Visitor Center and at the Old Mission Dam site. Stores and restaurants are nearby in Santee and Mission Gorge Road near I-8.

Trip F6 – Suycott Wash

Starting Point	Mission Trails Regional Park Visitor Center
Distance	5.5 miles
Elevation Gain/Loss	1020'/1020'
Riding Time	2 hours
Difficulty	Moderate, slightly technical in spots
Road Conditions	Rough dirt roads and trails
Season	Fall, Winter, and Spring
Equipment	Mountain bike
Optional Topo Map	La Mesa, CA

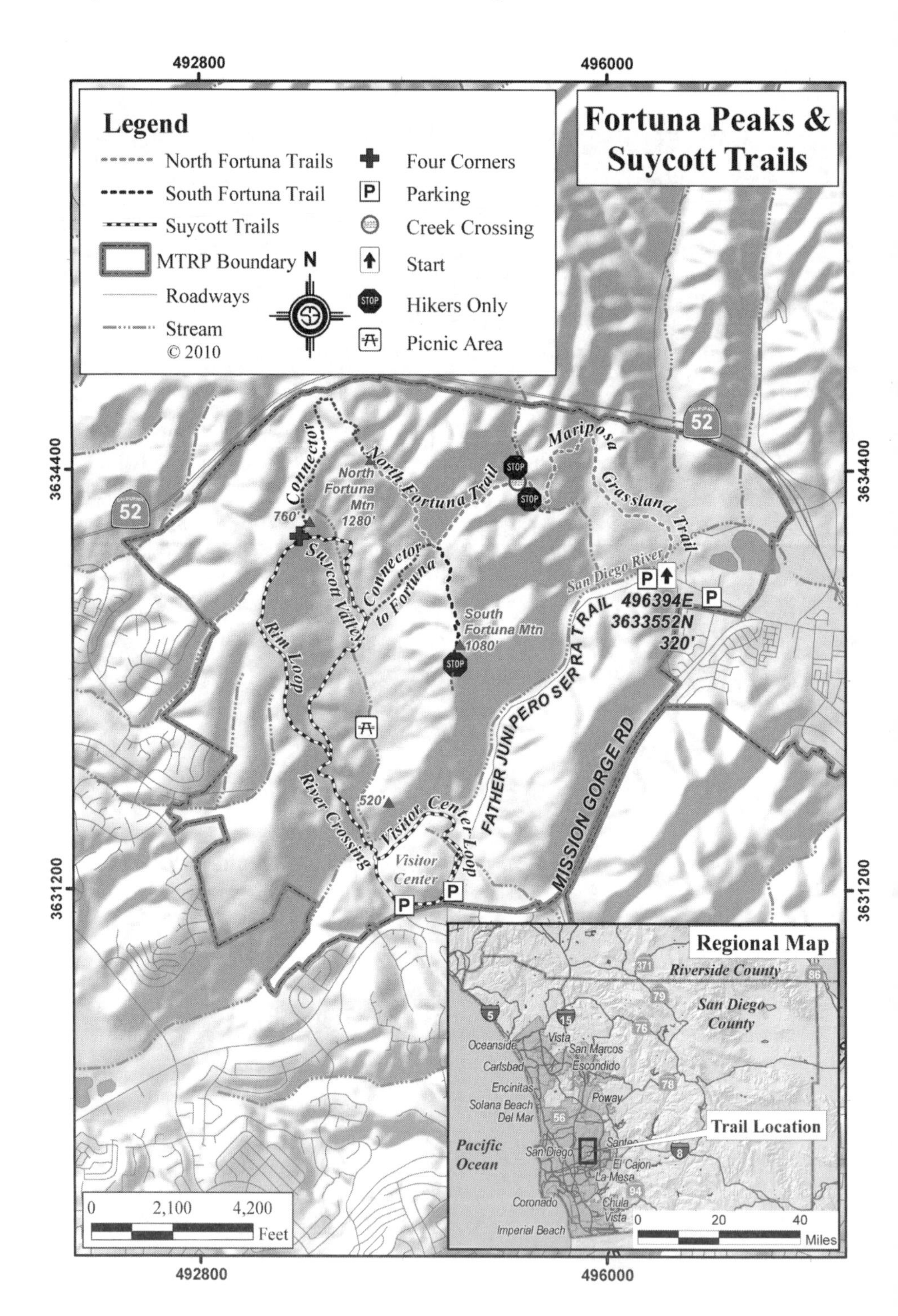

Fortuna Peaks & Suycott Trails
Legend
North Fortuna Trails
South Fortuna Trail
Suycott Trails
MTRP Boundary
Roadways
Stream
© 2010
Four Corners
Parking
Creek Crossing
Start
Hikers Only
Picnic Area
N
492800
496000
3634400
3631200
Connector
North Fortuna Mtn 1280'
North Fortuna Trail
Mariposa
Grassland Trail
760'
Suycott Valley
Connector to Fortuna
Rim Loop
South Fortuna Mtn 1080'
San Diego River
496394E
3633552N
320'
FATHER JUNIPERO SERRA TRAIL
MISSION GORGE RD
River Crossing
520'
Visitor Center Loop
Visitor Center
0 2,100 4,200 Feet
Regional Map
Riverside County
San Diego County
Oceanside
Vista
San Marcos
Carlsbad
Escondido
Encinitas
Solana Beach
Del Mar
Poway
Pacific Ocean
San Diego
Santee
El Cajon
La Mesa
Coronado
Chula Vista
Imperial Beach
Trail Location
0 20 40 Miles

This ride starts near the informative visitor center and takes you through scenic Suycott Wash.

From the visitor center, head northeast on Father Junipero Serra Trail a short distance, and turn left on a trail that becomes the Visitor Center Loop Trail. Follow the trail as it descends through chaparral, and swings south to the seasonal San Diego River crossing. If the water is deep, go slightly left and cross on a concrete slab. The road starts ascending fairly steeply for about 0.5 mile. Follow it right, and then left as it continues climbing to the Rim Loop Trail.

Soon you can enjoy the flat ride across the chaparral dotted mesa, with great views into Suycott Wash below. Ignore several trails to the left, and descend to the four corners junction. Just past the junction, turn right on the Suycott Wash Trail. This fun trail dips and climbs through several small drainages, and joins the graded road from the left descending from the Fortuna Saddle. Stay right, and follow the road as it heads southwest, and then south and climbs up to meet the end of the rim trail.

The road then sharply descends toward the seasonal San Diego River crossing. Stay to the right, and walk your bike across the concrete slab if the water is deep. Once across the river, ascend the road to the right, and follow the Visitor Center Loop Trail past the Jackson Drive Trailhead on your right and north around the hill to the visitor center.

GETTING THERE

This ride starts at Mission Trails Regional Park Visitor Center, just north of Mission Gorge Road and east of Jackson Drive. From I-8, take the Mission Gorge/Fairmount Avenue exit. Head east 4.2 miles on Mission Gorge Road and look for the large wooden Mission Trails Regional Park sign on the left. From I-52, take the Mast Boulevard exit east to West Hills Parkway, and right onto Mission Gorge Road. Proceed south 2.4 miles and look for the large wooden Mission Trails Regional Park sign on the right. Park on Father Junipero Serra Trail before the gate, or in the visitor center parking lot.

OPTIONS

Once on the Suycott Wash Trail from the four corners junction, you can head left at a wide graded road and ascend east to Fortuna Saddle. From there, the steep rocky climb to North Fortuna Peak is left, and the gentler climb to South Fortuna Peak is right. Stay straight to fly down “Blood Hill” to Oak Creek, and a moderate climb to the power lines and down to the Grasslands Loop. You will have to ride up the paved Father Junipero Serra Trail to return to the visitor center.

AMENITIES

Restrooms and water are available at the Mission Trails Regional Park Visitor Center and at the Old Mission Dam site. Stores and restaurants are nearby in Santee and Mission Gorge Road near I-8.

Trip F7 – Cowles Mountain

Starting Point	Mission Trails Regional Park
Distance	5.5 miles out and back
Elevation Gain/Loss	1190'/1190', 8.5% grade
Riding Time	2 hours
Difficulty	Difficult, technical in spots
Road Conditions	Rough dirt roads and trails
Season	Fall, Winter, and Spring
Equipment	Mountain bike
Optional Topo Map	La Mesa, CA

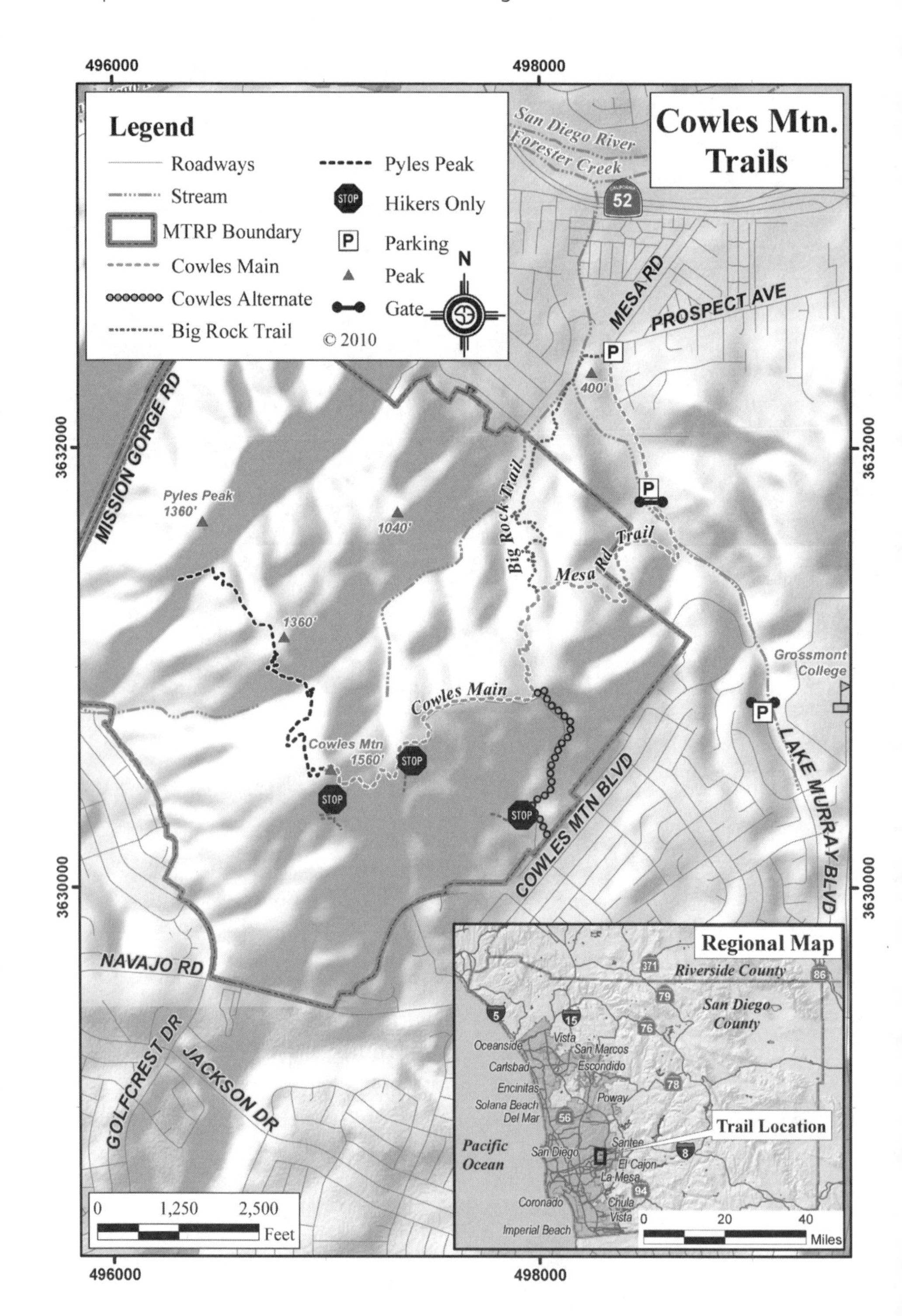

Cowles Mtn. Trails
Legend
Roadways
Stream
MTRP Boundary
Cowles Main
Cowles Alternate
Big Rock Trail
Pyles Peak
Hikers Only
Parking
Peak
Gate
© 2010
N
San Diego River
Forester Creek
52
MESA RD
PROSPECT AVE
MISSION GORGE RD
400'
Pyles Peak 1360'
1040'
Big Rock Trail
Mesa Rd Trail
1360'
Grossmont College
Cowles Main
Cowles Mtn 1560'
STOP
COWLES MTN BLVD
LAKE MURRAY BLVD
NAVAJO RD
GOLFCREST DR
JACKSON DR
0 1,250 2,500 Feet
Regional Map
Riverside County
San Diego County
Oceanside
Vista
San Marcos
Carlsbad
Escondido
Encinitas
Poway
Solana Beach
Del Mar
Trail Location
Pacific Ocean
San Diego
Santee
El Cajon
La Mesa
Coronado
Chula Vista
Imperial Beach
0 20 40 Miles
496000
498000
3632000
3630000

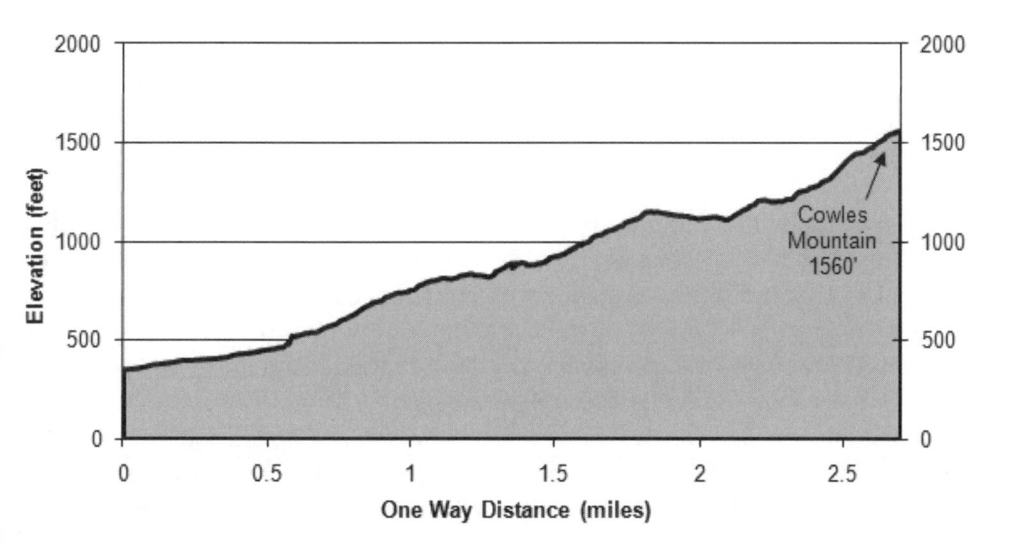

Mission Trails Regional Park, comprised of rugged hills, valleys, and open areas is a reminder of what southern California was like before urban sprawl. With some 5,800 acres of natural and developed land, and 40 miles of trails, it's one of the largest urban parks in the country. It's a wonderful place to ride and get away from it all for a few hours. This ride takes you to the top of Cowles Mountain from the northeast side where you will find it less crowded, but this route still affords great views of the surrounding area.

Start riding south on Mesa Road, and soon it turns to dirt. At 0.4 mile, a gate marks the beginning of the Mesa Road Trail. Look for a rock area on the right where a small waterfall cascades over boulders during wetter times. At 0.6 mile, the signed Mesa Road Trail to the peak heads right and descends across the small creek. The trail then begins to climb easily in places, and across more difficult rocky sections in others. A few water bars installed to stem erosion, make the climb more of a challenge. At 1.0 mile, the trail enters a chaparral tunnel that is fun to ride through. Once through the tunnel, the views to the north are worth pausing for.

The trail soon descends a bit and then keeps climbing, and at 1.3 miles you reach the junction of Big Rock Road Trail. Right descends quickly over many rocks and water bars and is an alternate, but more difficult descent on your return (see Options). Stay left, and in 0.5 mile you'll reach the wide graded dirt access road to the summit, and most likely more people. Don't let the wide easy-looking trail fool you, the real climbing will begin soon.

Remember what this junction looks like, because you will want to turn left here on your way down. Turn right, and enjoy the flat and slightly downhill section passing the hiking-only Barker Trail on your left. This trail marks the beginning of the real climbing to the peak. The road starts fiercely uphill and no doubt will keep you looking down for one more gear. When you stop to let your heart slow down, don't miss the great views north and east of the Palomar range and the Cuyamaca peaks.

The trail becomes more rutted, and begins to curve right where the hiking trail joins from the left with great views of Point Loma and the Coronado Islands. Thankfully, the peak is a short distance away, and with one more big push, the climbing is over at 2.7 miles. It's time for a rest and a snack at the 1560-foot summit, with spectacular views in all directions. You can see the ant-like people working their way up the hiking-only trail below. An optional rough ride to nearby Pyles Peak starts near here. When you are rested, begin the fast descent, but watch your speed and yield to other trail users. Watch for the Big Rock Trail junction on the left, where you exited earlier. Turn left there, and in 0.5 mile at the Mesa Road Trail junction, turn right to return the easier way, or straight ahead for the more rugged alternative (see Options).

GETTING THERE

This ride starts on Mesa Road, just south of Mission Gorge Road in west Santee. From I-8, take the Mission Gorge/Fairmount Avenue exit and head east 7.4 miles past Jackson Drive, and over the hill into west Santee. Turn right on Mesa Road, and drive 0.4 mile to Big Rock Park and park along the road just past Prospect Avenue.

From I-52, take the Mast Boulevard exit east to West Hills Parkway, and left onto Mission Gorge Road. Proceed 0.8 mile to Mesa Road and turn right. Drive 0.4 mile to Big Rock Park, and park along the road just past Prospect Avenue.

Another approach is to take the Lake Murray Blvd. exit from I-8 in La Mesa and proceed left (northeast) several miles to its end at a locked gate near Grossmont College. Pass around gate and ride down to the Mesa Road Trail noted above.

OPTIONS

Big Rock Park Trail is an alternate 1.1 mile way down (not recommended for going uphill), but it is rocky in places and has many water bars to negotiate, some dropping six inches or more. To return on this trail, stay straight at the junction with Mesa Road Trail. You exit at Big Rock Park where you parked your car.

AMENITIES

Restrooms and water are available at Big Rock Park near the start. Stores and restaurants are nearby in Santee. Camping is available near Kumeyaay Lake on Father Junipero Serra Trail.

Trip S1 – Lagoon Trail

Starting Point	San Andres Road, Del Mar
Distance	2.7 miles out and back
Elevation Gain/Loss	10'/10'
Riding Time	30 minutes
Difficulty	Easy, not technical
Road Conditions	Dirt roads
Season	Year-round
Equipment	Hybrid or mountain bike
Optional Topo Map	Del Mar, CA

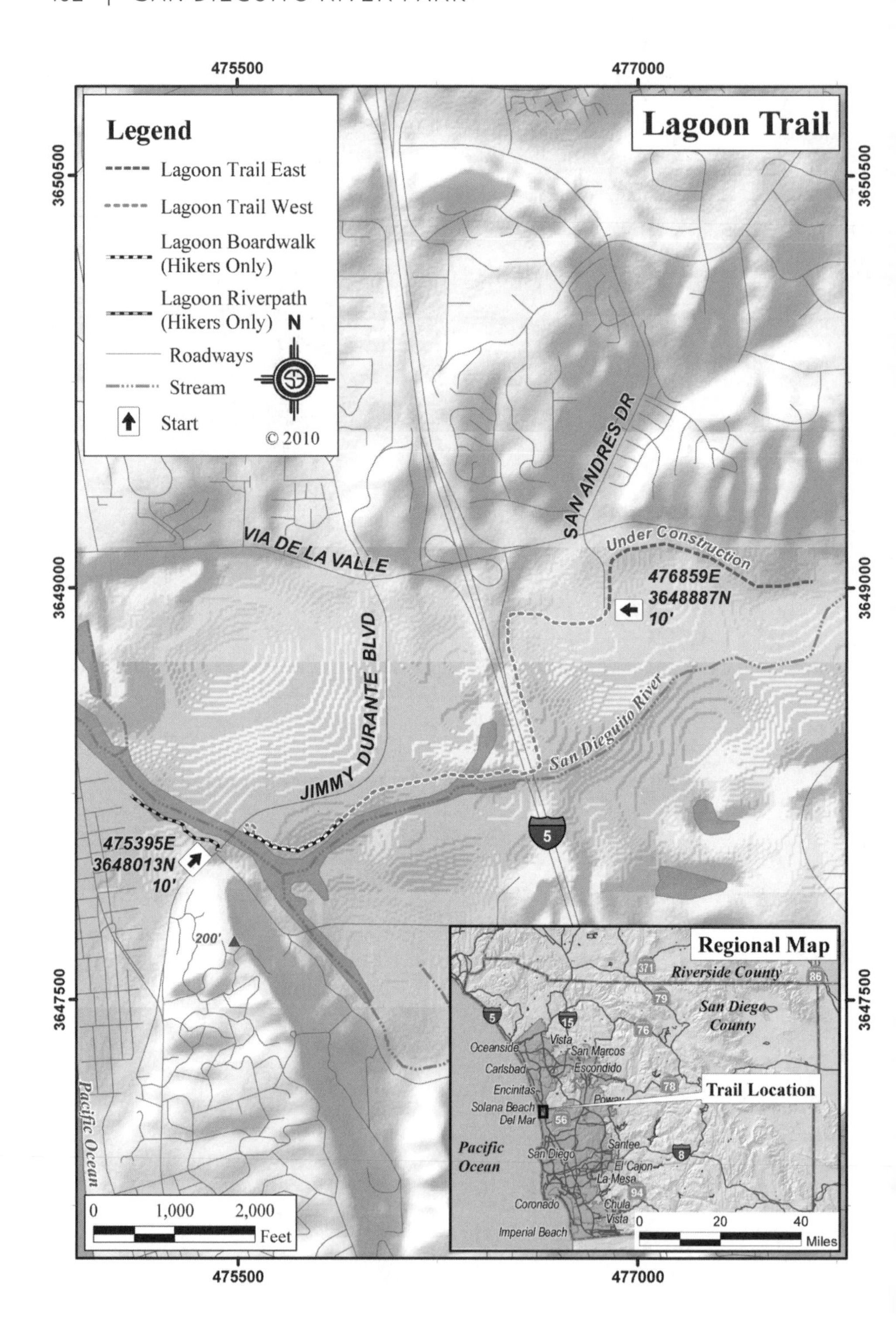
Lagoon Trail
Legend
Lagoon Trail East
Lagoon Trail West
Lagoon Boardwalk (Hikers Only)
Lagoon Riverpath (Hikers Only)
Roadways
Stream
Start
N
© 2010
475500
477000
3650500
3649000
3647500
VIA DE LA VALLE
SAN ANDRES DR
Under Construction
476859E
3648887N
10'
JIMMY DURANTE BLVD
San Dieguito River
475395E
3648013N
10'
200'
5
Pacific Ocean
0
1,000
2,000
Feet
Regional Map
Riverside County
San Diego County
Trail Location
Oceanside
Vista
San Marcos
Carlsbad
Escondido
Encinitas
Poway
Solana Beach
Del Mar
Pacific Ocean
San Diego
Santee
El Cajon
La Mesa
Coronado
Chula Vista
Imperial Beach
0
20
40
Miles

The Lagoon Trail in the sleepy coastal town of Del Mar is nearly the western-most link in the San Dieguito River Park Coast-to-Crest corridor. When completed, the San Dieguito River Park will extend along a 55-mile corridor that begins at the mouth of the San Dieguito River in Del Mar and ends at Volcan Mountain near Julian.

The Lagoon Trail is a short, but scenic trail that provides wonderful views of the San Dieguito River and tidal marshes, and is a great place for bird viewing. Work on extending the trail to Horseman Park is underway with extensions east to other sections of the trail planned for the future.

From the parking area, circle around the kiosk and follow the dirt road west as it skirts behind the Albertsons's shopping center. As the trail nears I-5, the din of traffic increases, but focus your attention to the tidal marsh on your left and look for wading and migratory birds.

The trail crosses under I-5, and follows a path between the San Dieguito River and a golf driving range. Watch out for rolling golf balls. At the pedestrian-only boardwalk, stay to the right on the dirt, and follow it to Jimmy Durante Boulevard. The current trail ends here, so retrace your route to return to the start.

GETTING THERE

From I-5, take the Via De La Valle exit and drive east a short distance to San Andres Drive, and turn right. Park toward the end of the road near the kiosk.

OPTIONS

From the starting point, the Lagoon Trail also heads east about 0.6 mile to Horseman's Park. Currently this section of trail is under construction but will eventually connect to other sections of the San Dieguito River Park corridor.

AMENITIES

Stores and restaurants are located near the starting point and farther west along the coast in Del Mar. Water and restrooms are available in some of these locations.

Trip S2 – Santa Fe Valley Trail

Starting Point	Del Dios Highway, Ranch Santa Fe
Distance	3.6 miles out and back
Elevation Gain/Loss	200'/110' one-way
Riding Time	1 hour
Difficulty	Easy, not technical, a few steep switchbacks at the end
Road Conditions	Dirt trails
Season	Year-round
Equipment	Mountain bike
Optional Topo Map	Rancho Santa Fe, CA

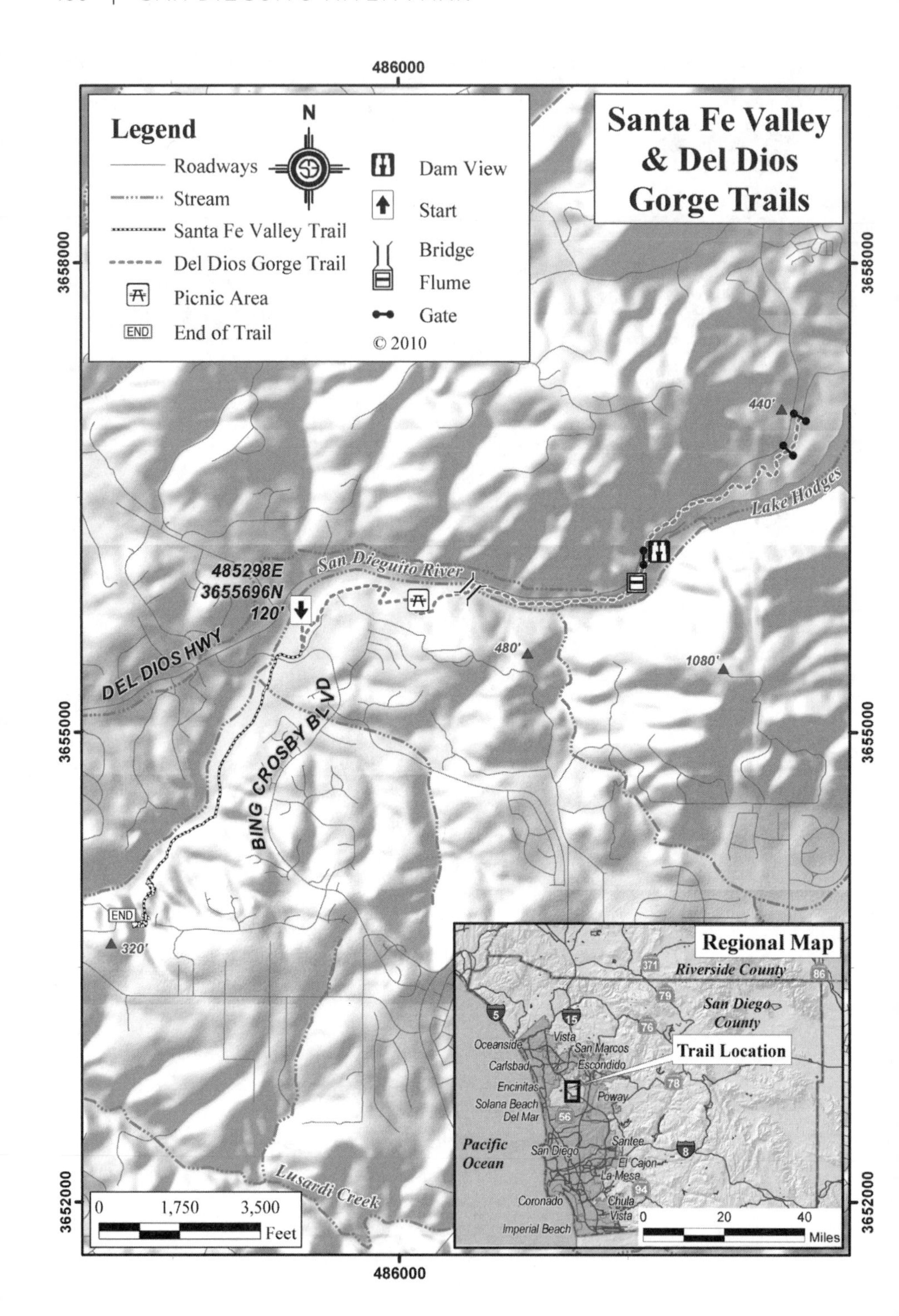

Santa Fe Valley & Del Dios Gorge Trails
Legend
Roadways
Stream
Santa Fe Valley Trail
Del Dios Gorge Trail
Picnic Area
End of Trail
Dam View
Start
Bridge
Flume
Gate
© 2010
N
486000
3658000
3655000
3652000
440'
Lake Hodges
San Dieguito River
485298E
3655696N
120'
480'
1080'
DEL DIOS HWY
BING CROSBY BLVD
END
320'
Lusardi Creek
0 1,750 3,500 Feet
Regional Map
Riverside County
San Diego County
Trail Location
Oceanside
Vista
San Marcos
Carlsbad
Escondido
Encinitas
Poway
Solana Beach
Del Mar
Pacific Ocean
San Diego
Santee
El Cajon
La Mesa
Coronado
Chula Vista
Imperial Beach
0 20 40 Miles

"Private Luxurious Peaceful" is the description for the Crosby at Rancho Santa Fe, a gated community in a natural setting with a golf course and luxurious homes. All this awaits you just past the gates, and over the bridge it goes on to say. This ride beckons you to find the real natural setting under the bridge, and along a short span of the San Dieguito River. Eucalyptus, oaks, and reeds guarding small river pools, line parts of the trail. Never far away of course, are the expensive homes and golf course.

The Santa Fe Valley Trail is a multi-use hiking, biking, and equestrian trail that connects to the Del Dios Gorge Trail to the east, and is part of the San Dieguito River Park Coast-to-Crest corridor. When completed, the San Dieguito River Park will extend along a 55-mile corridor that begins at the mouth of the San Dieguito River in Del Mar and ends at Volcan Mountain near Julian.

From the parking area, ascend the paved road south and just before the locked gate, turn right on the signed trail. Note that that Del Dios Gorge Trail starts from the left here, if you want to extend your ride eastward later.

The trail heads under Bing Crosby Boulevard and follows the golf course for a short distance. It crosses several bridges that span small drainages, and at about 1 mile the trail swings closer to the San Dieguito River and zigzags through an area bounded by river rocks. Burned remnants from the October 2007 Witch Creek Fire that swept through this area, can be seen along the trail.

At 1.25 miles, the trail begins to switchback upward to the hill above, and then begins to curve southward with a great view of the river valley below and horse farms across the river. The trail crosses the head of a canyon, descends quickly to a bridge and follows more switchbacks up the other side of the canyon. The official trail ends at the top of the hill by the power lines at this time. Turn around, and retrace your route to return to the starting point.

GETTING THERE

From I-15, take Via Rancho Parkway or West Valley Parkway west to Del Dios Highway and just before Calle Ambiente, and across from the fire station, turn left into an unmarked road by the rebuilt fruit stand, burned in the 2007 Witch Fire. The road descends and crosses a concrete ford. Park in the gravel lot.

From I-5, take Via De La Valle east 5 miles to Paseo Delicias. Turn right, and in 3 miles just after Calle Ambiente, and across from the fire station turn right into an unmarked road by the rebuilt fruit stand, burned in the 2007 Witch Fire. The road descends and crosses a concrete ford. Park in the gravel lot.

OPTIONS

Del Dios Gorge and Santa Fe Valley trails both start from the same location. You can do both rides to see this whole section of the San Dieguito River. In addition, since these trails are part of the San Dieguito River Trail system, the Santa Fe Valley Trail continues to the Del Dios Gorge Trail, and then becomes the North Lake Hodges Trail and so on, so you can extend this ride quite a distance.

AMENITIES

A few stores are located in the Cielo Village shopping center, and downtown Rancho Santa Fe has a few stores and restaurants for after ride nourishment. Hernandez Hideaway restaurant is located on Lake Drive by Lake Hodges (turn right on Rancho Drive). Portable toilets are located in several places around Lake Hodges.

Trip S3 – Del Dios Gorge Trail

Starting Point	Del Dios Highway, Ranch Santa Fe
Distance	6.3 miles out and back
Elevation Gain/Loss	410'/150' one-way
Riding Time	1.5 hours
Difficulty	Easy, not technical
Road Conditions	Dirt and gravel trails
Season	Year-round
Equipment	Mountain bike
Optional Topo Map	Rancho Santa Fe, CA

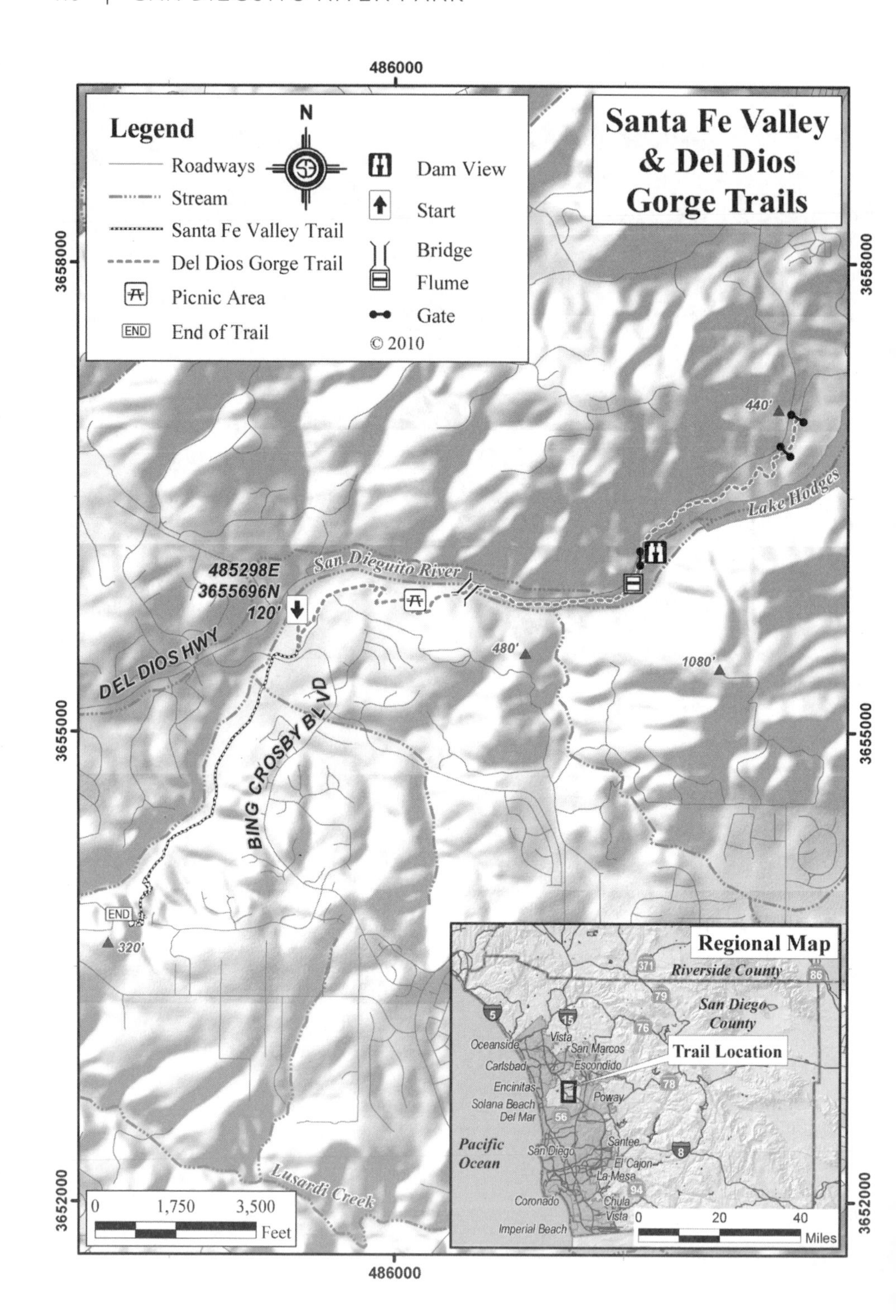
Santa Fe Valley & Del Dios Gorge Trails
Legend
Roadways
Stream
Santa Fe Valley Trail
Del Dios Gorge Trail
Picnic Area
END End of Trail
N
Dam View
Start
Bridge
Flume
Gate
© 2010
486000
3658000
3655000
3652000
485298E
3655696N
120'
San Dieguito River
Lake Hodges
DEL DIOS HWY
BING CROSBY BLVD
440'
480'
1080'
320'
END
Lusardi Creek
0 1,750 3,500 Feet
Regional Map
Riverside County
San Diego County
Trail Location
Oceanside
Vista
San Marcos
Carlsbad
Escondido
Encinitas
Solana Beach
Del Mar
Poway
Pacific Ocean
San Diego
Santee
El Cajon
La Mesa
Coronado
Chula Vista
Imperial Beach
0 20 40 Miles

The Del Dios Gorge Trail is a short, but beautiful trail that provides wonderful views of Del Dios Gorge and the San Dieguito River. It opened in early 2009, and is one more link in the San Dieguito River Park Coast-to-Crest corridor. When completed, the San Dieguito River Park will extend along a 55-mile corridor that begins at the mouth of the San Dieguito River in Del Mar and ends at Volcan Mountain near Julian.

The Del Dios Gorge Trail is a multi-use hiking, biking, and equestrian trail that connects the Santa Fe Valley Trail to the North Shore Lake Hodges Trail. Two of the highlights of the trail are getting a close-up view of the Lake Hodges dam, and crossing the 180-foot-long steel truss bridge that crosses the San Dieguito River. The bridge was shipped from Colorado in three pieces, and took three cranes to hoist into position (see the San Dieguito River Park website listed in the Appendix for pictures of the construction).

From the parking area, ascend the paved road south and just before the locked gate, turn left on the signed trail. Note that that Santa Fe Valley Trail starts from the right here, if you want to extend your ride westward later.

The trail follows SDG&E maintenance roads above the river for a short distance, with nice views of the river and surrounding hills. At 0.8 mile you'll reach a picnic area and a sign explaining the Lake Hodges flume you can see in segments across the valley. Pass by the bat houses, as the trail quickly descends to the river and the steel truss bridge.

Cross the bridge, and continue up the valley passing stands of cattails guarding cool pools of water and numerous oak and eucalyptus trees. The eucalyptus and other non-native plants will be removed to reduce the competition for the natural habitat. Soon the trail drops below road level, and the noise from Del Dios Highway fades somewhat into the background.

At 2 miles, the quiet is over and you start climbing. Stay left at the gate, cross over the flume and enjoy the great view of the dam. W.E Hodges of the Santa Fe Railroad joined Colonel Ed Fletcher to build a dam to provide water and protect agricultural areas below from flooding. Built in 1918, it continues to meet its original needs as well as provide recreational space for fisherman and boaters.

You can follow the trail as it curves left and then ascends to the dirt parking area, where people congregate to watch the spillway overflow in times of high water. The trail then heads east and joins with the North Shore Lake Hodges Trail as it descends and follows the lake north. The ride ends here unless you want to stretch your legs a bit and continue. See The North Shore Lake Hodges ride for details.

GETTING THERE

From I-15, take Via Rancho Parkway or West Valley Parkway west to Del Dios Highway and just before Calle Ambiente, and across from the fire station, turn left into an unmarked road by the rebuilt fruit stand, burned in the 2007 Witch Fire. The road descends and crosses a concrete ford. Park in the gravel lot.

From I-5, take Via De La Valle east 5 miles to Paseo Delicias. Turn right, and in 3 miles just after Calle Ambiente, and across from the fire station turn right into an unmarked road by the rebuilt fruit stand, burned in the 2007 Witch Fire. The road descends and crosses a concrete ford. Park in the gravel lot.

OPTIONS

Del Dios Gorge and Santa Fe Valley trails both start from the same location. You can do both rides to see this whole section of the San Dieguito River. In addition, since these trails are part of the San Dieguito River Trail system, the Del Dios Gorge Trail continues on to become the North Lake Hodges Trail, which becomes Mule Hill Trail and so on, so you can extend this ride quite a distance.

AMENITIES

A few stores are located in the Cielo Village shopping center, and downtown Rancho Santa Fe also has a few stores and restaurants for after ride nourishment. Hernandez Hideaway restaurant is located on Lake Drive by Lake Hodges (turn right on Rancho Drive). Portable toilets are located in several places around Lake Hodges.

Trip S4 – North Shore Lake Hodges

Starting Point	Lake Boulevard, Escondido
Distance	11.5 miles out and back
Elevation Gain/Loss	180'/180'
Riding Time	2–2 1/2 hours
Difficulty	Easy, not technical
Road Conditions	Dirt trails and roads
Season	Year-round, but can be warm in summer
Equipment	Mountain bike
Optional Topo Maps	Escondido, Rancho Santa Fe, CA

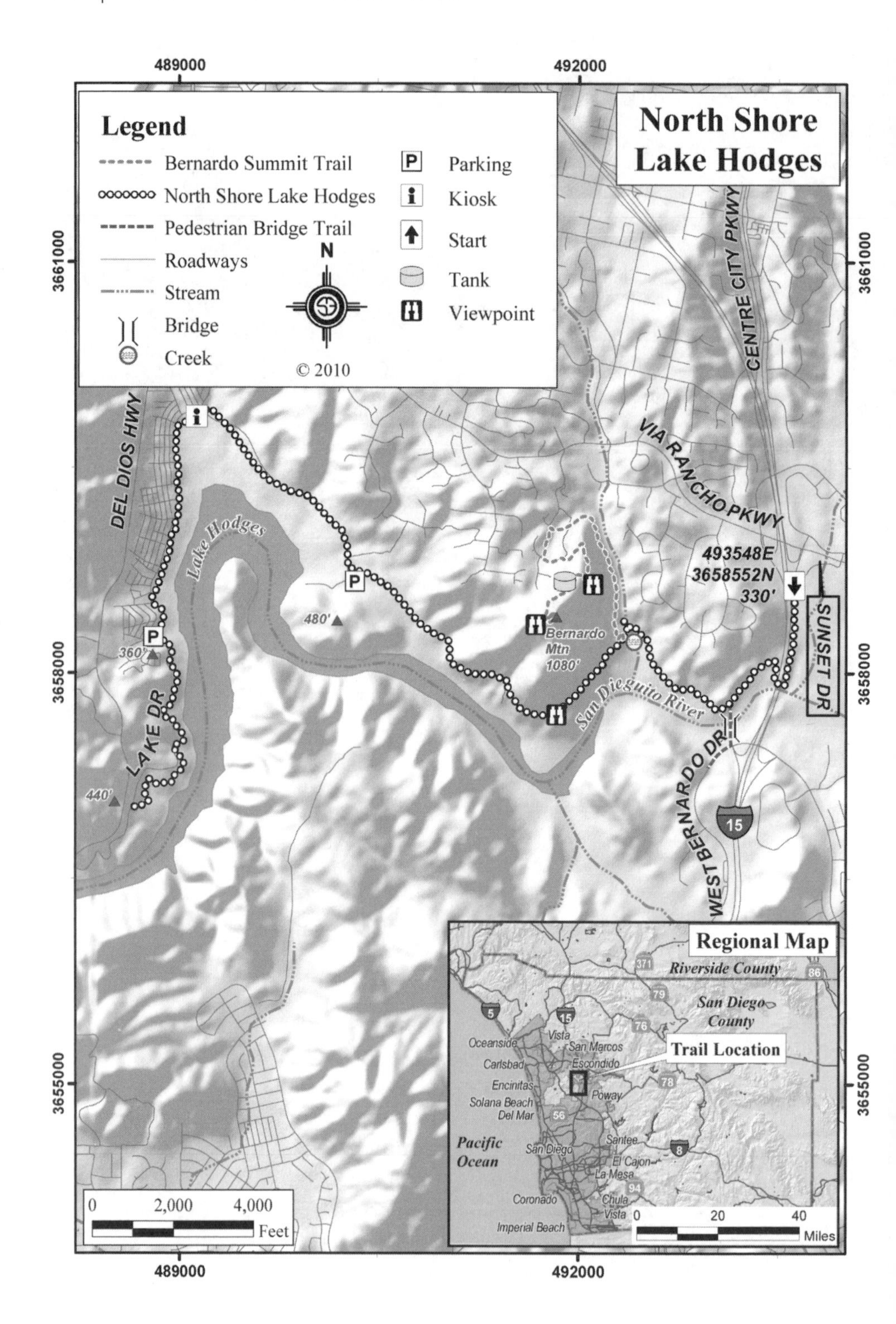
North Shore Lake Hodges
Legend
Bernardo Summit Trail
North Shore Lake Hodges
Pedestrian Bridge Trail
Roadways
Stream
Bridge
Creek
Parking
Kiosk
Start
Tank
Viewpoint
N
© 2010
489000
492000
3661000
3658000
3655000
DEL DIOS HWY
LAKE DR
Lake Hodges
480'
360'
440'
Bernardo Mtn 1080'
San Dieguito River
VIA RANCHO PKWY
CENTRE CITY PKWY
493548E
3658552N
330'
SUNSET DR
WEST BERNARDO DR
15
Regional Map
Riverside County
San Diego County
Trail Location
Oceanside
Vista
San Marcos
Carlsbad
Escondido
Encinitas
Poway
Solana Beach
Del Mar
Pacific Ocean
San Diego
Santee
El Cajon
La Mesa
Coronado
Chula Vista
Imperial Beach
0 20 40 Miles
0 2,000 4,000 Feet

Lake Hodges is a man made reservoir, completed in 1918 by the San Dieguito Water District and purchased by the City of San Diego in 1925. W.E Hodges of the Santa Fe Railroad joined Colonel Ed Fletcher to build the dam to provide water and protect agricultural areas below from flooding. It continues to meet its original needs as well as provide recreational space for fisherman and boaters. Diverse natural plant communities including coastal sage scrub, chaparral, and riparian oak woodland surround the lake making it a perfect place for hiking and biking. It's also an important link in the San Dieguito River Park Coast-to-Crest Trail that follows the San Dieguito River corridor for 55 miles from Del Mar to Volcan Mountain near Julian. This ride will take you on part of that trail, following the north shoreline of Lake Hodges.

From the west end of Lake Hodges near Hernandez Hideaway, follow the dirt trail heading north along the lake and through some sharp little drainages. Soon you'll reach a eucalyptus-shaded park, and the north parking area. Follow the road a short distance east and drop onto the dirt trail along the right side of the road as it hugs Lake Hodges' north shoreline.

The trail passes a gate where fishermen line up early in their vehicles, waiting to have a chance to try their luck. Continue on to a parking area and boat ramp, and ride southeast through a gate onto a dirt road. Scattered oak and pepper trees and lots of buckwheat and laurel sumac dot the hills in this area. In the warmer months, the prickly pear cacti may be in bloom. The road ascends easily as it follows the shore of the lake and circles around the base of 1150-foot Bernardo Mountain on your left.

You'll pass by the left turn to Bernardo Peak (see Options) and after a rough, rutty, downhill section, the road crosses a small creek where oaks and sycamores provide cool shade. Watch out for poison oak in this area. The road heads closer to the shoreline for a short distance, and passes a new pedestrian and bike bridge across Lake Hodges. The innovative new bridge is 900 feet long and is constructed using a unique stressed-ribbon design that uses only two piers allowing for a thin profile minimizing visual impact (see Options to extend your ride to the Piedras Pintadas area).

Soon the road runs into an old section of highway in use before I-15. When you reach the fence just short of I-15, turn right on a relatively new section of paved trail and continue under I-15. The trail continues on the other side of I-15 to the east parking area and kiosk off of Sunset Drive. The Mule Hill and San Pasqual Valley trail starts from this point and heads east. From here it's time to turn around and retrace your path.

Just past the east trail staging area by I-15, is the Sikes Adobe Farmhouse, a state point of historic interest. It was burned in the October 2007 Witch Creek Fire that left only the adobe walls standing. The one-room adobe was constructed in 1870, just after Zenas Sikes and his wife Eliza moved to the site. They soon added onto the original adobe, the additional rooms made of wooden framing. The farmhouse needs repairs and the River Park is restoring it. When complete, the farmhouse will be open to the public for docent-led tours.

When you return to your starting point near Hernandez Hideaway restaurant, don't stop there. The trail continues to the south end of the lake and the dam. Follow the dirt trail signed coast to crest. (This is not the dirt road to the right of the parking area.) Continue to a picnic area and a dock where windsurfers launch their craft. Climb a small hill, and follow the road along the lake and up to the dam where the trail connects to the Del Dios Gorge Trail and Santa Fe Valley Trails, also part of the San Dieguito River Park. This route is currently blocked by construction to connect the city of San Diego's Hodges Reservoir to the Water Authority's Olivenhain Reservoir. When this project is completed in late 2010, water will be transferred downhill from Olivenhain Reservoir into Hodges Reservoir and will generate up to 40-megawatts of peak hydroelectric energy, enough power to annually sustain nearly 26,000 homes.

OPTIONS

A moderately strenuous option is the climb to Bernardo Peak. This 765-foot, 4 mile round-trip climb circles the north side of Bernardo Mountain, and ascends the western slope with great views of the lake below. There are several steep loose sections and a few rocky areas, so this trail is not for beginners. From the summit you get a 360-degree view of the area, and you can clearly see the Bernardo Bay Trail and Piedras Pintadas Trail on the south side of Lake Hodges for one of your future rides.

Near I-15, is the newly built bike and pedestrian bridge across the lake. No longer do bicyclists have to negotiate the busy I-15 bridge to reach West Bernardo Drive and the Piedras Pintadas trails. The 900 foot bridge was dedicated in May 2009 by the San Dieguito Park Joint Powers Authority. You can extend your ride by crossing the impressive bridge and turning right onto West Bernardo Drive and ride a short distance to the trailhead on your right. See the Piedras Pintadas ride for details.

GETTING THERE

There are multiple places to start this ride. From the west side of the lake, take Via Rancho Parkway or West Valley Parkway west from I-15 to Del Dios Highway, and turn left at Rancho Drive and park in the dirt parking area near Hernandez Hideaway restaurant.

To start from the north end of the lake, from Del Dios Highway, turn southeast on Date Lane to where it intersects Lake Drive. From Via Rancho Parkway, turn south on Lake Drive to reach the same intersection. The parking lot there is open Wednesday, Saturday, and Sunday (dawn to dusk); otherwise just park your car alongside the road.

Now that the San Dieguito River Park bike trail passes under I-15, an alternate starting point is the parking area at the end of Sunset Drive. Exit I-15 at Via Rancho Parkway, and drive a short distance east to Sunset Drive and turn right. Follow Sunset to the end and park.

AMENITIES

Hernandez Hideaway restaurant is located by the west starting point. Restaurants are near the I-15 start as well. Portable toilets are located in several places around Lake Hodges.

Trip S5 – Piedras Pintadas Trail

Starting Point	West Bernardo Drive, Escondido
Distance	2.3–5.3 miles, varies depending on route
Elevation Gain/Loss	120'/120', varies
Riding Time	1 hour
Difficulty	Easy, not technical
Road Conditions	Dirt trails and roads
Season	Year-round, but can be warm in summer
Equipment	Mountain bike
Optional Topo Map	Escondido, CA

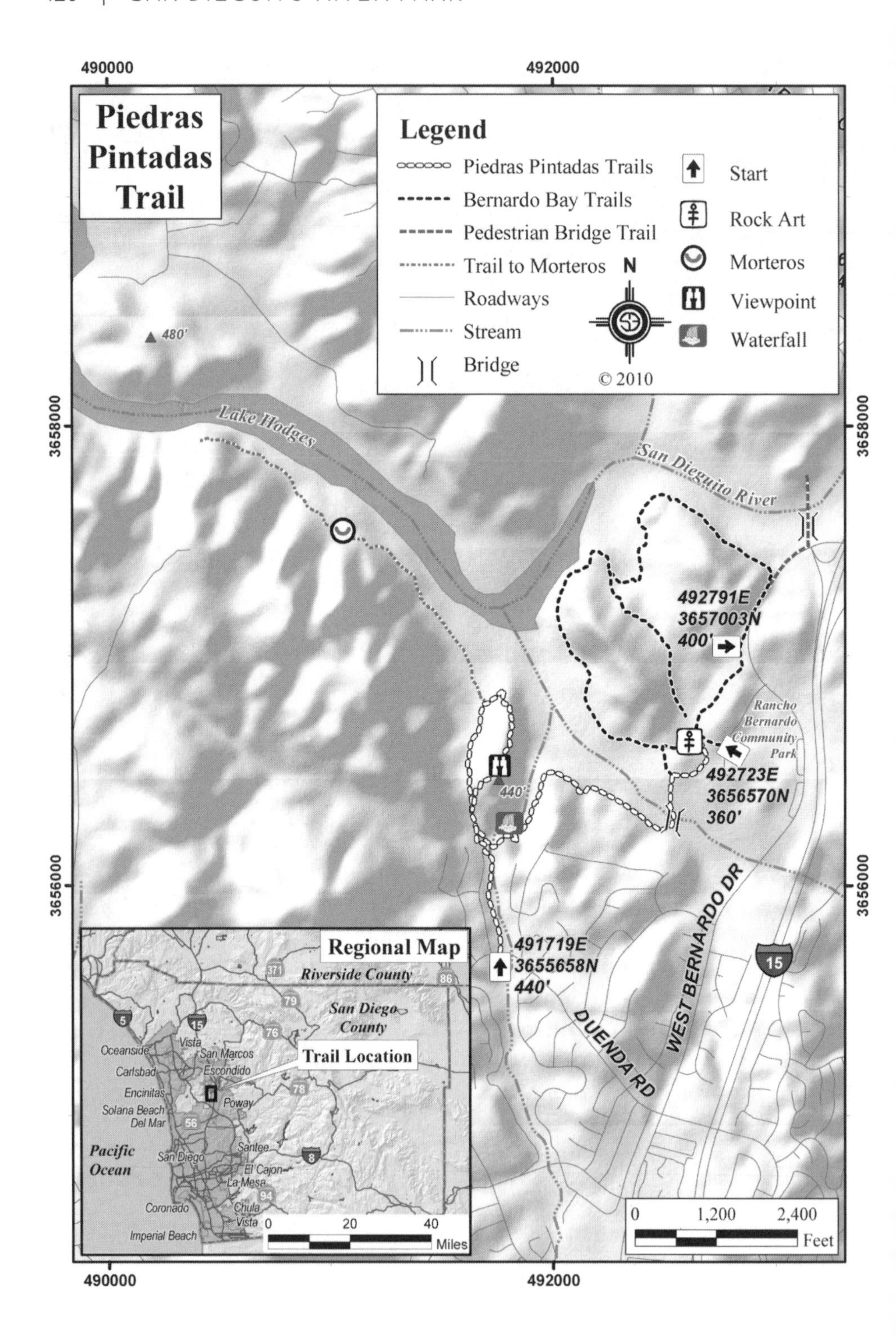

Piedras Pintadas Trail
Legend
Piedras Pintadas Trails
Bernardo Bay Trails
Pedestrian Bridge Trail
Trail to Morteros
Roadways
Stream
Bridge
Start
Rock Art
Morteros
Viewpoint
Waterfall
N
© 2010
490000
492000
3658000
3656000
480'
Lake Hodges
San Dieguito River
492791E
3657003N
400'
Rancho Bernardo Community Park
492723E
3656570N
360'
440'
491719E
3655658N
440'
WEST BERNARDO DR
DUENDA RD
15
Regional Map
Riverside County
San Diego County
Trail Location
Oceanside
Vista
San Marcos
Carlsbad
Escondido
Encinitas
Solana Beach
Del Mar
Poway
Pacific Ocean
San Diego
Santee
El Cajon
La Mesa
Coronado
Chula Vista
Imperial Beach
0 20 40 Miles
0 1,200 2,400 Feet

The Piedras Pintadas and Bernardo Bay Trails on the south side of Lake Hodges, like the north shore trail, are part of the San Dieguito River Park set of trails, and it's a fun area to explore. The Kumeyaay people lived in this area starting about 500 years ago, hunting small game and harvesting plants. Piedras Pintadas literally means "Painted Rocks" in Spanish, and the area is known for its rock art. The Kumeyaay rock art site is off limits, but you can ride the trails in the area and get a sense of what it might have been like a few hundred years ago, before the roads and homes crept into the region. There are a number of trails in this area, including an interpretive trail that provides information about the Kumeyaay and the many plants they used for medicinal and nutritional purposes.

The Bernardo Bay Trail is a loop that circles the small hill in the middle of the area, providing great views of Lake Hodges and Bernardo Mountain to the north. Follow the loop trail west toward the lake, and then north as it swings alongside the lake and clockwise around the hill. Many birds can be seen along this route, and wildflowers provide color along the trail in spring. The trail narrows around the north end of the hill, and is rocky in a few places. You can take the next trail south, as soon as you round the hill or keep following the shoreline as it winds toward I-15, and the ever increasing din of traffic. When you reach West Bernardo Drive, stay right on the dirt shoulder back to the starting point.

To explore the wetlands along Green Valley Creek on beautiful Piedras Pintadas Trail, follow the trail south from the kiosk. Soon the trail crosses Green Valley Creek, on a bridge reconstructed by Northrop Grumman Corporation after the 2007 wildfires. The interpretive trail curves west, through colorful native vegetation. The trail bends around the head of a small canyon, and passes some slick rocks with a gurgling waterfall. Follow the switchbacks to the top of a small ridge, and turn right at the next junction (left at this spot follows a small creek with heavy riparian vegetation to Poblado Road which becomes Duenda Road, an alternate parking spot).

As the trail curves right and begins to climb a small hill, an optional side trip, not part of the Piedras Pintadas Trail, heads left (see Options). Climb the hill, and enjoy the nice view of the lake and creek drainage. Trace your route back to the starting point.

OPTIONS

A moderate level trail that is not part of the Piedras Pintadas Trail follows the south side of Lake Hodges for a mile or so, and starts from the Piedras Pintadas

Trail described above. The trail descends toward the lake, and then begins climbing the hillside through thick chaparral above the lake, steeply dipping across several small drainages. The trail passes some morteros, and then becomes increasing difficult to ride as it continues to climb. Turn around at that point to return to the trailhead. Keep your eye out for deer on this seldom-traveled trail.

GETTING THERE

Parking is available in or near the Rancho Bernardo Community Park on West Bernardo Drive, south of where it crosses I-15. There is also a San Dieguito River Park gravel parking lot on the right, before you reach the right turn into Rancho Bernardo Community Park.

You can also extend the ride a bit by parking at the staging area at the end of Sunset Drive by I-15, and ride the new pedestrian and bike bridge across Lake Hodges. Exit I-15 at Via Rancho Parkway, and head a short distance east to Sunset Drive and turn right. Follow Sunset Drive to the end and park. Head south on the paved trail and under I-15. Follow the trail west to the pedestrian bridge and cross the lake. Turn right on West Bernardo Drive, and turn onto the trail when you see it on your right.

AMENITIES

Stores and restaurants are located south on West Bernardo Drive. A portable toilet is located at the San Dieguito River Park gravel parking lot before you reach Rancho Bernardo Community Park.

Trip S6 – Mule Hill and San Pasqual Valley

Starting Point	Sunset Drive, Escondido
Distance	10.3 miles one-way
Elevation Gain/Loss	560'/465' one-way
Riding Time	2–2 1/2 hours
Difficulty	Easy to moderate, not technical
Road Conditions	Dirt trails and well-graded roads
Season	Fall, Winter, and Spring
Equipment	Mountain bike
Optional Topo Maps	Escondido, San Pasqual, CA

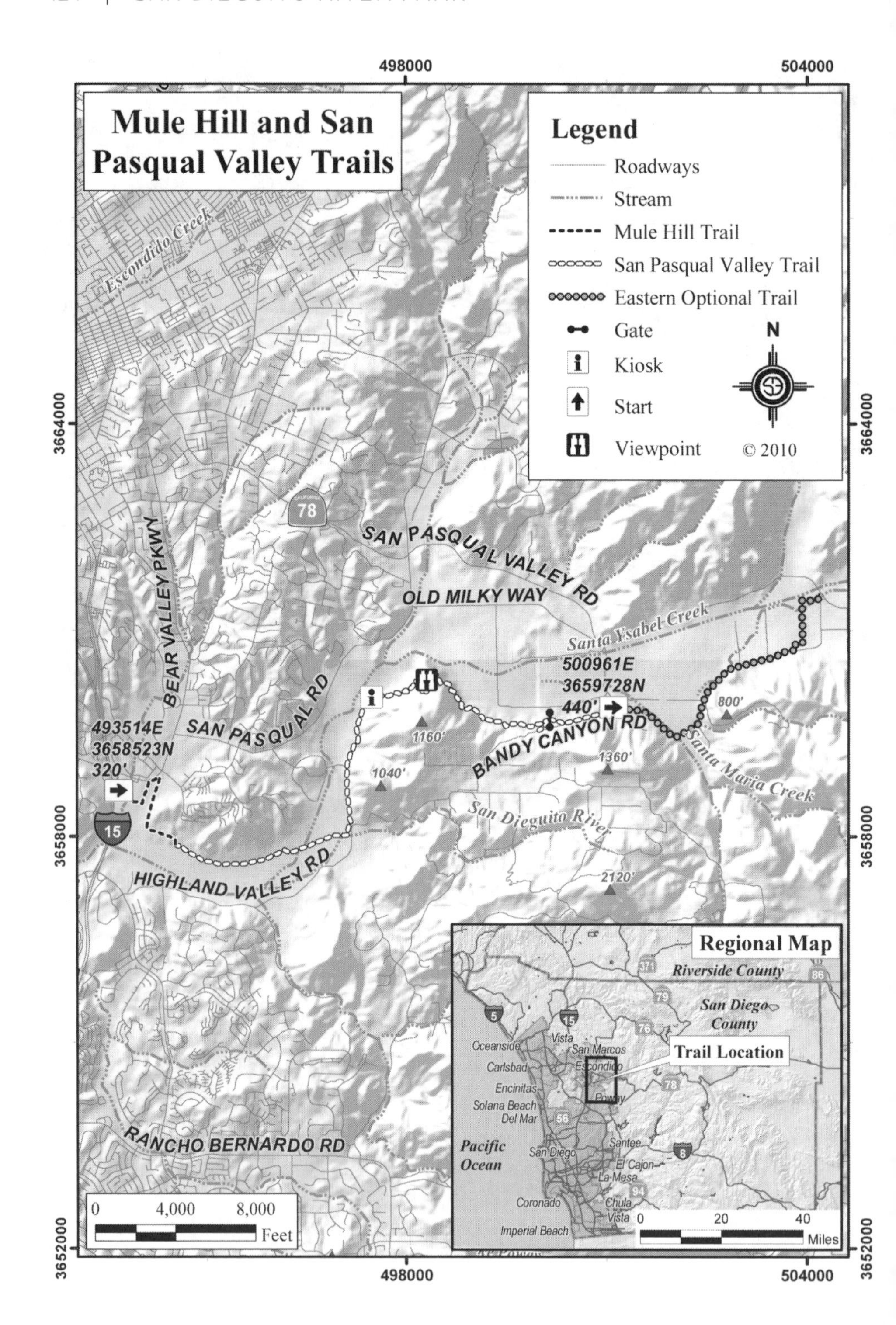

Mule Hill and San Pasqual Valley Trails
Legend
Roadways
Stream
Mule Hill Trail
San Pasqual Valley Trail
Eastern Optional Trail
Gate
Kiosk
Start
Viewpoint
N
© 2010
498000
504000
3664000
3658000
3652000
Escondido Creek
78
SAN PASQUAL VALLEY RD
OLD MILKY WAY
BEAR VALLEY PKWY
SAN PASQUAL RD
Santa Ysabel Creek
500961E
3659728N
440'
800'
1160'
BANDY CANYON RD
1360'
Santa Maria Creek
493514E
3658523N
320'
1040'
San Dieguito River
15
HIGHLAND VALLEY RD
2120'
RANCHO BERNARDO RD
0 4,000 8,000
Feet
Regional Map
Riverside County
San Diego County
Trail Location
Oceanside
Carlsbad
Encinitas
Solana Beach
Del Mar
Vista
San Marcos
Escondido
Poway
Pacific Ocean
San Diego
Santee
El Cajon
La Mesa
Coronado
Chula Vista
Imperial Beach
0 20 40
Miles

The Mule Hill and San Pasqual Valley trails are part of the trail system extending from the mouth of the San Dieguito River in Del Mar to Volcan Mountain near Julian. The proposed San Dieguito River Park's Coast-to-Crest Trail will follow the San Dieguito River corridor for 55 miles. This ride connects to the North Shore Lake Hodges ride from the west, and heads east through farmlands in Highland Valley and San Pasqual Valley to Highway 78 east of the San Diego Wild Animal Park.

San Pasqual Valley, designated as an agricultural preserve, is characterized by pasture, farms, fields, and citrus groves. The City of San Diego leases the land for farming to help preserve the rural character of the valley. The In-ke-pah tribe lived here and called the valley *Mo-culoch-culoch* meaning "one stone on top of another." The Spanish Franciscans renamed it in the late eighteenth century for Saint Pascal.

Start riding east by the circa 1870 Sikes Adobe Farmhouse, a state point of historic interest. It was burned in the October 2007 Witch Creek Fire that left only the adobe walls standing. The one-room adobe was constructed in 1870, just after Zenas Sikes and his wife Eliza moved to the site. They soon added onto the original adobe, the additional rooms made of wooden framing. The farmhouse needs repairs and the River Park is restoring it. When complete, the farmhouse will be open to the public for docent-led tours.

Follow the trail as it swings north along Via Rancho Parkway and then begins heading south on the Mule Hill Historic Trail. A number of signs explain the small town of Bernardo that flourished near here from 1872 to 1917, but was inundated by the Lake Hodges reservoir project. Another explains about the Mule Hill Standoff of the Mexican War in December 1846. The Americans, short of food, resorted to eating their mules, hence the name "Mule Hill." Hopefully you remembered to bring your own snacks along.

At 1.3 miles, the Mule Hill Trail easily reaches the top of a small rise where it becomes the San Pasqual Valley Agricultural Trail. This section of the ride winds through the San Pasqual Agricultural Preserve and across Highland Valley. During the spring, if you pause for a moment, the loud buzz of bees can be heard among the various sweet-smelling plants along the trail.

At 3.25 miles, the trail reaches the eastern edge of the valley and heads north alongside the base of the hills. Highland Valley road is just to your right and where an optional return on the pavement ends (see Options). At 4.4 miles, the trail descends slightly to a small picnic spot; keep your eye out for deer in this area. From here the trail becomes much more challenging as it ascends along Raptor Ridge on a winding single track trail. This is a good turnaround point if you are not up to steep, narrow dirt trails.

If you've continued on, the trail steeply ascends across several small drainages among scattered oak trees. At 5.2 miles, you'll reach the first of several viewpoints alternately looking west and east. The views into the scenic San Pasqual Agricultural Preserve are wonderful.

At 5.3 miles, the trail begins to quickly descend east around the 1460' summit on your right. This is a good turnaround point if you want to enjoy the fast descent back on the trail you just climbed. Continuing down the road brings you to the eastern part of the preserve, and across an open field to a wooden gate at 6.75 miles. The trail continues on the other side of the small road. An optional exit here is to turn right, and ascend to Bandy Canyon Road (see Options).

Continuing on, the trail stays close to Bandy Canyon Road, and soon you cross Ysabel Creek Road to a small staging area. Follow the trail east, as it continues to parallel Bandy Canyon Road. The trail ascends slightly to the bridge across Santa Maria Creek opposite the Bandy Canyon Ranch. The trail parallels the road, passing grazing cows and horses and then the Verger Dairy, where you'll ride on the west shoulder of the road a short distance. The trail then resumes on the left, and soon curves north between an orange grove and a sod farm. Follow the trail 0.4 mile and veer right along the Santa Ysabel Creek another 0.4 mile to the Ysabel Creek staging area. For the roundtrip route, return the way you came.

OPTIONS

Where the San Pasqual Valley Agricultural Trail nears Bandy Canyon Road, an option is to turn right and climb paved Bandy Canyon Road. Turn right on Highland Valley Road, and enjoy a fast descent to Highland Valley. When the road flattens out and begins to swing left, turn right, negotiate the gate, and join back up with the trail you took earlier. Turn left and head back across Highland Valley to the starting point. This optional section of pavement is 2.4 miles long with an elevation gain of 176 feet and a loss of 435 feet.

GETTING THERE

The starting point is the parking area at the end of Sunset Drive. Exit I-15 at Via Rancho Parkway, and head a short distance east to Sunset Drive and turn right.

Follow Sunset to the end and park. It's also possible to do a car shuttle by leaving one car at Sunset Drive and the other on Bandy Canyon Road at the Ysabel Creek Staging Area. From I-15, take Bear Valley Parkway east 0.6 mile and turn right on San Pasqual Road. It soon becomes Via Rancho Parkway. Turn right on Highway 78 (San Pasqual Valley Road) heading east toward the Wild Animal Park. In 4.3 miles, turn right on Bandy Canyon Road and then immediately right onto a dirt road that turns right into the staging area. A second staging area is 2.5 miles farther west on Bandy Canyon Road at Ysabel Creek. These are also optional starting points, if you want to just ride the eastern section of trail to Raptor Ridge.

Note that the section of trail from east Highland Valley over Raptor Ridge is moderately steep with several slightly technical sections.

AMENITIES

Restaurants are located near the starting point. A portable toilet is on your left as you pass by Sikes Adobe near the start of the ride.

Trip S7 – Santa Ysabel Preserve

Starting Point	Farmer Road, Julian
Distance	7 miles Kanaka Loop, 15 miles Kanaka and West Vista Loops
Elevation Gain/Loss	925'/925' Kanaka Loop, 2300'/2300' Kanaka and West Vista Loops, 9% grade in places
Riding Time	2–3 hours depending on route
Difficulty	Moderate to Difficult, not technical
Road Conditions	Well-graded roads
Season	Fall, Winter, and Spring
Equipment	Mountain bike
Optional Topo Maps	Julian, Santa Ysabel, Warners Ranch, CA

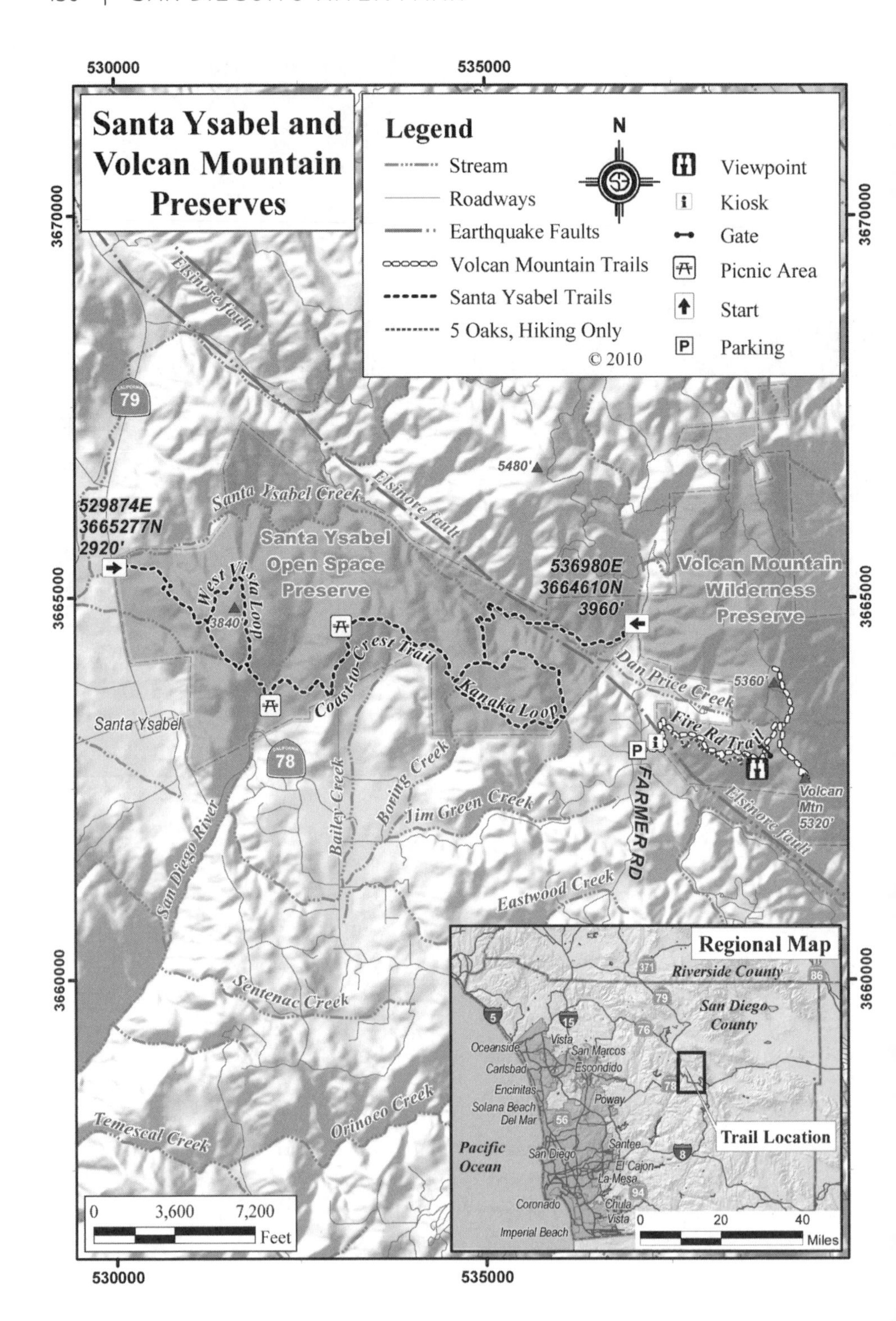

Santa Ysabel and Volcan Mountain Preserves
Legend
Stream
Roadways
Earthquake Faults
Volcan Mountain Trails
Santa Ysabel Trails
5 Oaks, Hiking Only
© 2010
N
Viewpoint
Kiosk
Gate
Picnic Area
Start
Parking
530000
535000
3670000
3665000
3660000
Elsinore fault
79
5480'
Santa Ysabel Creek
529874E
3665277N
2920'
Santa Ysabel Open Space Preserve
West Vista Loop
3840'
536980E
3664610N
3960'
Volcan Mountain Wilderness Preserve
Coast-to-Crest Trail
Kanaka Loop
Dan Price Creek
5360'
Fire Rd Trail
Santa Ysabel
78
FARMER RD
Boring Creek
Bailey Creek
Jim Green Creek
Volcan Mtn 5320'
San Diego River
Eastwood Creek
Sentenac Creek
Orinoco Creek
Temescal Creek
0
3,600
7,200
Feet
Regional Map
Riverside County
San Diego County
Oceanside
Vista
San Marcos
Carlsbad
Escondido
Encinitas
Poway
Solana Beach
Del Mar
Pacific Ocean
San Diego
Santee
El Cajon
La Mesa
Coronado
Chula Vista
Imperial Beach
Trail Location
20
40
Miles

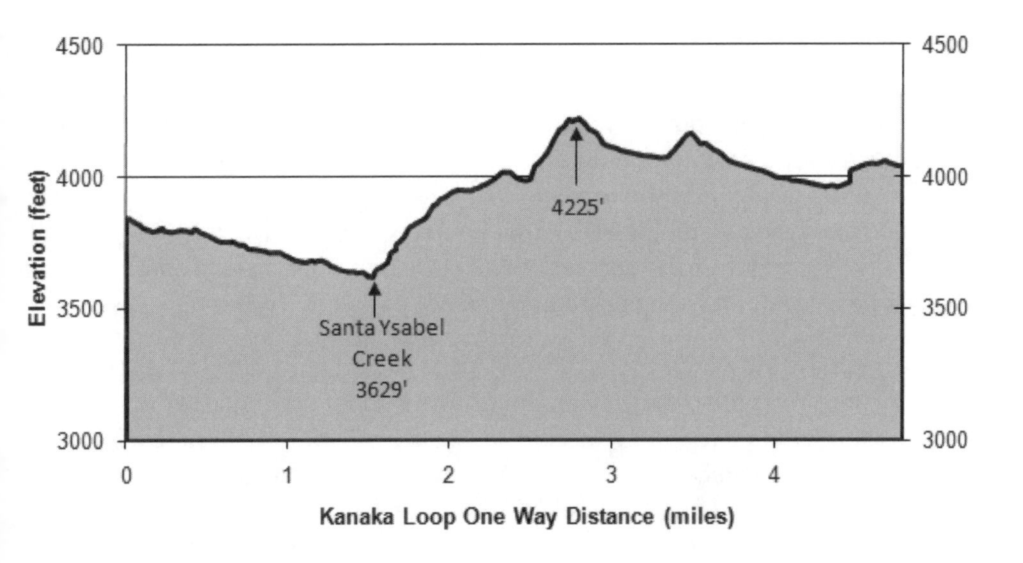

The Santa Ysabel Preserve just north of Julian, contains 3800 acres of oak woodlands, native grasslands, and beautiful fields of wildflowers. There are more than 13 miles of multi-use hiking, equestrian, and mountain biking trails in the preserve which is part of the San Dieguito River Park Coast-to-Crest corridor. When completed, the San Dieguito River Park will extend along a 55-mile corridor that begins at the mouth of the San Dieguito River in Del Mar and ends at Volcan Mountain just east of the preserve. This ride will help you explore the Kanaka Loop and the optional West Vista Loop and see the preserve first hand. This area can be hot and dry in the summer, so carry plenty of water and stay on the old ranch roads—any single track trail is off limits.

From the staging area on Farmer Road, negotiate the gate and follow the trail through a grassy meadow complete with grazing cows. Soon the trail nears Santa Ysabel Creek that runs along the northern boundary of the preserve. Sycamore trees line the river as the road slowly descends west. At 0.7 mile, a nice live oak tree grove provides some shade. When you reach a gated road ahead, bear left and descend to the Santa Ysabel Creek crossing at 1.6 miles.

Once past the creek, the road turns sharply right and begins a steep ascent on the south side of the creek. The road swings left and ascends a ridge, until it reaches Kanaka Flat, and its rolling grasslands at 2 miles. You can spot the Palomar Observatory domes from here, and great views of the hills in between. The 2003 Cedar Fire burned much of Cuyamaca Rancho State Park, but luckily spared this area, so it's worth seeing.

When you reach the Kanaka Loop junction, the recommended route is left, around the loop in a clockwise direction. Quickly you'll reach a very steep ascent at 2.6 miles that tops out with a great view of the staging area to the east, the three Cuyamaca Peaks to the south, and the Palomar domes to the northwest. Enjoy the fast descent, as the road heads east and then swings south gently descending alongside an orchard. The trail begins ascending again, and levels out at Kanaka Flat and then the second Kanaka junction. Turn right to complete the Kanaka Loop, and return to the staging area for a total of 7 miles.

To continue on the much more difficult West Vista Loop, turn left at the second junction. You are now following the Coast-to-Crest trail. Stay left at the next junction and begin a moderate ascent to the top of a hill at 5.8 miles. A picnic area here is a good place to grab a snack before the trail begins its steep descent. The road begins descending quickly, somewhat rocky in places, with great views to the west (heed the Watch Your Downhill Speed sign). At 6.5 miles, turn right at a junction and continue shedding more elevation. The road begins to ascend and descend as most of the elevation loss is behind you.

Stay right at the next junction with a picnic table and a Coast-to-Crest sign, at 7.2 miles. Soon you'll reach the West Vista Loop junction. Follow it right, as it ascends and descends through chaparral and manzanita. At 8 miles, it begins descending sharply with great views of the Santa Ysabel Valley. When you reach the next junction right to Highway 79 at 8.9 miles, stay straight and begin the moderate ascent to the West Vista Loop junction. Considering how much elevation you shed, you'll reach the junction sooner than you think at 9.5 miles.

Retrace your route, and begin the steep ascent back to Kanaka Flat and the Kanaka Loop junction. Turn left to return to the staging area for a total of 15 miles. Have a piece of apple pie in Julian, you deserve it.

OPTIONS

An optional starting point is the trailhead on Highway 79, 1.25 miles north of Santa Ysabel. The 1.1 mile road to the West Vista Loop is extremely steep and can be hot. It ascends 640 feet of elevation in less than a mile. However, it's a great place for a car shuttle. Park the first car here, and drive to the staging area on Farmer Road, and enjoy the great downhill ride and have a snack at Dudley's Bakery afterward.

GETTING THERE

Take Highway 78/79 into Julian to Main Street. Turn left onto Farmer Road, and drive 2 miles to Wynola Road and jog right, then left back onto Farmer Road. Pass the Volcan Mountain Wilderness Preserve on your right. Santa Ysabel Preserve will be on the left side, about one mile from the Volcan Preserve. Parking is available in the staging area.

For a car shuttle, drop the first car at the trailhead just north of Santa Ysabel. From Highway 79/79 turn left at Santa Ysabel and drive 1.25 miles to the trailhead. Park on the side of the road. Follow the directions above to the Farmer Road staging area and ride start.

AMENITIES

Restaurants are located in Julian. Public restrooms and water are available on Highway 78/79 as you enter Julian by the Julian Pioneer Museum at 4th Street.

Trip S8 – Volcan Mountain Preserve

Starting Point	Farmer Road, Julian
Distance	5 miles
Elevation Gain/Loss	1200'/1200', 9% grade
Riding Time	2–3 hours
Difficulty	Difficult, not technical
Road Conditions	Well-graded, steep road
Season	Fall, Winter, and Spring
Equipment	Mountain bike
Optional Topo Map	Julian, CA

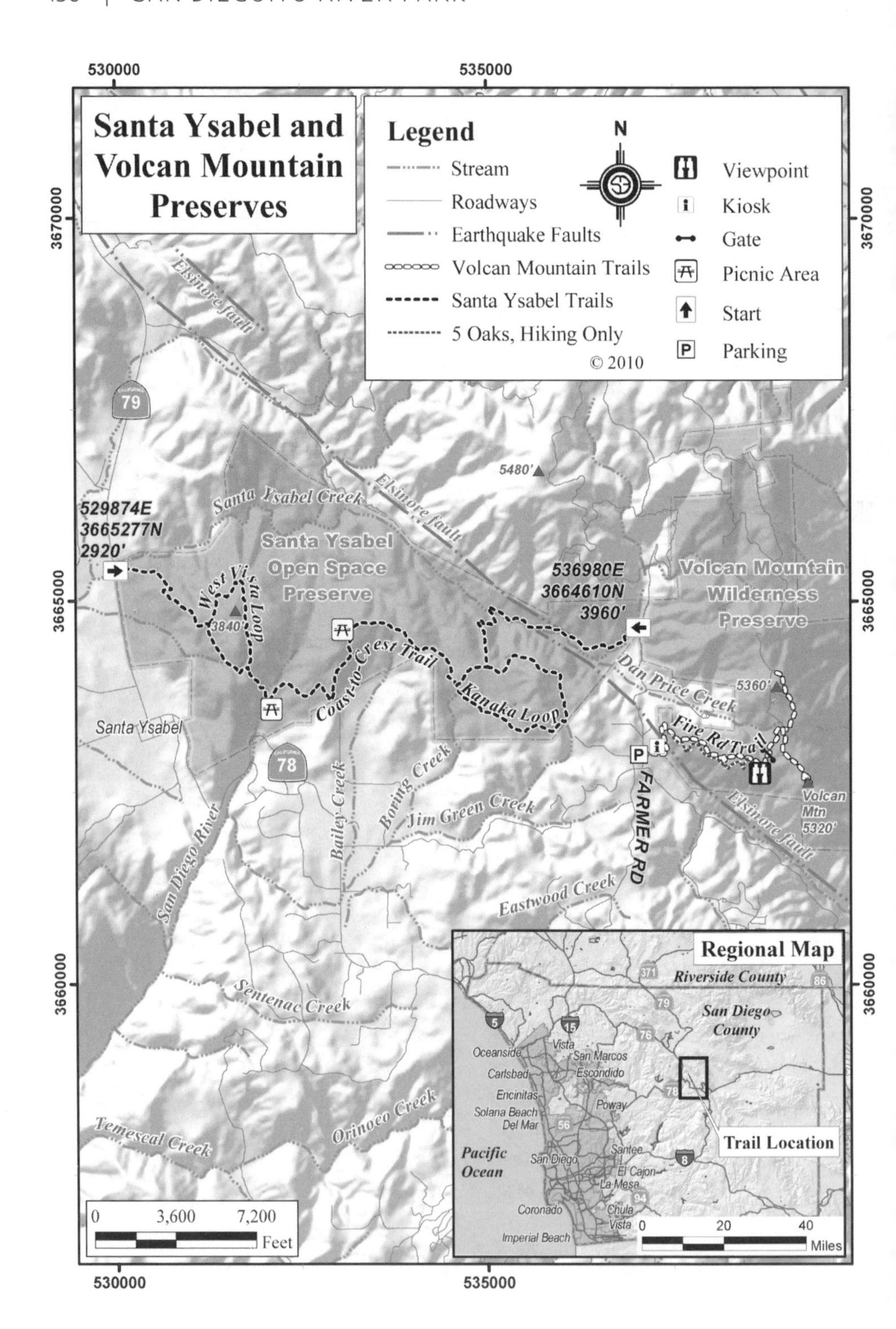

Santa Ysabel and Volcan Mountain Preserves
Legend
Stream
Roadways
Earthquake Faults
Volcan Mountain Trails
Santa Ysabel Trails
5 Oaks, Hiking Only
© 2010
N
Viewpoint
Kiosk
Gate
Picnic Area
Start
Parking
530000
535000
3670000
3665000
3660000
Elsinore fault
79
5480'
Santa Ysabel Creek
529874E
3665277N
2920'
Santa Ysabel Open Space Preserve
West Vista Loop
3840'
Coast-to-Crest Trail
Kanaka Loop
536980E
3664610N
3960'
Volcan Mountain Wilderness Preserve
Dan Price Creek
Fire Rd Trail
5360'
Volcan Mtn 5320'
Santa Ysabel
78
FARMER RD
Bailey Creek
Boring Creek
Jim Green Creek
San Diego River
Eastwood Creek
Sentenac Creek
Temescal Creek
Orinoco Creek
0
3,600
7,200
Feet
Regional Map
Riverside County
San Diego County
Oceanside
Carlsbad
Encinitas
Solana Beach
Del Mar
Vista
San Marcos
Escondido
Poway
Santee
El Cajon
La Mesa
San Diego
Coronado
Imperial Beach
Chula Vista
Pacific Ocean
Trail Location
20
40
Miles

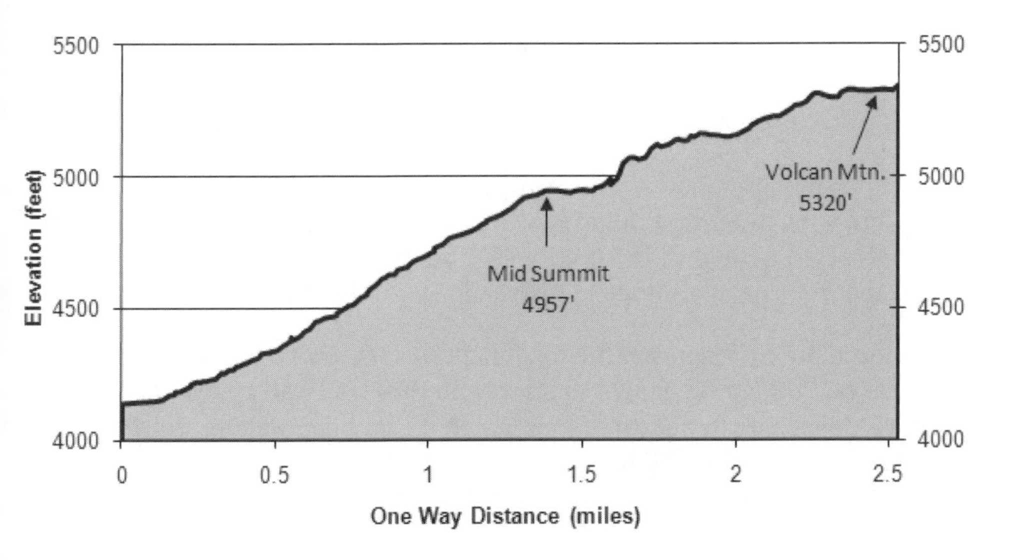

The Volcan Mountain Preserve is the proposed end of the San Dieguito River Park Coast-to-Crest corridor. When completed, the San Dieguito River Park will extend along a 55 mile corridor that begins at the mouth of the San Dieguito River in Del Mar and ends here at Volcan Mountain, just north of Julian. Volcan Mountain rises over 5,000 feet in San Diego County's backcountry, and is home to a wide diversity of vegetation and wildlife and is the location of Ironside Spring, the headwaters of the San Dieguito River.

Volcan Mountain is part of the Peninsular Ranges extending from Los Angeles to Baja that tipped up due to movements along the Pacific and North American tectonic plates. Heading east from San Diego, the top of Volcan Mountain is the end of the upturned slab, and quickly drops down to the desert below and the Salton Sea depression. From a viewpoint on the old fire road at mid summit, you can peer down into Banner Canyon, and spot the old mining roads and Chariot Canyon heading southeast. Until the early 1990s it was under ownership of the Rutherford Ranch that extended into the desert to San Felipe Valley. Native Americans crossed this area traveling back and forth from the desert to the mountains following the weather and seasonal vegetation.

The road is quite steep, and best ridden by those in great shape. Remember to bring plenty of water and snacks. If you've eaten a little too much apple pie, it's also a fine hike, and you can enjoy the Five Oaks Trail on the way down that is off limits to bikes. From Farmer Road, follow the dirt road east past the ranger station and through the interesting gateway designed by Julian artist James

Hubbell. The road begins its moderate ascent with great views of the orchards below. Soon it curves right and sharply ascends through a mix of live oaks, sycamores, and manzanita.

At 0.5 mile, the lower end of the hiking-only Five Oaks Trail joins from the right. The road switchbacks several times at 1.1 miles, flattens out a bit, and then continues its steep assault of the mountain. The lower sections of the trail are exposed and hot, but as you ascend the shade increases helping to cool you a bit.

You'll reach mid summit, and the top junction of the Five Oaks Trail on the right at 1.3 miles. This is a great spot to stash your bike, and walk a short distance on the Five Oaks Trail, to a lookout and bench. From here, Banner Canyon is visible below. The Elsinore, Earthquake Valley, and Chariot Canyon faults all run through this area, no doubt causing much of the linear nature of the canyons below.

When you return to the fire road you can continue the ascent to the top, passing the Mid Summit Gate in 0.3 mile, and finally reach the summit in 1.2 more miles. Return the way you came if you're riding, watching your downhill speed. If you're hiking, enjoy the narrow, winding Five Oaks Trail as it passes alternately through chaparral and sage and black oak trees. When it reaches the fire road again, turn left to return to the start.

GETTING THERE

Take Highway 78/79 into Julian to Main Street. Turn left onto Farmer Road and drive 2 miles to Wynola Road and jog right, then left back onto Farmer Road. The Volcan Mountain Wilderness Preserve is immediately on your right. Park alongside the road, no parking is available in the preserve. The preserve is open weekends only.

AMENITIES

Restaurants are located in Julian. Public restrooms and water are available on Highway 78/79 as you enter Julian by the Julian Pioneer Museum at 4th Street.

Trip M1 – Nate Harrison Grade

Starting Point	Highway 76, Pauma Valley
Distance	29 miles
Elevation Gain/Loss	5625'/5625', 8.5% grade
Riding Time	5 hours
Difficulty	Strenuous, not technical
Road Conditions	Graded dirt roads, 22 miles paved roads
Season	Year-round
Equipment	Mountain bike
Optional Topo Maps	Boucher Hill, Palomar Observatory, CA

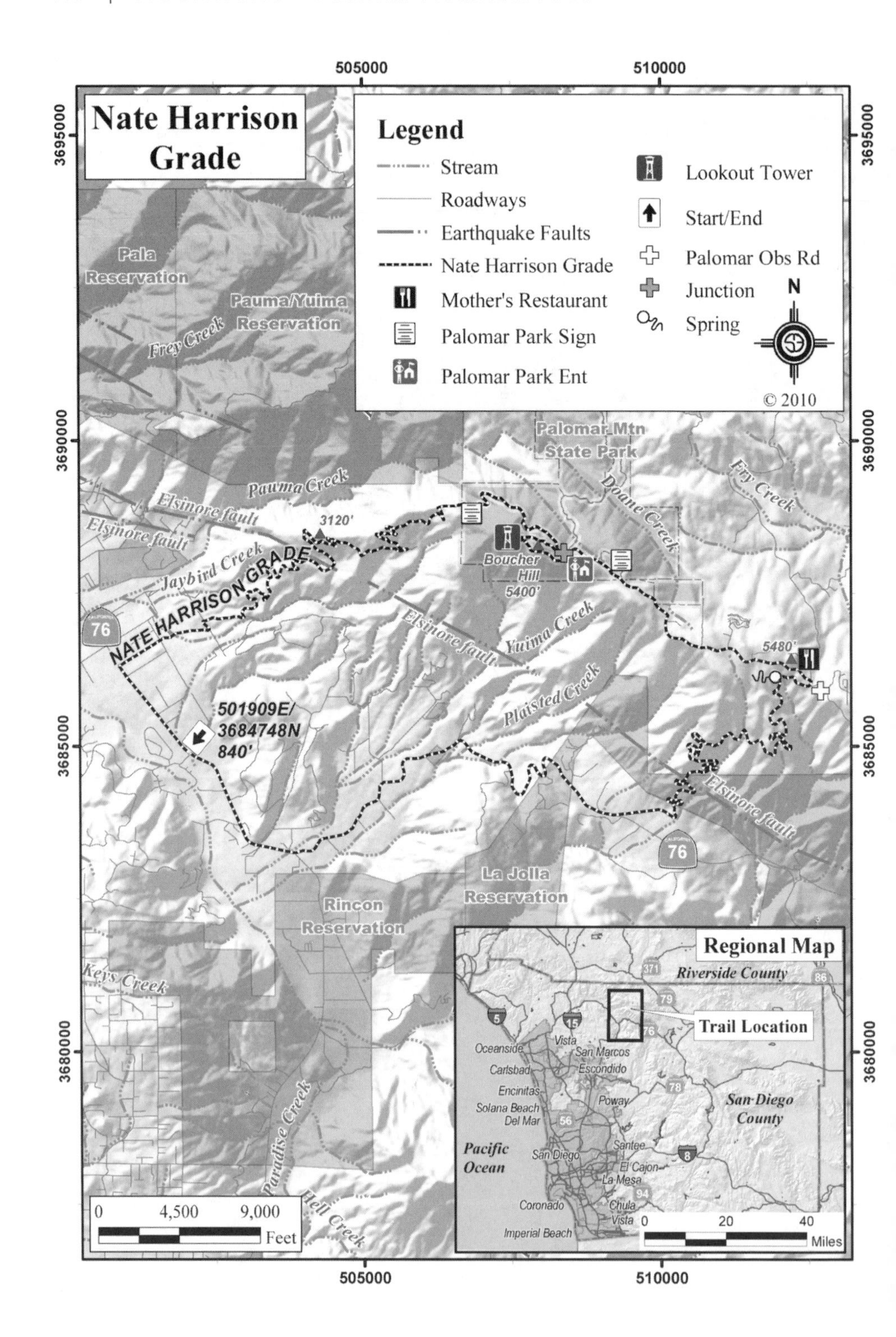
Nate Harrison Grade
Legend
Stream
Roadways
Earthquake Faults
Nate Harrison Grade
Mother's Restaurant
Palomar Park Sign
Palomar Park Ent
Lookout Tower
Start/End
Palomar Obs Rd
Junction
Spring
N
© 2010
505000
510000
3695000
3690000
3685000
3680000
Pala Reservation
Pauma/Yuima Reservation
Frey Creek
Palomar Mtn State Park
Doane Creek
Fry Creek
Pauma Creek
Elsinore fault
3120'
Jaybird Creek
NATE HARRISON GRADE
Boucher Hill 5400'
Yuima Creek
76
5480'
Plaisted Creek
501909E/
3684748N
840'
La Jolla Reservation
Rincon Reservation
Keys Creek
Paradise Creek
Hell Creek
0 4,500 9,000 Feet
Regional Map
Riverside County
Trail Location
Oceanside
Vista
San Marcos
Carlsbad
Escondido
Encinitas
Solana Beach
Del Mar
Poway
San Diego County
Pacific Ocean
San Diego
Santee
El Cajon
La Mesa
Coronado
Chula Vista
Imperial Beach
0 20 40 Miles

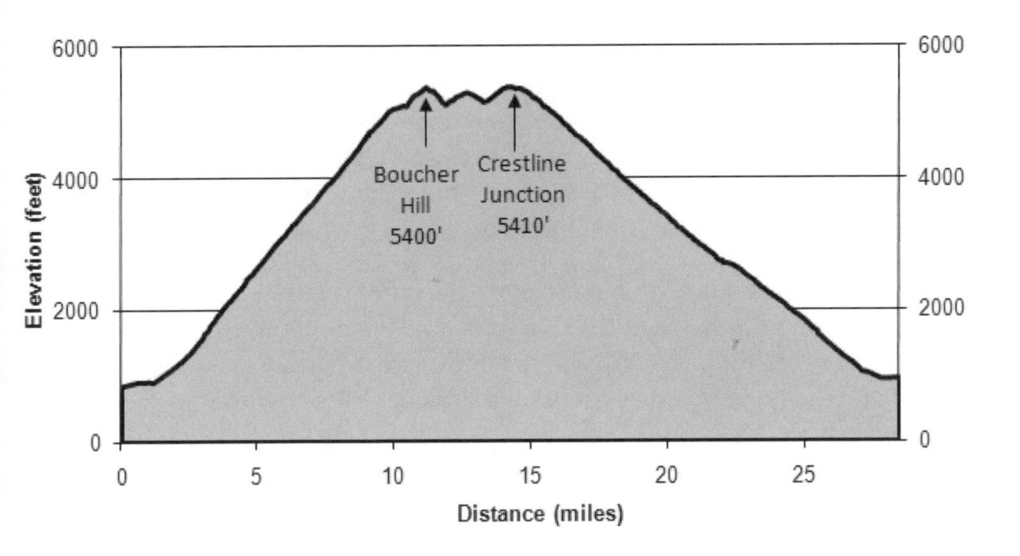

Nate Harrison Grade provides an alternate route up Palomar Mountain from the typical paved roads most people use. The graded dirt road climbs almost 3600 feet in 7 miles, winding its way up the steep, sun-exposed south-facing slopes. Starting in warm citrus groves and ending in cool oak and conifer forests, the contrast will be quite pleasant on a warm day. The panoramic view from the Boucher Hill Lookout at 5438 feet is well worth the climb.

The circa-1900 Nate Harrison Grade, originally a wagon route, predated South Grade Road ("Highway to the Stars") by at least 35 years. The road was named after Nathan Harrison, a freed slave who homesteaded a small ranch part way up the grade. Nate graciously provided water for thirsty travelers and horses heading up the mountain. Since then, Nate's road has been widened and the switchbacks rounded somewhat, but its wild character is still evident.

Start by riding west on Highway 76 for 1 mile, where you'll reach the bottom of the Nate Harrison Grade. Turn right and the road starts heading uphill, on pavement at first, through orderly rows of sweet-smelling citrus trees. The Pauma Indian Reservation lies just west of here. Pauma is an Indian word meaning "place of little water," which is evident in the area's sparse native vegetation—mostly white sage at this elevation.

Soon the incline steepens as the pavement turns to dirt at 2.3 miles. The unrelenting climb will have you searching for just one more gear, but also brings increasingly better vantage points of the beautiful citrus covered valley below. At

3.5 miles, the road swings left with a nice spot to stop and enjoy the great view. When you reach 4.8 miles the grade lets up a bit at Tin Can Flat, and a small road joins from the right. As you swing left and continue climbing, you'll cross the Elsinore Fault. It's not really noticeable here and continues along the south side of Palomar Mountain, crossing the paved South Grade Road, past the south end of Lake Henshaw and down Banner Grade.

As you continue climbing, the aromatic sage-scrub vegetation slowly gives way to oaks. Around 6.6 miles, a few oak trees provide some much-needed shade and a great place for a snack. Soon firs and cedars, burned in a recent fire, can be seen on the ridge above as well as the Boucher Hill Fire Tower where you will be soon.

The road swings around to the north side of the mountain with a nice view of the valley to the north. At 9 miles you reach the boundary of Palomar Mountain State Park where the firs and cedars become more abundant, and the air decidedly cooler. The road continues its ascent, and at 9.2 miles you're back on pavement, though potholed in several places. When you reach the five-point junction at 10.4 miles, you have the option of climbing to Boucher Hill Lookout (highly recommended), or continuing on (see Options).

Continuing on, follow the road straight through the park and exit the main entrance to join East Grade Road. It's a nice, easy cruise along the southern rim of the mountain to Crestline, the main Palomar Mountain crossroads. Mother's Kitchen is on the left at 15.1 miles, a great place to grab a bite to eat before the big descent.

From here it's mostly downhill on smooth pavement, 4400 feet to be exact. Watch your downhill speed through some of the deceptively sharp turns, and keep an eye and ear out for fast motorcycles that sometime cross over the center line or hug the shoulder too closely. The Palomar Artesian Spring is on the right 0.5 mile down the grade, with cool spring water.

Keep straight when South Grade Road merges with Highway 76, and continue the wonderful 14 mile downhill run past Rincon Springs and back to the starting point in Pauma Valley.

GETTING THERE

Park near the general store in Pauma Valley on Highway 76, 14.5 miles east of Interstate 15 and 1.5 miles east of Cole Grade Road.

OPTIONS

The climb to Boucher Hill Lookout is steep and gains 285 feet of elevation, but is well worth it for the view. A tower has been located on Boucher Hill since 1921. The current 30-foot tower was constructed in 1948, but was last in service in 1983. From the five-point junction, turn sharply right and follow the one-way road 0.7 mile to the top. Picnic tables and a composting toilet are available here. Follow the road back down to the five-point junction and turn right to continue.

AMENITIES

A general store is located near the starting point and Mother's Kitchen is at the Palomar Mountain crossroads before the long downhill ride. Bathrooms can be found at the Boucher Hill Lookout. Camping is available on Palomar Mountain.

Trip M2 – East Palomar Mountain

Starting Point	Highway 79, near Warner Springs
Distance	35 miles
Elevation Gain/Loss	4650'/4650', 6% grade
Riding Time	6 hours
Difficulty	Strenuous, not technical
Road Conditions	Graded and rough dirt roads, 19 miles paved roads
Season	Year-round
Equipment	Mountain bike
Optional Topo Maps	Aguanga, Palomar Observatory, Warner Springs, CA

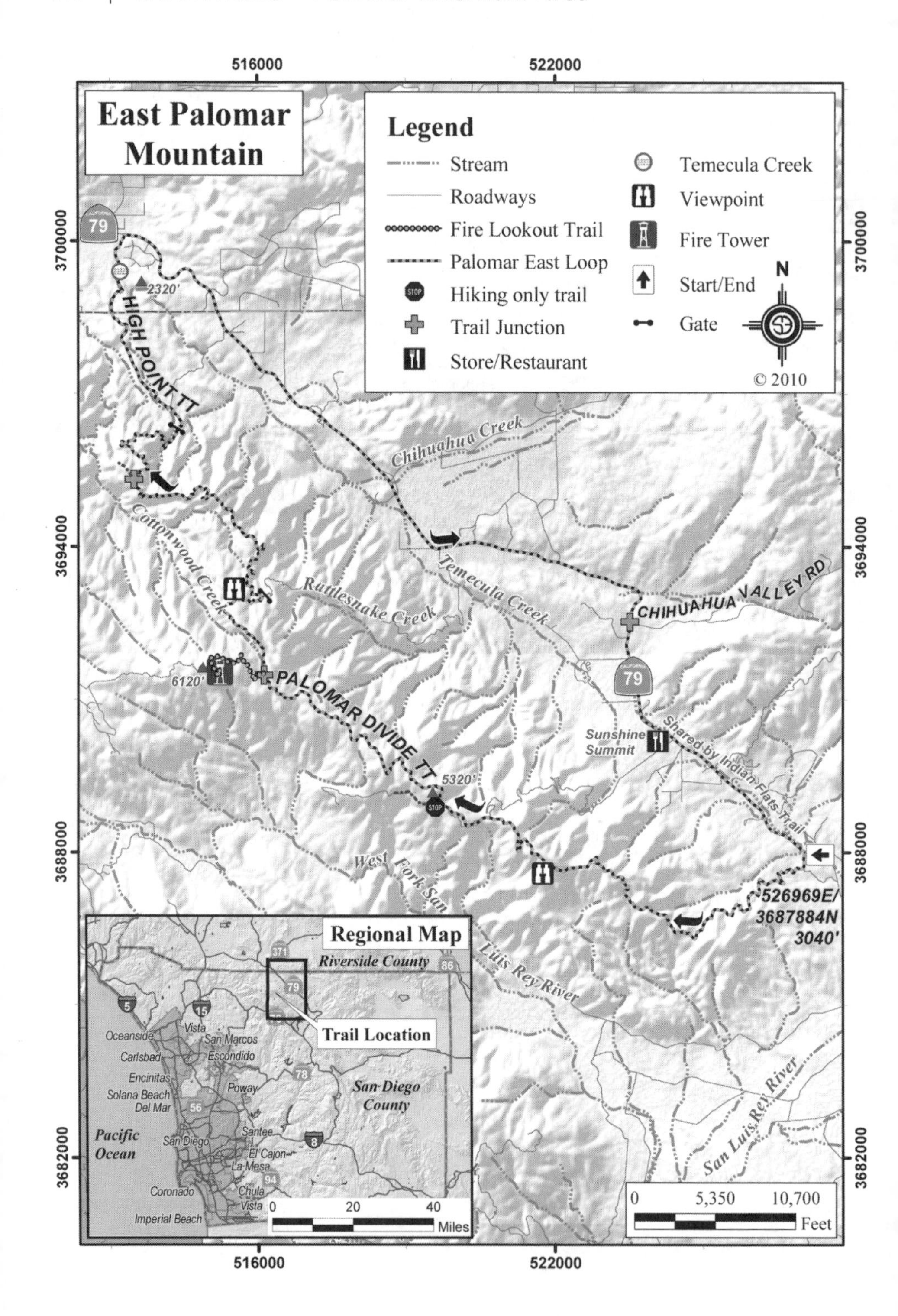
East Palomar Mountain
Legend
Stream
Roadways
Fire Lookout Trail
Palomar East Loop
Hiking only trail
Trail Junction
Store/Restaurant
Temecula Creek
Viewpoint
Fire Tower
Start/End
Gate
N
© 2010
516000
522000
3700000
3694000
3688000
3682000
79
2320'
HIGH POINT TT
Chihuahua Creek
Cottonwood Creek
Rattlesnake Creek
Temecula Creek
CHIHUAHUA VALLEY RD
6120'
PALOMAR DIVIDE TT
Sunshine Summit
Shared by Indian Flats Trail
5320'
West Fork San Luis Rey River
526969E/
3687884N
3040'
San Luis Rey River
Regional Map
Riverside County
Trail Location
Oceanside
Vista
San Marcos
Carlsbad
Escondido
Encinitas
Solana Beach
Del Mar
Poway
San Diego County
Pacific Ocean
San Diego
Santee
El Cajon
La Mesa
Coronado
Chula Vista
Imperial Beach
0
20
40
Miles
5,350
10,700
Feet

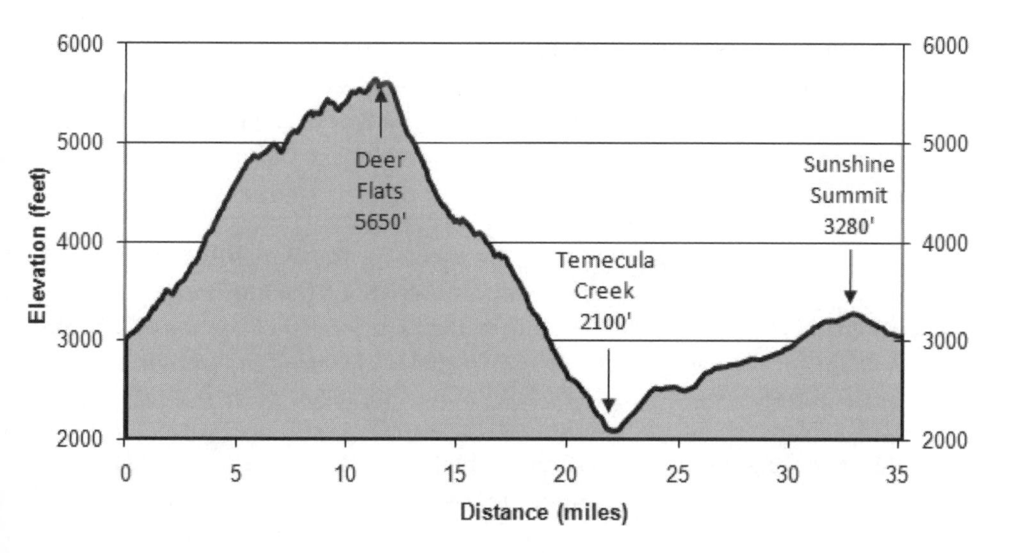

Another challenging dirt-road route up Palomar Mountain is the Palomar Divide Road. (TT for Truck Trail on the map.) Although not quite as steep as the Nate Harrison Grade ride, 11 miles and 2600 feet of elevation gain will get you to the saddle near the top of the east side of Palomar Mountain. If you're feeling extra strong, Palomar's "High Point," another 525 feet higher, and 91 steps to the top of a 60-foot fire tower, provides an even more commanding view of Lake Henshaw to the south and the San Jacinto and San Bernardino Mountains to the north.

During the warmer months, make sure you take plenty of water along, since none is available until you reach Aguanga at mile 22. Winter may bring snow to the higher slopes several times a year, making the route practically impassable.

Start riding up the dirt road 9507, the Palomar Divide TT. Sometimes the gate is shut, closed to motor vehicles, but open to non-motorized travelers. The dirt gives way to pavement at 1.5 miles making the somewhat tedious climb a little easier. The road flattens a bit and then resumes climbing at mile marker 2. As the road continues to climb, ever-widening views appear, first to the east and then the west. During the springtime beautiful patches of lupine and other wildflowers grace the roadside.

At 5 miles the road traverses a ridge where views on both sides are possible and the first glimpse of the San Bernardino Mountains to the north. Soon you'll pass a small, round water tank on the right—a source of water for fire fighting. Around the next bend you'll notice a large paved area that collects rainwater for the tank.

At 6 miles, the pavement turns to dirt, rough in some places. Soon you'll enjoy a slight downhill run with great views in both directions, as well as views of the Palomar Observatory domes and the High Point fire tower. The Halfway Truck Trail (9506, locked gate)intersects from the right at 7 miles—stay left and cross the cattle guard. The road begins ascending again, perhaps the steepest incline so far.

Ahead a little farther, at mile 7.8 is the trailhead for the Barker Valley Trail that descends to the West Fork of the San Luis Rey River (hiking only). Once you reach about 5400 feet elevation at mile 9, the temperature is noticeably cooler and the road flattens out again. Once you reach the oak trees at 11.4 miles, you've come to Deer Flats and a nice spot to rest in the shade and have a snack.

The High Point road (9S07) continues to the left just past this spot. You can follow it 1.3 miles up to High Point (veer left on the road to the lookout. Straight ahead is Palomar Observatory land which is off limits to the public).

Continuing on to the north, the Palomar Divide Road changes briefly to the Oak Grove Truck Trail (9S09) and begins descending around the north side of the mountain. In fall, sycamore trees provide a colorful frame for the fire tower visible in the distance above you. Now the fun downhill descent begins that will take you 11 miles down the High Point Road (TT) to Aguanga. At 13.3 miles the road is 8S05. Stay left on 8S05, now ignoring the Oak Grove road to the right with a locked gate.

Watch your downhill speed through some rough sections of road. During the late spring, yerba santa bushes color the hillsides purple on this side of the mountain. At 17.3 miles the Cutca Trail (1E01) heads left. It is rideable, but dead ends at the Agua Tibia Wilderness. The road continues to shed elevation quickly, and then heads across a flat ridge with rolling ascents and descents.

At 22 miles, you end the long descent by crossing the normally dry Temecula Creek. Shortly after that the road turns to pavement which is a right-of-way for both the Rancho California RV Resort and High Point Road. At Highway 79, a short 0.5 mile detour left takes you to the rustic Aguanga General Store, where cold drinks and snacks await. When you've stocked up, continue back southeast on Highway 79.

After climbing for several miles, you'll pass the Oak Grove Stage Station. The historic marker there commemorates the Butterfield Overland Stage, which linked San Francisco to the Midwest from 1858 to 1861. A short distance farther is another sign marking Camp Wright that was established to protect the lines of communication in this area. Chihuahua Valley Road intersects from the left at mile 31.7, and after a little more climbing; you will finally reach Sunshine Summit at 33 miles. The Summit Center General Store and a Mexican restaurant are here in case you need more sustenance. But the word "summit" may entice you to keep going, since it's only 2.3 miles—all downhill, from here to your car.

GETTING THERE

The start of the ride is at the foot of Palomar Divide Road (TT on the map, signed 9S07), near mile marker 41.9 on Highway 79. This is 6.5 miles northwest of Warner Springs. Park in the clearing just off the highway.

OPTIONS

To shorten this trip by 13 paved miles, you can set up a car shuttle between the starting point near Warner Springs and the town of Aguanga.

AMENITIES

The Summit Center General Store and a Mexican restaurant are located at Sunshine Summit, 2.3 miles north from the starting point. A restaurant, bathrooms, and water are also available at the Warner Springs golf course.

Trip M3 – Indian Flats

Starting Point	Highway 79, Warner Springs
Distance	24 miles
Elevation Gain/Loss	2220'/2220', 4.7% grade
Riding Time	4 hours
Difficulty	Moderate to difficult (due to length), not technical
Road Conditions	Graded and rough dirt roads, 20 miles paved roads
Season	Year-round, but can be hot in summer
Equipment	Mountain bike
Optional Topo Maps	Beauty Mountain, Warner Springs, CA

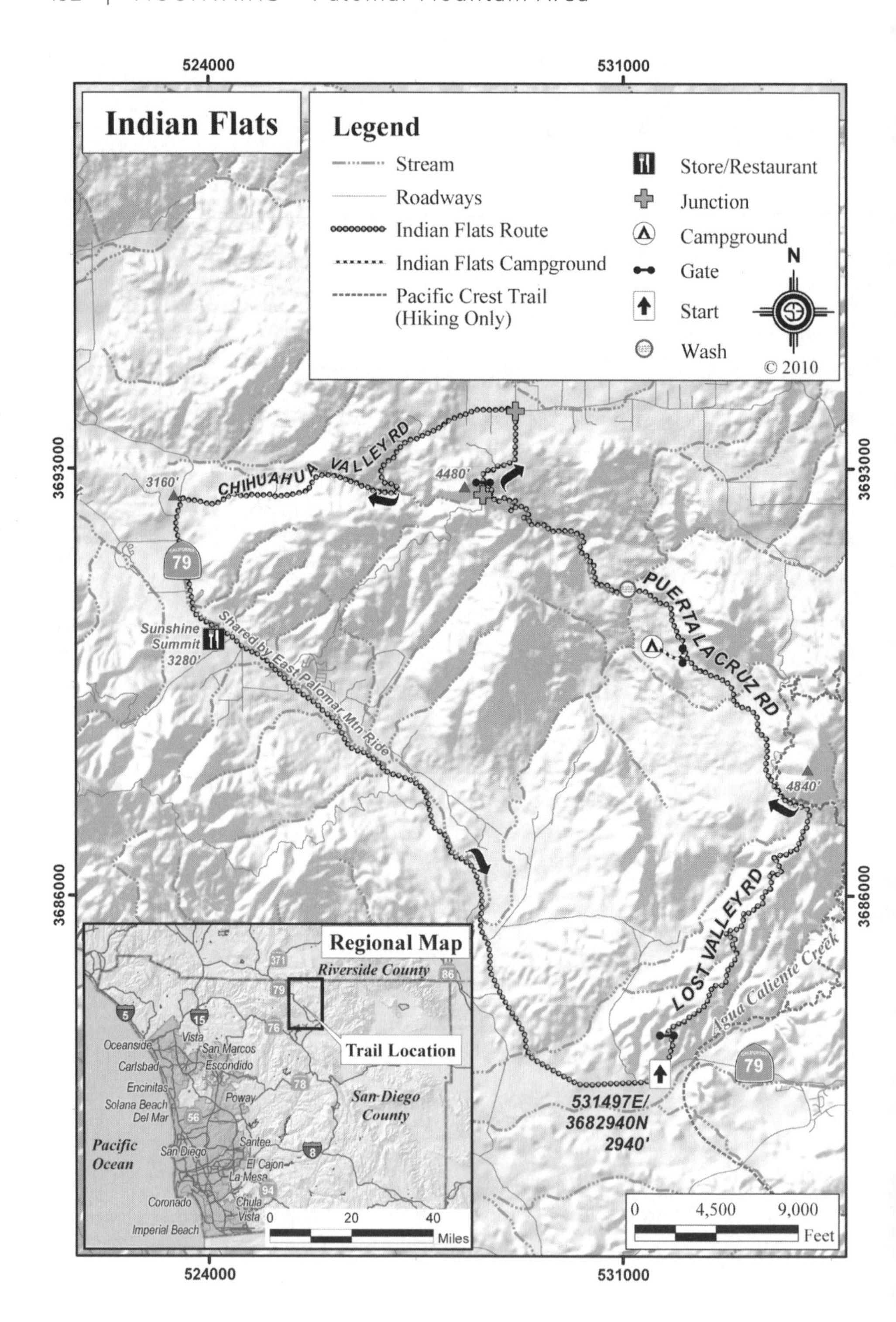
Indian Flats
Legend
Stream
Roadways
Indian Flats Route
Indian Flats Campground
Pacific Crest Trail (Hiking Only)
Store/Restaurant
Junction
Campground
Gate
Start
Wash
N
© 2010
524000
531000
3693000
3686000
CHIHUAHUA VALLEY RD
PUERTA LA CRUZ RD
LOST VALLEY RD
Shared by East Palomar Mtn Ride
Sunshine Summit 3280'
3160'
4480'
4840'
79
Agua Caliente Creek
531497E/ 3682940N 2940'
0 4,500 9,000 Feet
Regional Map
Riverside County
Trail Location
San Diego County
Pacific Ocean
Oceanside
Carlsbad
Encinitas
Solana Beach
Del Mar
Vista
San Marcos
Escondido
Poway
Santee
San Diego
El Cajon
La Mesa
Coronado
Chula Vista
Imperial Beach
0 20 40 Miles

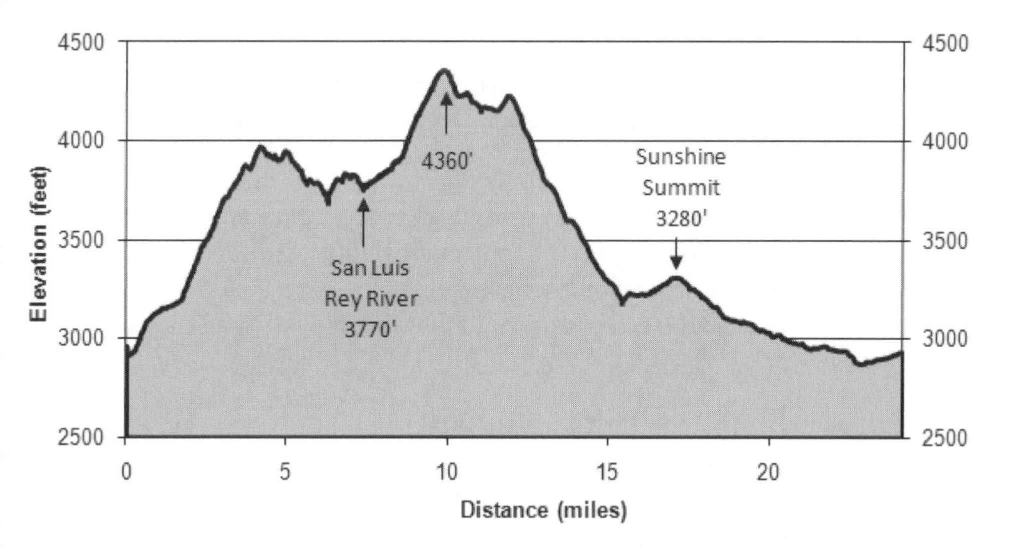

If you're not quite up to the arduous East Palomar Mountain ride, the Indian Flats loop provides a taste of the remote Palomar area countryside with great views of the surrounding peaks, without all of the climbing. Much of the ride is on pavement, but Lost Valley Road has enough climbing and is rough enough to qualify as a mountain bike ride.

Start riding north on the narrow, roughly paved Lost Valley Road (previously called Indian Flats Road). The beginning of the road ascends through low scrub that slowly turns to a mix of manzanita and ribbonwood, both with their distinctive bark. As the road continues to climb you might notice glider planes soaring across the hills after being towed to release elevation by struggling tow planes. Look northeast for a fine view of 6533-foot Hot Springs Mountain, the highest in San Diego County, and the old fire lookout tower.

The climb lessens a bit around 3.6 miles then resumes its upward march through magnificent boulders and passes the gated Pacific Crest Trail on your right at 4.5 miles (no bikes allowed). When the road starts to level out somewhat, you are nearing the oak-shaded Indian Flats Campground that can be a blessing on a hot day. At 6.3 miles the paved road veers left and descends quickly to the campground. The ride continues straight onto the rough, dirt Lost Valley Truck Trail here if you detour left to the campground. Pit toilets are available in the campground, but no water.

Returning to the truck trail, continue northwest and ignore the left fork 0.3 mile ahead. The road descends to the sycamore-lined San Luis Rey River and crosses on a concrete ford. You may need to cross carefully if the water is deep.

The road becomes rougher as it continues northwest over rolling terrain across a small, secluded valley. You begin to ascend easily along an oak-shaded ravine, and then more steeply when the road curves right, eventually heading to a 4368-foot summit. Pause for a moment and enjoy the vista, including 6000-foot Bucksnort Mountain and Hot Springs Mountain to the east. The Palomar range is to the west.

Just past 10 miles, ignore the left and veer right through an open gate and start a one mile descent that ends at paved Chihuahua Valley Road and back to civilization. Few people in San Diego know of the quiet community of Chihuahua Valley, which is probably why the local inhabitants live here.

Turn left on Chihuahua Valley Road, and enjoy a wonderful 4.3-mile descent to Highway 79. Turn left and begin a two mile climb south to Sunshine Summit. Then it's easy going as the remaining 7 miles back to Lost Valley Road effortlessly glide by.

GETTING THERE

Park at the Lost Valley Road turnoff (previously called Indian Flats Road) along Highway 79, 1.6 miles west of Warner Springs.

AMENITIES

A general store and restaurant are located at Sunshine Summit on Highway 79. A public restaurant and bathrooms can be found at the golf course at Warner Springs. Camping is available at Indian Flats Campground with pit toilets, but no water.

Trip M4 – Anderson Truck Trail

Starting Point	Peutz Valley Rd, Alpine
Distance	8 miles out and back or 13 mile loop
Elevation Gain/Loss	1000'/1000' out and back, 4.7% grade, 1800'/1800' loop
Riding Time	2–3 hours out and back, 3–5 hours loop
Difficulty	Difficult, technical in spots
Road Conditions	Rough trails and dirt roads, 5 miles paved on loop route
Season	Fall, Winter, and Spring
Equipment	Mountain bike
Optional Topo Maps	Alpine, El Cajon Mtn., Viejas Mtn. CA

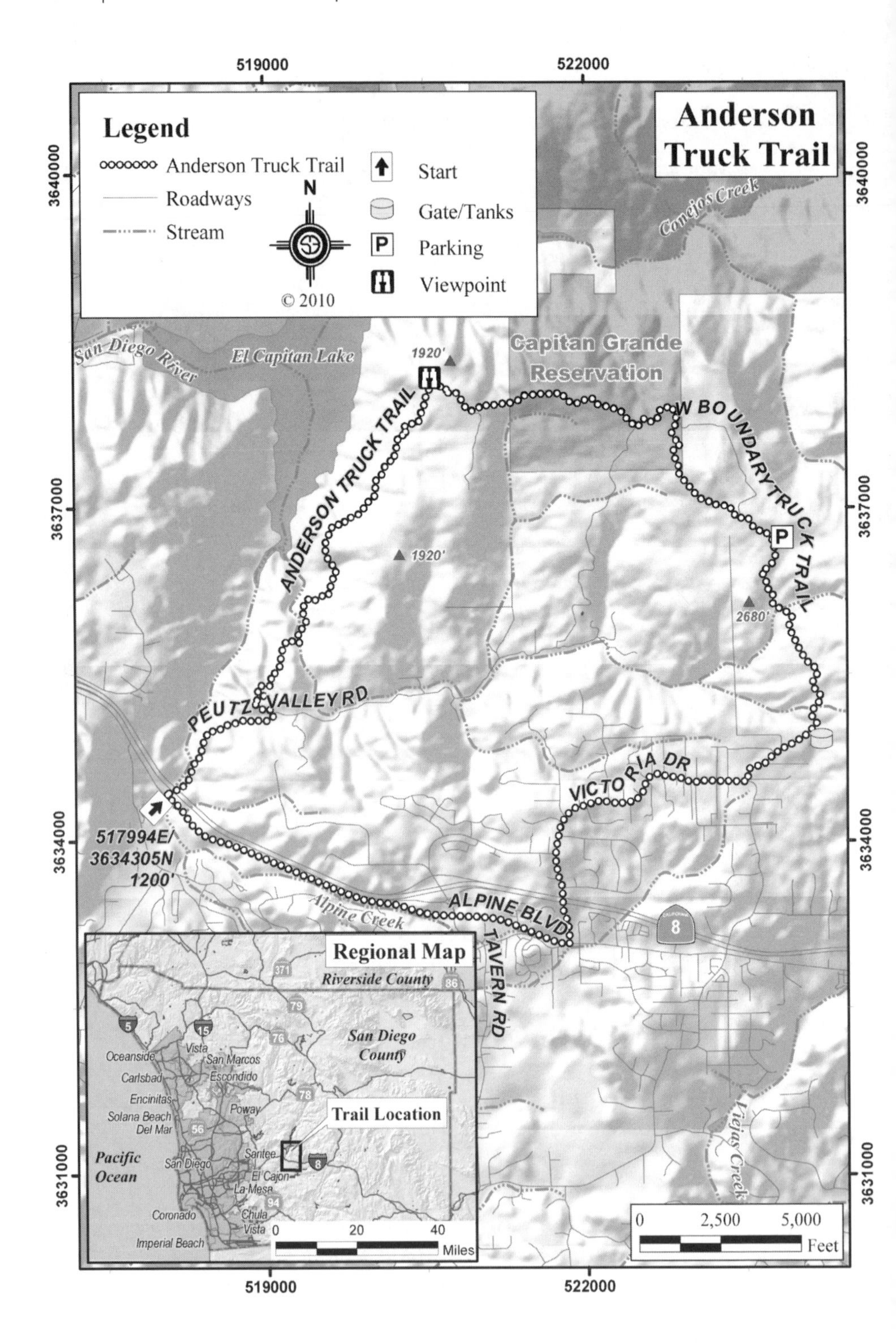
Anderson Truck Trail
Legend
Anderson Truck Trail
Roadways
Stream
Start
Gate/Tanks
Parking
Viewpoint
N
© 2010
519000
522000
3640000
3637000
3634000
3631000
San Diego River
El Capitan Lake
Capitan Grande Reservation
Conejos Creek
1920'
1920'
2680'
ANDERSON TRUCK TRAIL
W BOUNDARY TRUCK TRAIL
PEUTZ VALLEY RD
VICTORIA DR
ALPINE BLVD
TAVERN RD
Alpine Creek
Viejas Creek
517994E/
3634305N
1200'
8
0
2,500
5,000
Feet
Regional Map
Riverside County
San Diego County
Trail Location
Pacific Ocean
Oceanside
Carlsbad
Encinitas
Solana Beach
Del Mar
San Diego
Coronado
Imperial Beach
Vista
San Marcos
Escondido
Poway
Santee
El Cajon
La Mesa
Chula Vista
0
20
40
Miles

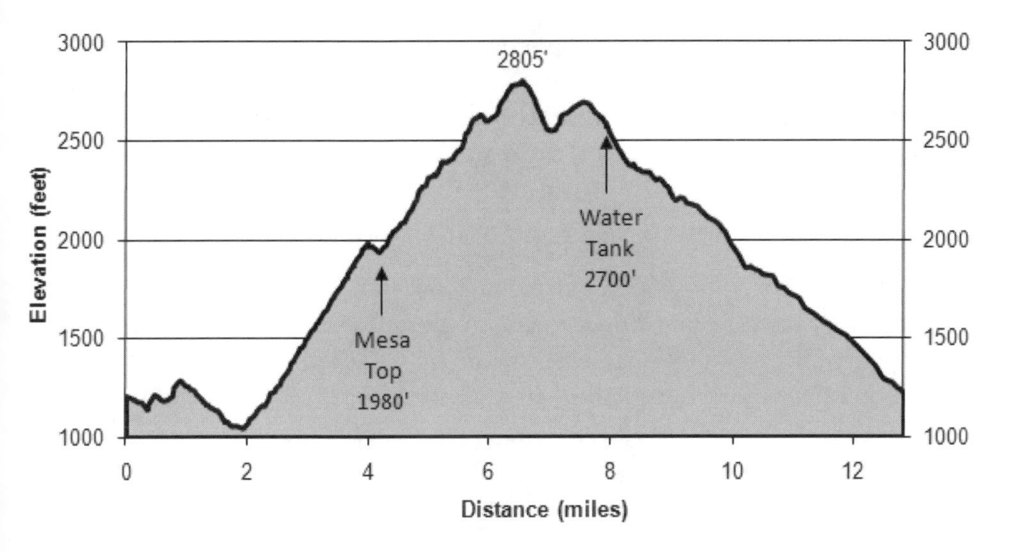

This ride takes you through the beautiful back country of Alpine and past the sparkling blue waters of the El Capitan Reservoir. El Capitan Reservoir has the largest capacity in the City of San Diego Lakes system. It's located approximately 30 miles northeast of San Diego, on the San Diego River which has its headwaters in the Cuyamaca Mountains. The dam, completed in 1934, is 237 feet high and when full has a maximum depth of 197 feet and 22 miles of shoreline. We will be riding above 2 miles of the shoreline.

Start off by heading north under I-8 on Peutz Valley Road. The road begins to climb and soon completely escapes the sounds of traffic. At 0.9 mile, look for the single track trail heading left from the pavement near 815 Peutz Valley Road. If you see the tank on the right you've gone too far. Follow the fun single track as it rises and dips, then swings north and passes narrowly by a steel barrier. There was some controversy about this part of the trail at one point and a local put in the illegal barrier. Just in case, an alternate entrance is on your left a little farther up Peutz Valley Road.

The trail then begins a nice downhill run with beautiful views of the reservoir and mountains and at 1.6 miles crosses a small creek. The trail then starts its unrelenting climb, hugging the western side of the slope. There are a few rocky sections to negotiate that will keep you watching the trail for the best track. During the spring, colorful flowers dress up the landscape.

At 3 miles, a small grove of oak trees provides the only shady section on the trail and is a great place to view the reservoir and have a snack.

Around 3.5 miles the trail eases up a bit, and soon there is a great lookout on the left with spectacular views of the reservoir below and El Cajon Mountain and Rock Mountain looming to the west. The trail then heads east up a red dirt slope where Cuyamaca Peak is visible in the distance through a dip in the hills. As the trail heads east, south, and then east again Cuyamaca, Middle, and North Peaks are all visible to the east.

At 4 miles into the ride you'll pass a guard rail that blocks vehicle access and then quickly reach the top open area with a great view in all directions. Trails head off in multiple directions here that can be explored. The out and back ride turns around here and returns the way you came, quickly losing all of the elevation you gained for an 8-mile total ride.

To continue the loop ride, stay straight ahead on the jeep trail heading southwest and then stay left at the next junction. The rough road curves eastward over rolling terrain with a few short, but steep rutted ascents. In about one mile stay left at the T intersection. San Miguel Mountain with the antennas on top is visible in the distance to the southwest. BMX-type trails wind their way through the chaparral in this area, but we stay left on the jeep trail. After the T intersection, you'll climb a steep rutted hill and then thankfully it levels out some.

At 5.5 miles you'll pass a fence on your left and then a house. Follow the road right past the house, ignoring the next left and begin another steep ascent. A small false summit gives you hope the climbing is over, with a great view back the way you came.

At about 6.5 miles, a small dirt parking area is on your left where another popular trail heads north. This is an optional parking spot for a car shuttle (see Options). Now you'll finally get some serious downhill. Watch for cars as you blast ahead. After a series of ascents and descents you reach the pavement and the tanks on your left at 8 miles. The gate here closes at dusk.

Stay straight on the pavement and at Victoria turn right. It's all downhill from here! At 10.5 miles turn right on Alpine Blvd. A bike and board shop is located near here. Follow Alpine Boulevard about 1.5 miles back to your car.

GETTING THERE

Take I-8 east to the Harbison Canyon/Dunbar Lane exit. Continue straight onto Alpine Blvd. heading east 1 mile and turn left on Peutz Valley Road. Park on the side of the road here under I-8.

OPTIONS

This ride can be done as an out and back to the big open area on top or as a complete loop returning on Alpine Boulevard. Another option is a car shuttle, parking somewhere near the end of the pavement on Anderson Road (take Alpine Blvd. to West Victoria Drive, then left on Anderson Road). There is also a dirt parking area on the rough unpaved Anderson Truck Trail about 1.3 miles past the gate and the tanks. This route is not recommended for low clearance vehicles. You will need a Forest Adventure Pass to park here. From either spot, the ride is all mostly downhill to Peutz Valley Road. Watch for slow cyclists and other trail users.

AMENITIES

After the ride there are a number of restaurants to pick from in downtown Alpine. Water and restrooms may be available in these locations.

Trip M5 – Sloan Canyon

Starting Point	Sequan Truck Trail, Alpine
Distance	6.3 miles one-way
Elevation Gain/Loss	400'/825' one-way
Riding Time	1 1/2-2 hours
Difficulty	Moderate, not technical
Road Conditions	Rough dirt trail, well-graded road
Season	Fall, Winter, and Spring
Equipment	Mountain bike
Optional Topo Map	Alpine, CA

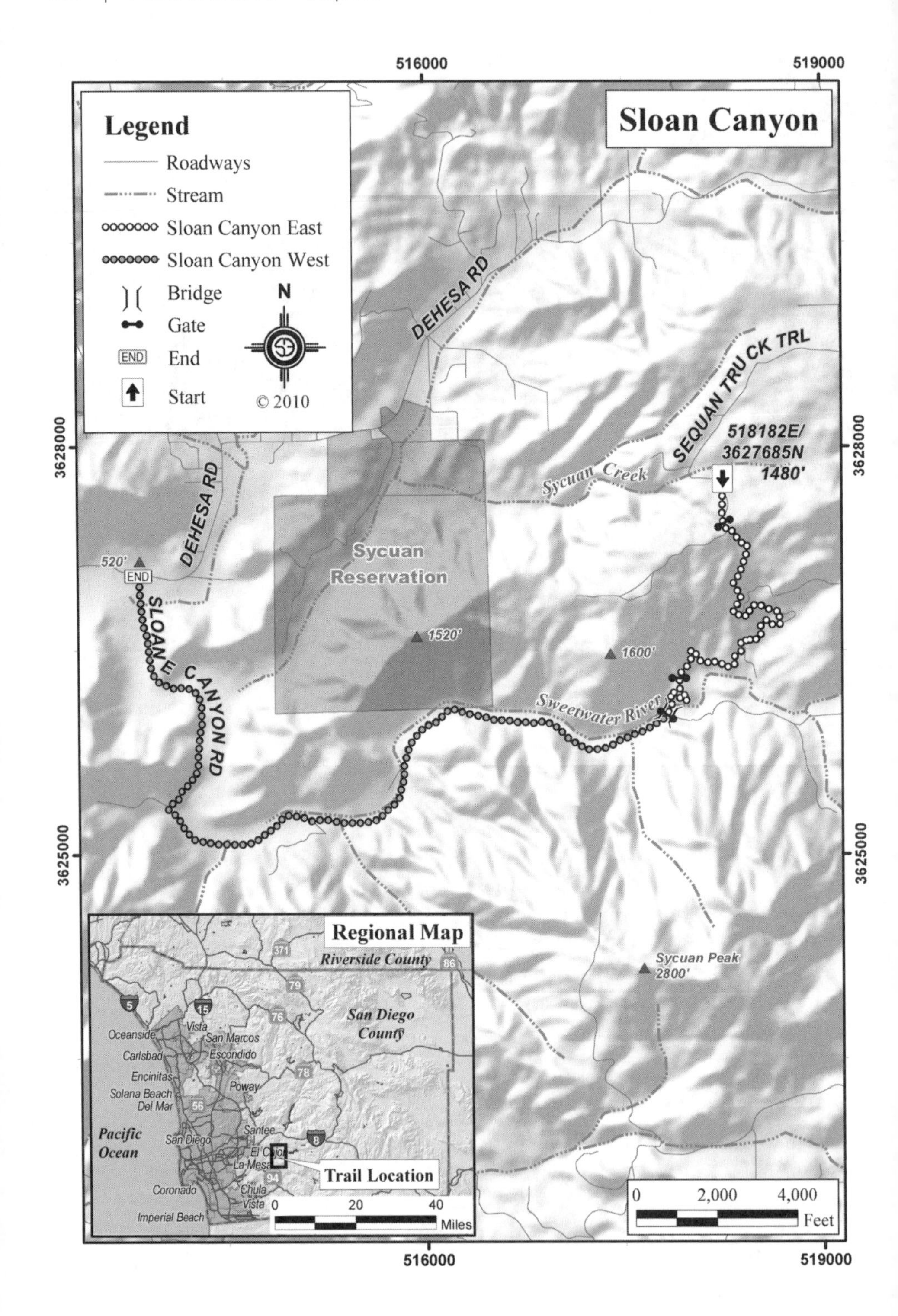
Sloan Canyon
Legend
Roadways
Stream
Sloan Canyon East
Sloan Canyon West
Bridge
Gate
End
Start
N
© 2010
516000
519000
3628000
3625000
DEHESA RD
SEQUAN TRUCK TRL
518182E/
3627685N
1480'
Sycuan Creek
Sycuan Reservation
1520'
1600'
520'
END
SLOANE CANYON RD
Sweetwater River
Sycuan Peak
2800'
Regional Map
Riverside County
San Diego County
Oceanside
Vista
San Marcos
Carlsbad
Escondido
Encinitas
Poway
Solana Beach
Del Mar
Pacific Ocean
San Diego
Santee
El Cajon
La Mesa
Coronado
Chula Vista
Imperial Beach
Trail Location
0 20 40
Miles
0 2,000 4,000
Feet

This ride takes you to Sloan Canyon near Alpine, where the Sweetwater River lazily flows through a beautiful stretch of oak-shaded riparian habitat. The first half of the ride follows the California Riding and Hiking Trail, a multi-use hiking, equestrian, and biking trail through much of San Diego County. The second half of the ride follows the well-graded Sloan Canyon Road, for an enjoyable ride near the river. The first part of the trail descends a sun-exposed, south-facing slope, so leave early while the air is still cool.

Follow the dirt road south a short distance, where it turns to pavement and passes several houses. Continue straight through the pole gate, with the California Riding and Hiking Trail stickers. In a short distance, look for a brown Riding and Hiking sign on the left, and follow it down the slope. The trail is steep and rutted in places as it cuts its way through the chaparral. At 0.75 mile you reach a wide, well-graded road. Turn right, and continue descending as the road curves east and then south. The Sweetwater River valley traversing Sloan Canyon is visible below and the nearby Sycuan Peak. To the southeast you can spot Lawson and Lyons peaks as well.

The road passes a few buildings and trailers, and an interesting small gorge where the river eroded its way through granite rock slabs. The road is sandy in a few places as it continues to descend, and soon reaches a wooden bridge across the Sweetwater River at 2.2 miles. Oak trees provide a nice shady spot for a snack. Cross the bridge and head through the gate to continue south on Sloan Canyon Road.

Sloan Canyon Road ascends and descends easily, as it follows along the Sweetwater River. Now and then it veers away slightly, but always returns to the beautiful riparian vegetation bordering the river.

The road ascends for a bit, then descends and passes the private Model A Ford Lane at 2.8 miles. The surface turns to pavement briefly as you cross a bridge over the river then continues to the junction of Dehesa Road.

GETTING THERE

This ride is best done as a car shuttle starting from Sequan Truck Trail and descending 6.3 miles to Sloan Canyon Road, where it intersects Dehesa Road. Take I-8 east, to the Tavern Road exit in Alpine. Follow Tavern Road 2.7 miles south to the junction with Dehesa Road. Turn sharply right on Dehesa Road, and follow it west past the Sycuan Indian Reservation Casino, and turn left where Harbison

Canyon Road intersects from the right. Just past the Dehesa School, turn left on Sloan Canyon Road and park the first car by the side of the road. Return to the Dehesa and Tavern Road junction, and stay straight onto Japatul Road. Follow it 0.3 mile to Sequan Truck Trail. Turn right, and drive 3 miles past the Loveland Reservoir on your left, to where the pavement turns to dirt, then park on the side of the dirt road where it bends right (south).

OPTIONS

This ride is best done as a car shuttle, but it's possible to start at Sequan Truck Trail, ride to the Sweetwater River and climb back to the top for a difficult 4.4 miles. Riding Sloan Canyon Road from Dehesa Road to the Sweetwater River and back would be a moderately flat 8.2 mile ride.

AMENITIES

After the ride there are a number of restaurants to pick from in downtown Alpine. Water and restrooms may be available in these locations.

Trip M6 – Boulder Creek

Starting Point	Perkins Store, Descanso
Distance	39 miles
Elevation Gain/Loss	4760'/4760', 3.5% grade
Riding Time	6 hours
Difficulty	Strenuous (due to length), not technical
Road Conditions	13 mi graded dirt roads, 26 miles narrow paved roads
Season	Spring, Summer, and Fall as snow permits
Equipment	Mountain bike
Optional Topo Maps	Cuyamaca Peak, Descanso, Julian, Santa Ysabel, Tule Springs, Viejas Mtn., CA

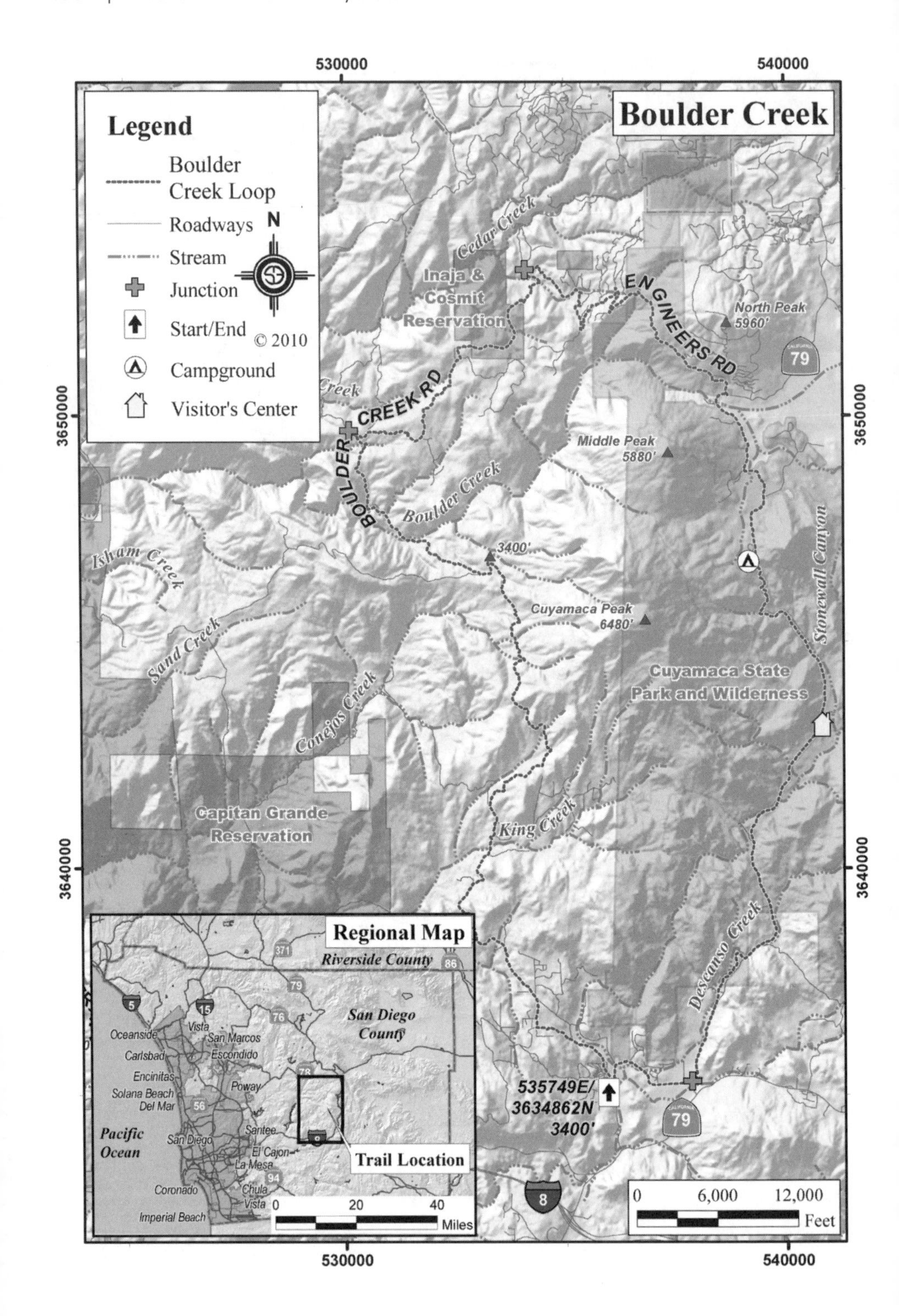
Boulder Creek
Legend
Boulder Creek Loop
Roadways
Stream
Junction
Start/End
Campground
Visitor's Center
N
© 2010
530000
540000
3650000
3640000
Cedar Creek
Inaja & Cosmit Reservation
ENGINEERS RD
North Peak 5960'
79
BOULDER CREEK RD
Middle Peak 5880'
Boulder Creek
3400'
Isham Creek
Sand Creek
Cuyamaca Peak 6480'
Stonewall Canyon
Cuyamaca State Park and Wilderness
Conejos Creek
Capitan Grande Reservation
King Creek
Descanso Creek
535749E/ 3634862N 3400'
8
0
6,000
12,000
Feet
Regional Map
Riverside County
San Diego County
Oceanside
Vista
San Marcos
Carlsbad
Escondido
Encinitas
Solana Beach
Del Mar
Poway
Pacific Ocean
San Diego
Santee
El Cajon
La Mesa
Coronado
Chula Vista
Imperial Beach
Trail Location
0
20
40
Miles

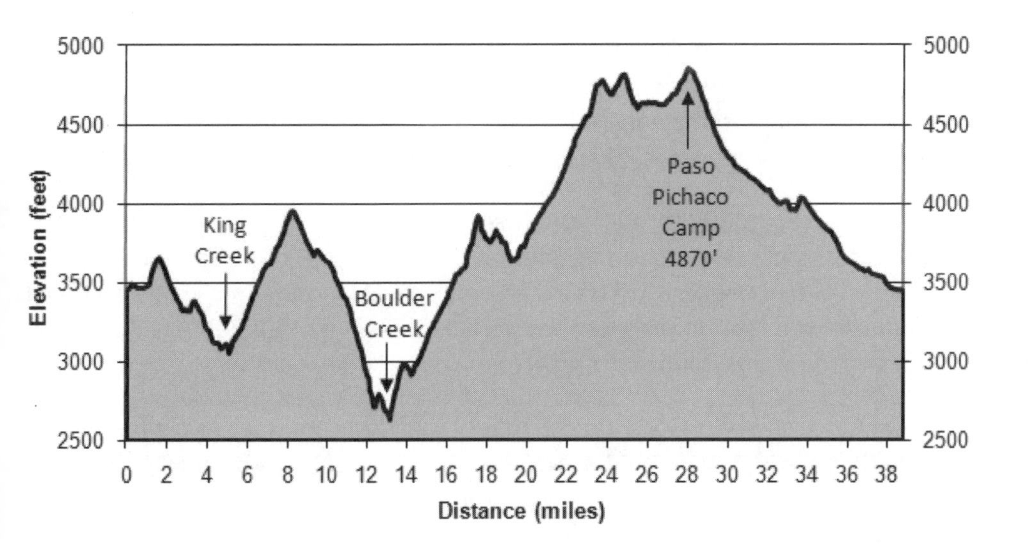

This ride has it all: dirt roads, paved roads, miles of hills, and spectacular vistas of the Cuyamaca Peaks and surrounding countryside. You will pass through scrub-covered hills on your way to mixed coniferous-oak forests as you do a complete circle around Cuyamaca and Middle Peaks. The distance makes it a difficult ride although there are no technical sections.

Begin by riding north on Oak Grove Drive. First a gradual climb and then a steeper section takes you past eclectic houses, corrals, and pastures. When you reach the first crest, turn right on Boulder Creek Road. As you start a rapid descent you can see Cuyamaca Peak in the distance.

At the bottom of the grade at 5.0 miles, you'll cross King Creek on a concrete ford. The road begins climbing here. At 6.5 miles, the pavement ends and the graded dirt road begins. As the road climbs, the panoramic view west toward the Capitan Grande Indian Reservation and Eagle Peak improves. Sage and manzanita cover the hillsides in this area and occasional clusters of oaks offer shade for grazing cattle, but little for the rider.

Soon you'll reach a 3934-foot summit, just two miles southwest of Cuyamaca Peak that continues to rise 2600 feet higher. The road then starts losing elevation until you cross Boulder Creek on a concrete ford at 12.2 miles. Cuyamaca Reservoir provides most of the water for Boulder Creek.

The road begins climbing again and passes the junction of Cedar Creek Road and the trailhead for Eagle Peak at 14.4 miles where, on a clear day you can see Woodson Mountain and Iron Mountain in the distance.

The road continues climbing into a thin forest of oak and pine trees. Middle Peak, once covered with forests of oak, incense-cedar, white fir, and several varieties of pine, is now visible to the east. The 2003 Cedar Fire swept through the area and destroyed most of the trees. The forest is slowly recovering.

The road passes briefly through the Inaja Indian Reservation and at about 19.5 miles you'll reach the junction of Engineers Road. The Pine Hills Fire Station is here with water, if needed. This is a starting point for mountain bikers who travel a tough, 21-mile loop to the west and south consisting of Eagle Peak Road, Cedar Creek Road, and Boulder Creek Road.

Turn right on Engineers Road at 25.2 miles. The road continues to climb through oaks and conifers. Soon you'll reach the boundary of Cuyamaca Rancho State Park where Incense cedar and oaks complement each other as you continue winding up a moderately steep hill. In several places you'll have a great view south and east toward Middle Peak and chaparral-covered Stonewall Peak.

After reaching a small crest, enjoy the nice gentle downhill ride toward Cuyamaca Reservoir. Turn right when you reach Highway 79, and ride around the shoreline to the store and picnic area on the left and enjoy a much-deserved break.

Past the lake, there's a moderate climb up to Paso Picacho Campground at 28.0 miles—the highest point of the ride at 4870 feet. The climbing is now over and you get paid back as the mostly downhill ride ahead starts with a quick section that includes a couple of very sharp curves. Watch your speed and lookout for cars. You'll zoom by the park headquarters and museum entrance on the left, glide through the meadows along the Sweetwater River, and climb a bit to a summit just beyond Green Valley picnic area. Continuing downhill through a number of tight turns leads you to Viejas Boulevard at 37.2 miles. Turn right at the country store and fruit stand to sail along the 1.6 mile, mostly flat road back to Descanso. Perkins Store with its food and cold drinks awaits you.

GETTING THERE

The starting point is the town of Descanso, accessed from Interstate 8, about 35 miles east of San Diego. Exit I-8 at the Cuyamaca/Highway 79 off ramp, go 1.3 miles north, and turn left at the Descanso Junction. Continue another mile and park near Perkins Store. This store, established in 1875, is a great place to get a cold drink after the ride.

You can do the ride in either direction, but clockwise allows you to do the uphill on the rough sections of Boulder Creek Road and downhill on the narrow paved highway. Carry plenty of water; there's no drinking water for the first 20 mostly uphill miles. Also, leave early to avoid the intense midday heat in warmer months.

AMENITIES

Perkins Store, at the starting point, has food and cold drinks. Around mile 26, near the highest point of the ride, is a store and picnic area by Cuyamaca Lake. Camping is available at Paso Picacho Campground or in the nearby Laguna Mountains.

Trip M7 – Cuyamaca Grand Tour

Starting Point	Sweetwater River Bridge, Cuyamaca Rancho State Park
Distance	18 miles
Elevation Gain/Loss	1925'/1925', 6% grade in places
Riding Time	5–6 hours
Difficulty	Moderate, not technical
Road Conditions	Graded and rough dirt fire roads, 2 miles paved roads
Season	Spring, Summer, and Fall as snow permits
Equipment	Mountain bike
Optional Topo Map	Cuyamaca Peak, CA

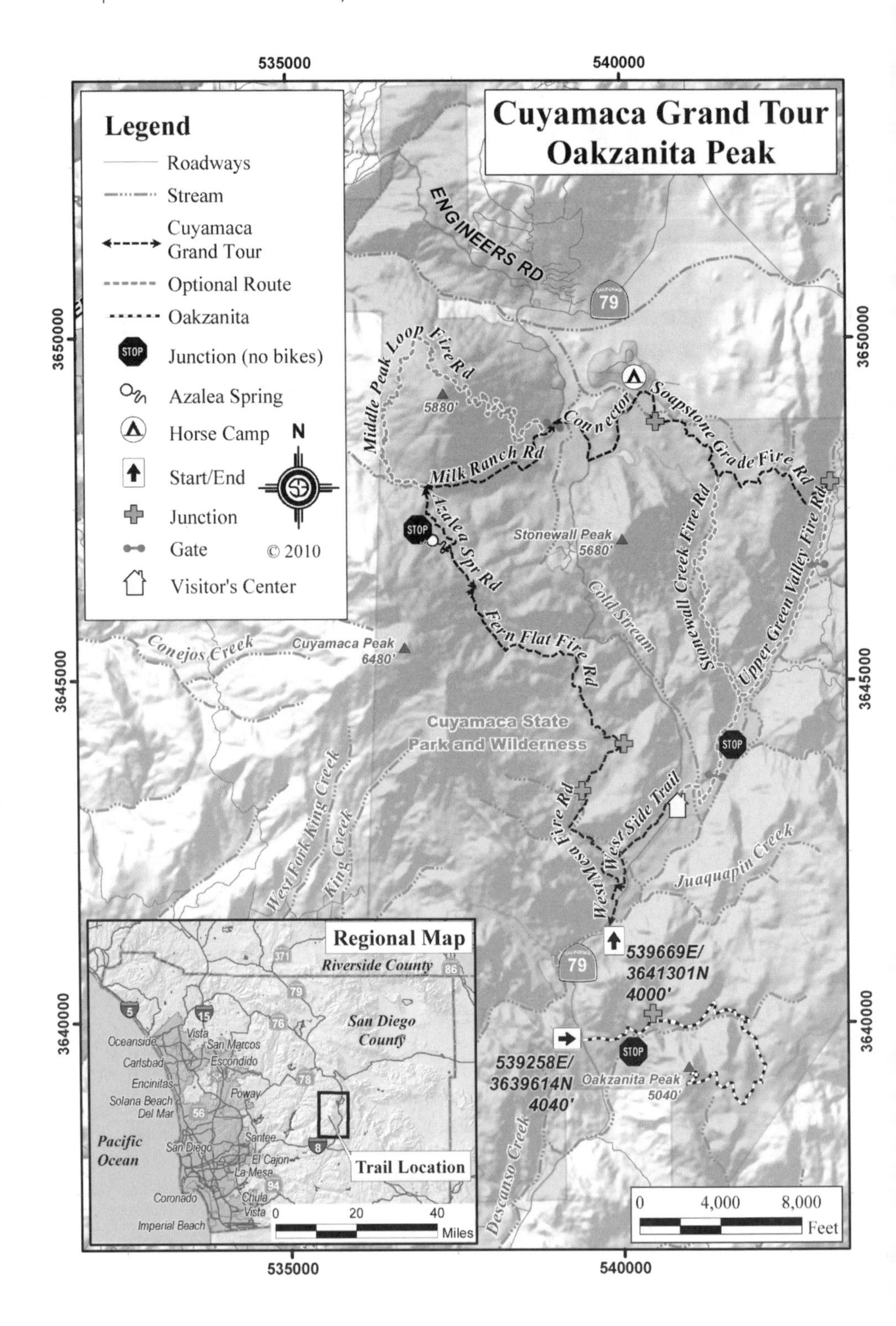

Cuyamaca Grand Tour
Oakzanita Peak
Legend
Roadways
Stream
Cuyamaca Grand Tour
Optional Route
Oakzanita
Junction (no bikes)
Azalea Spring
Horse Camp
Start/End
Junction
Gate
Visitor's Center
N
© 2010
535000
540000
3650000
3645000
3640000
ENGINEERS RD
79
Middle Peak Loop Fire Rd
5880'
Connector
Soapstone Grade Fire Rd
Milk Ranch Rd
Azalea Spr Rd
Stonewall Peak
5680'
Stonewall Creek Fire Rd
Upper Green Valley Fire Rd
Cold Stream
Fern Flat Fire Rd
Conejos Creek
Cuyamaca Peak
6480'
Cuyamaca State
Park and Wilderness
West Fork King Creek
King Creek
West Mesa Fire Rd
West Side Trail
Juaquapin Creek
539669E/
3641301N
4000'
539258E/
3639614N
4040'
Oakzanita Peak
5040'
Descanso Creek
0
4,000
8,000
Feet
Regional Map
Riverside County
San Diego
County
Oceanside
Vista
San Marcos
Carlsbad
Escondido
Encinitas
Poway
Solana Beach
Del Mar
Pacific
Ocean
San Diego
Santee
El Cajon
La Mesa
Coronado
Chula
Vista
Imperial Beach
Trail Location
0
20
40
Miles

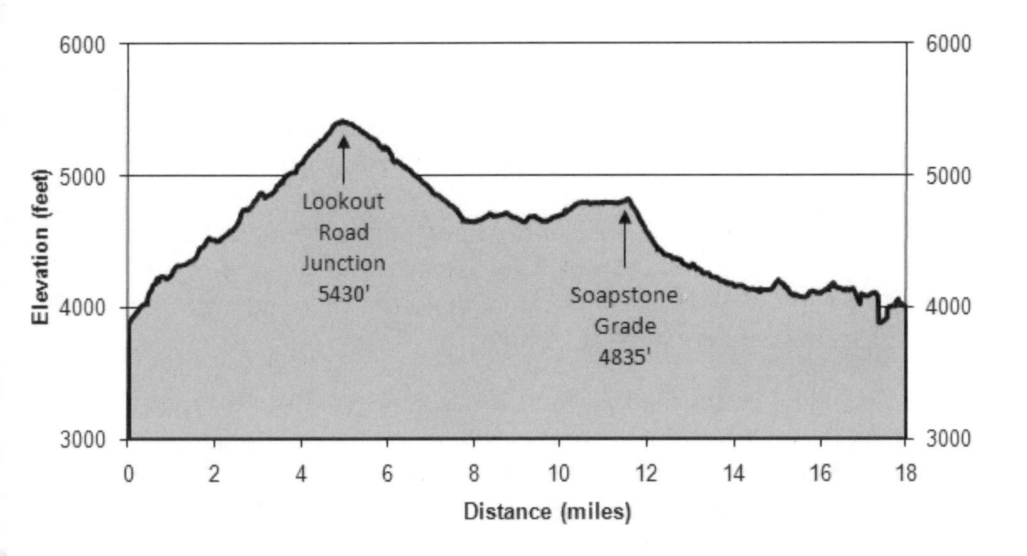

Cuyamaca Rancho State Park spreads across roughly 45 square miles of east San Diego County, a short hour's drive from downtown San Diego. Near the park's western edge, Cuyamaca Peak, at 6480 feet, is the county's second highest point. The park is well known for its 100-mile trail system that allows hikers, equestrians, and mountain bikers to enjoy its beautiful meadows and forests. The Indian name Cuyamaca, "Behind the clouds," is a good name since the area receives about 40 inches of precipitation—enough to sustain beautiful forests of oaks, pines, firs, and cedars.

Nearly half of the park is reserved as state wilderness, where policy prohibits the use of any vehicles including bicycles. This moderately challenging ride however, is on old fire roads that stay clear of the prohibited areas. To explore further, you can obtain a map from the park headquarters that indicates the various trails and roads and which are suitable for each kind of use.

Begin by riding north a short distance, then carefully cross the highway when you spot the gated fire road on the left. Once on the fire road, you'll turn right almost immediately and continue north on Japacha Fire Road. Notice the West Side Trail on your right, you will return via that trail in a few hours. You climb sometimes easily, sometimes moderately through pines and oaks. As you near trickling Japacha Creek, the forest begins to thin in places where the 2003 Cedar Fire swept through the area destroying many of the standing trees. The forest is slowly recovering. Near Japacha Spring, you'll cross the creek and continue climbing along the lower edge of Cuyamaca Peak.

At 2.3 miles, turn left on Fern Flat Fire Road and continue uphill. Stay right as several trails join from the left, including the California Riding & Hiking Trail (no bikes allowed). When you reach the paved Lookout Road, sometimes called Cuyamaca Peak Fire Road, jog right briefly then left, to resume your northwest journey along Cuyamaca Peak's flank. You're now working your way downhill, gently at first then more steeply, past Azalea Spring where water is available. Continue on to the junction of Milk Ranch Road at 6.3 miles. Turn right on Milk Ranch Road and enjoy a nice, rather smooth ride down to Highway 79 at the former Boy Scout Camp entrance at 7.9 miles.

Turn right and follow the highway for 0.5 mile, then go left on the road to Stonewall Mine. One mile later, just short of the mine site, stay right, go around the log gate and take the road to Los Vaqueros Group Horse Camp. After another 0.4 mile, turn left, off the pavement, onto the CA Hiking and Riding Trail, Soapstone Grade Fire Road.

You're now crossing a beautiful, grassy area with a view of the three summits of the Cuyamaca range—North Peak, Middle Peak, and Cuyamaca Peak. In about a mile (at 9.8 miles), make a left on Soapstone Grade Fire Road. In the late spring, blooming lupine brightens up an otherwise dry and rough stretch of road. At 10.8 miles, the Stonewall Creek Fire Road heads right that will shorten the ride about 1.5 miles. To continue, head straight and soon the Soapstone Grade descends quickly, and you'll have to pay attention to make it safely to the bottom of the rough, rutted road. Watch out for riders walking their bikes up the hot, sun-exposed road.

The big effort is all behind you now. When you reach the foot of Soapstone Grade, turn right and enjoy the easy ride along Upper Green Valley Fire Road. You'll cross the trickling upper Sweetwater River several times and enjoy the benefit of shade from live oak trees.

At 13.2 miles, ignore the ascent to a road and locked gate for the Cima State Prison, and stay right (south) on the wide gravel road. Soon you'll pass the Stonewall Creek Fire Road joining from the right and pass through the gate into Camp Cuyamaca (school district camp). Stay straight through the camp and head up a small hill and curve right onto the pavement. Pass the park headquarters and museum to reach Highway 79. Restrooms and water are located near the headquarters.

When safe, head straight across the highway and onto the West Side Trail. It is a delightful trail that meanders through the pines and oaks, crosses Japacha Creek, and joins Japacha Fire Road that you passed a few hours ago. Turn left and it's a short ride back to Highway 79 and your car at the Sweetwater River Bridge.

OPTIONS

At the cost of about 4.5 extra miles and an extra 700 feet of elevation gain, you can loop around the north shoulder of Middle Peak. Middle Peak's slopes had the largest coniferous trees in the park—sugar pines for the most part before the Cedar Fire. Now most are just charred remains. When you reach Milk Ranch Road at 6.1 miles, turn left, coast downhill, staying right at the next two intersections, and then start your climb up the switch backing Middle Peak Fire Road.

You can also shorten ride by about 1.5 miles by staying on Stonewall Creek Fire Road instead of using Soapstone Grade Fire Road to get to Upper Green Valley Fire Road.

GETTING THERE

Exit I-8 at the Cuyamaca/Highway 79 off ramp and continue north about 7.5 miles. Start at the Sweetwater River Bridge parking area at mile 4.8-4.9 on Highway 79 (just north of Green Valley picnic area) about 35 miles east of San Diego. Remember to display your National Forest Adventure Pass in your parked vehicle.

AMENITIES

Perkins Store, established in 1875 in Descanso (1 mile west at the Descanso Junction) has food and cold drinks as well as the small country store and fruit stand at Descanso Junction. Bathrooms and water can be found at the Paso Picacho Campground and the park headquarters/museum just north of the parking area.

Camping is available at Paso Picacho Campground or in the nearby Laguna Mountains.

Trip M8 – Oakzanita Peak

Starting Point	Highway 79, Cuyamaca Rancho State Park
Distance	8.6 miles out and back
Elevation Gain/Loss	1060'/1060', 4.7% grade
Riding Time	2 hours
Difficulty	Moderate, some technical rocky sections near the peak
Road Conditions	Graded fire road, trails
Season	Spring, Summer, and Fall as snow permits
Equipment	Mountain bike
Optional Topo Map	Cuyamaca Peak, CA

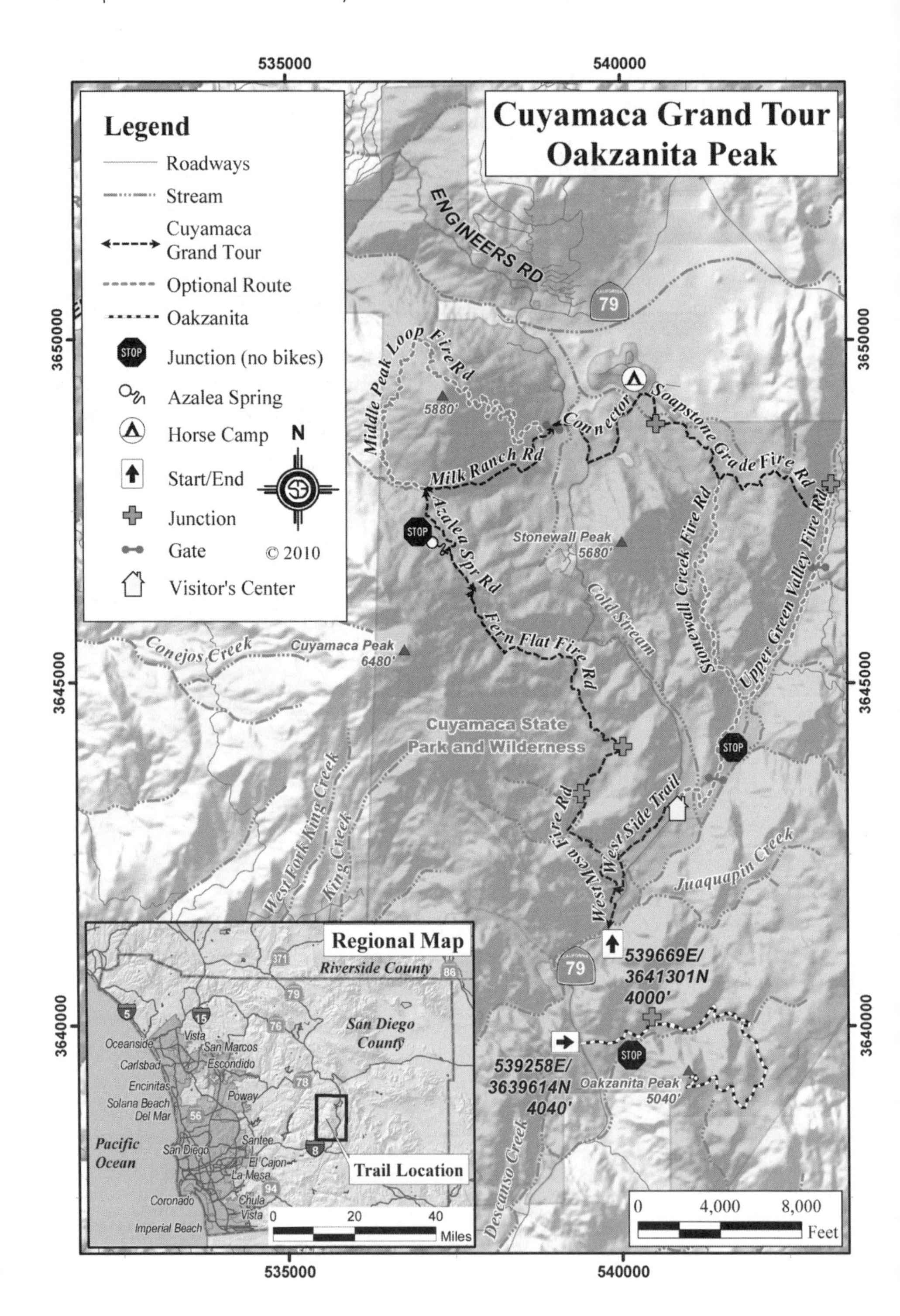
Cuyamaca Grand Tour
Oakzanita Peak
Legend
Roadways
Stream
Cuyamaca Grand Tour
Optional Route
Oakzanita
Junction (no bikes)
Azalea Spring
Horse Camp
Start/End
Junction
Gate
Visitor's Center
N
© 2010
535000
540000
3650000
3645000
3640000
ENGINEERS RD
79
Middle Peak Loop Fire Rd
5880'
Connector
Soapstone Grade Fire Rd
Milk Ranch Rd
Azalea Spr Rd
Stonewall Peak
5680'
Stonewall Creek Fire Rd
Upper Green Valley Fire Rd
Cold Stream
Fern Flat Fire Rd
Conejos Creek
Cuyamaca Peak
6480'
Cuyamaca State
Park and Wilderness
West Fork King Creek
King Creek
West Mesa Fire Rd
West Side Trail
Juaquapin Creek
539669E/
3641301N
4000'
539258E/
3639614N
4040'
Oakzanita Peak
5040'
Descanso Creek
Regional Map
Riverside County
San Diego
County
Oceanside
Vista
San Marcos
Carlsbad
Escondido
Encinitas
Poway
Solana Beach
Del Mar
Pacific
Ocean
San Diego
Santee
El Cajon
La Mesa
Coronado
Chula
Vista
Imperial Beach
Trail Location
0
20
40
Miles
0
4,000
8,000
Feet

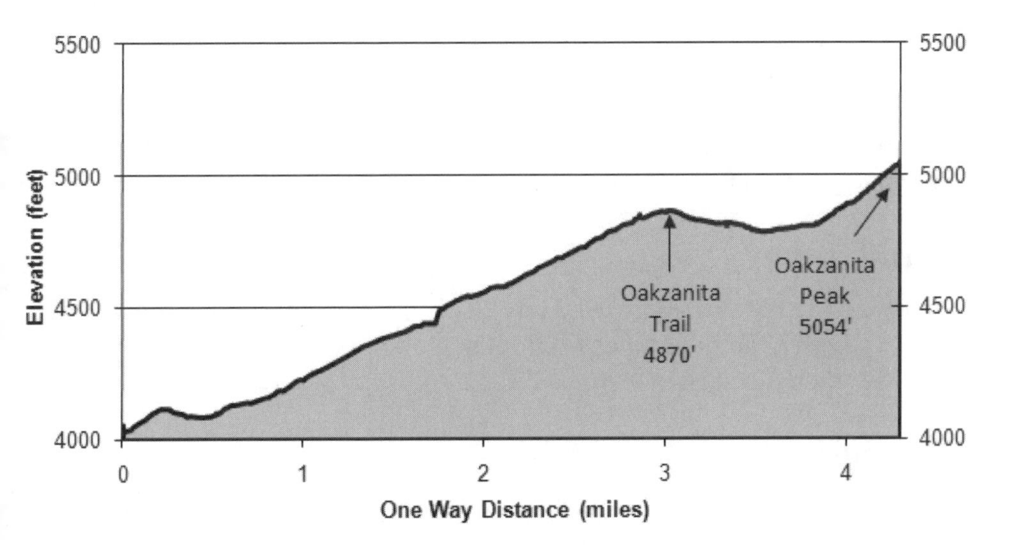

Oakzanita Peak, located in Cuyamaca Rancho State Park, is part of the 45 square miles of wonderful back-country waiting to be explored—and just an hour's drive from San Diego. At 5040 feet above sea level, it's not remarkably high, yet the view from the top is wonderful. This ride takes you on the well-graded East Mesa Fire Road most of the way, with a fun single track trail the last 1.3 miles. The name Oakzanita was derived from the oaks and manzanita found on the hill-sides in the area.

Ride past the gate, and continue on the East Mesa Fire Road as it ascends easily, and then descends northward. At 0.4 mile you'll pass the Lower Descanso Creek Trail and soon after the Upper Descanso Trail, both hiking only. The road begins to slowly ascend, passing the Harvey Moore connector trail and enters a nice oak-shaded area that will provide some relief on a warm day. Follow the road, as it passes over a seasonal creek at 2.1 miles with lots of vegetation nearby. Press on, as the road continues its moderate uphill grade and soon reaches a saddle at 2.9 miles. The signed Oakzanita Trail intersects from the right—left continues on about 1.5 miles to Granite Springs.

Turn right, and enjoy the generally flat single track trail as it winds around boulders and trees. When you reach the hiking-only Upper Descanso Trail (straight ahead), turn left to continue on the Oakzanita Trail. Oakzanita Peak is now in full view, with the three Cuyamaca Peaks visible as well. The trail soon begins ascending and zigzags through dense vegetation. As you near the peak, the trail turns very rocky, so you may want to park your bike and walk the short distance to the peak. Sign the peak register, and enjoy the wonderful view of the southern part of the park. Cuyamaca and Stonewall Peaks are visible to the north.

Reverse your route to return to the starting point. Descending on the East Mesa Fire Road is a lot of fun and you will reach the bottom very quickly.

GETTING THERE

Take I-8 east to the Cuyamaca/Highway 79 off ramp and continue north about 6 miles, or south about 16.8 miles from Julian, to a small parking area on the east side of the road just past mile marker 3 at the East Mesa Fire Road.

AMENITIES

Perkins Store, established in 1875 in Descanso (1 mile west at the Descanso Junction) has food and cold drinks as well as the small country store and fruit stand at Descanso Junction. Bathrooms and water can be found at the Paso Picacho Campground and the park headquarters and museum just north of the parking area.

Camping is available at Paso Picacho Campground or in the nearby Laguna Mountains.

Trip M9 – Big Laguna Trail

Starting Point	Penny Pines/Noble Canyon Trailhead, Laguna Mtns.
Distance	6 miles
Elevation Gain/Loss	300'/300'
Riding Time	1–2 hours
Difficulty	Easy, not technical
Road Conditions	Dirt trails
Season	Spring, Summer, and Fall as snow permits
Equipment	Mountain bike
Optional Topo Map	Monument Peak, CA

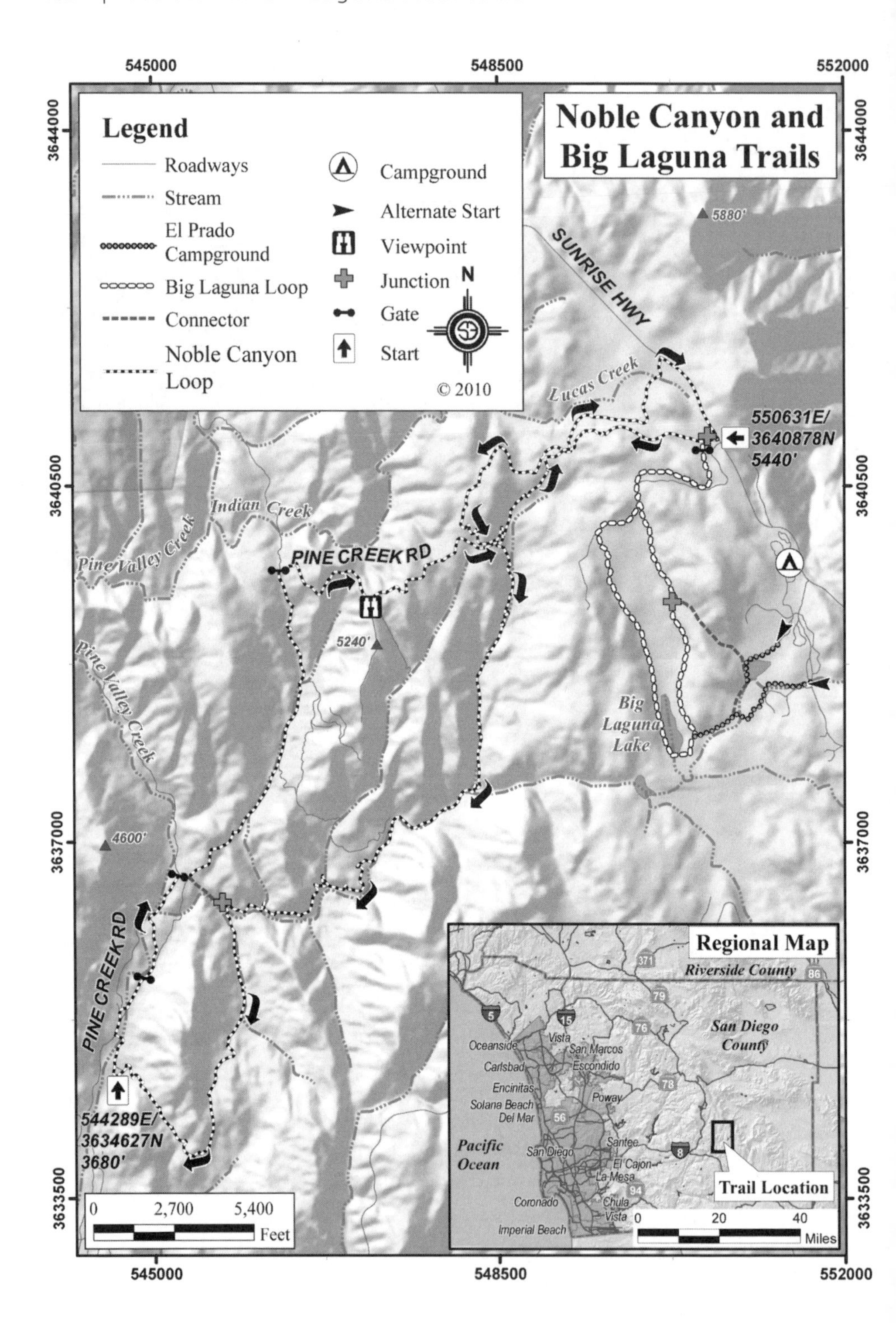

Noble Canyon and Big Laguna Trails
Legend
Roadways
Stream
El Prado Campground
Big Laguna Loop
Connector
Noble Canyon Loop
Campground
Alternate Start
Viewpoint
Junction
Gate
Start
N
© 2010
545000
548500
552000
3644000
3640500
3637000
3633500
SUNRISE HWY
5880'
Lucas Creek
550631E/
3640878N
5440'
Indian Creek
Pine Valley Creek
PINE CREEK RD
5240'
Big Laguna Lake
4600'
544289E/
3634627N
3680'
0 2,700 5,400 Feet
Regional Map
Riverside County
San Diego County
Oceanside
Vista
San Marcos
Carlsbad
Escondido
Encinitas
Solana Beach
Del Mar
Poway
Pacific Ocean
San Diego
Santee
El Cajon
La Mesa
Coronado
Chula Vista
Imperial Beach
Trail Location
0 20 40 Miles

This ride appears deceptively simple and it is, but the real treasure is not the difficulty, but the beauty of the Big Laguna Meadow area that will appeal to riders of all levels. Grassy meadows, wildflowers, pine trees, and gorgeous vistas await you. Longer rides can be created by linking together a number of trails in the area. There are many other trail users in this area, so please be courteous and yield to hikers and equestrians so the trails will remain open to cyclists.

From the Penny Pines/Noble Canyon Trailhead follow the trail south and turn at the first left—the Big Laguna Trail junction. Pass through a gate and the trail starts gradually ascending through an area burned out by the Laguna Fire. The vegetation is recovering nicely.

At 0.9 mile you'll pass the Sunset Trail on your right which is off limits to bikes. At 1 mile you reach the signed loop around Big Laguna Meadow. Turn right and begin riding across the northern end of the meadow. If you follow the loop as written you'll return to this junction on your way back.

At 1.4 miles the hiking-only Sunset Trail joins from the right; just continue going straight and then veer left (south) as the trail begins to follow along the grassy western side of the meadow. The trail hugs the fence rolling through the edge of the lumpy meadow. The trail gradually bends this way and that around tree snags and stumps providing a very fun, slightly downhill ride. As the trail nears the end of the large meadow, there may be water in the lake on your left during wetter times.

At 2.9 miles you'll reach a berm crossing the southern end of the lake and a trail junction. You can explore straight ahead, but the loop described here turns left and crosses the lumpy berm. Now and then the sounds of grazing cows may echo across the meadow.

At 3.1 miles, a junction from the Laguna/El Prado Campground area joins from the right. This is one of the alternate routes you can take to lengthen the ride (see Options). Stay straight to continue the loop. The trail climbs into the pine trees on the eastern side of the meadow where you delightfully dodge around the trees and over the roots enjoying the view of the peaceful meadow below.

At 4 miles you reach another trail from the Laguna/El Prado Campground area that joins from the right. Continuing on, the trail begins to veer away from the meadow. At 4.7 miles, the junction at the north end of the meadow should look familiar. You went west here on the way in; continue straight and enjoy the mostly downhill, fun ride back to the start.

GETTING THERE

Take I-8 east to Pine Valley and exit at Sunrise Highway. Turn left, and head north 14 miles through the Laguna Recreation Area of the Cleveland National Forest and park at the Noble Canyon/Penny Pines parking area just past mile marker 27.0. Display your Forest Adventure Pass here.

OPTIONS

The main ride is a lollipop starting at the trailhead and heading around Big Laguna Meadow and back. But there are many trail connectors and optional extensions you can add to make a longer ride. The map shows a few. You may also park in the Laguna/El Prado Campground near the north end or the group camp area at the south end and enter the trails from there ($5 day use fee, in lieu of the Forest Adventure Pass). It is also possible to enter from the Penny Pines/Noble Canyon Trailhead and exit via Laguna/El Prado and return for about 1.1 miles on the pavement (turn left on Sunrise Highway from the campground). Watch for vehicles on this route.

AMENITIES

Water and restrooms are available in the nearby Laguna/El Prado Campground. The General Store at Laguna Mountain Lodge is sometimes open. There is a public restroom and water at the visitor center next door that is open Friday, Saturday, and Sunday weather permitting.

Additional restaurants and stores are in Julian or Pine Valley. Public restrooms and water are available in both locations.

There are many opportunities for camping in the Laguna Recreation Area. Laguna/El Prado Campground is the closest. Burnt Rancheria Campground is about 4.5 miles south on Sunrise Highway. The Laguna Mountain Lodge is a service partner with the Cleveland National Forest and provides cabins and motel rooms. Several locations for dispersed camping are also found in the area and require a Forest Adventure Pass.

Trip M10 – Noble Canyon

Starting Point	Noble Canyon Trailhead, Pine Valley
Distance	18.3 miles
Elevation Gain/Loss	2825'/2825', 7% average grade
Riding Time	5 hours
Difficulty	Strenuous, technical
Road Conditions	Dirt trails, very rocky in places, 8.5 miles pavement
Season	Spring, Summer, and Fall as snow permits
Equipment	Mountain bike
Optional Topo Maps	Cuyamaca Peak, Descanso, Monument Peak, Mount Laguna, CA

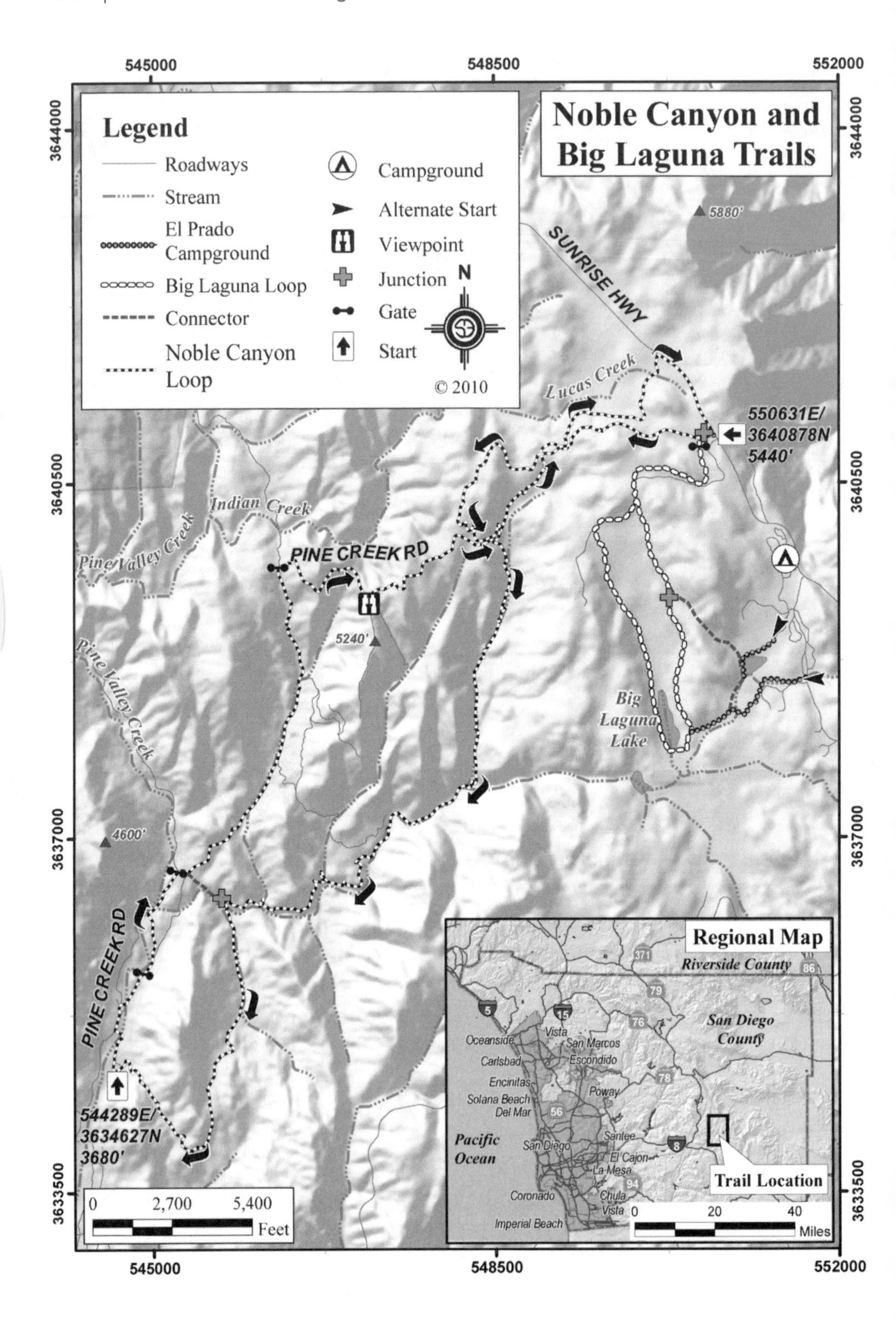
Noble Canyon and Big Laguna Trails
Legend
Roadways
Stream
El Prado Campground
Big Laguna Loop
Connector
Noble Canyon Loop
Campground
Alternate Start
Viewpoint
Junction
Gate
Start
N
© 2010
545000
548500
552000
3644000
3640500
3637000
3633500
SUNRISE HWY
5880'
Lucas Creek
550631E/
3640878N
5440'
Indian Creek
Pine Valley Creek
PINE CREEK RD
5240'
Big Laguna Lake
4600'
544289E/
3634627N
3680'
0
2,700
5,400
Feet
Regional Map
Riverside County
San Diego County
Oceanside
Vista
San Marcos
Carlsbad
Escondido
Encinitas
Poway
Solana Beach
Del Mar
Pacific Ocean
San Diego
Santee
El Cajon
La Mesa
Coronado
Chula Vista
Imperial Beach
Trail Location
20
40
Miles

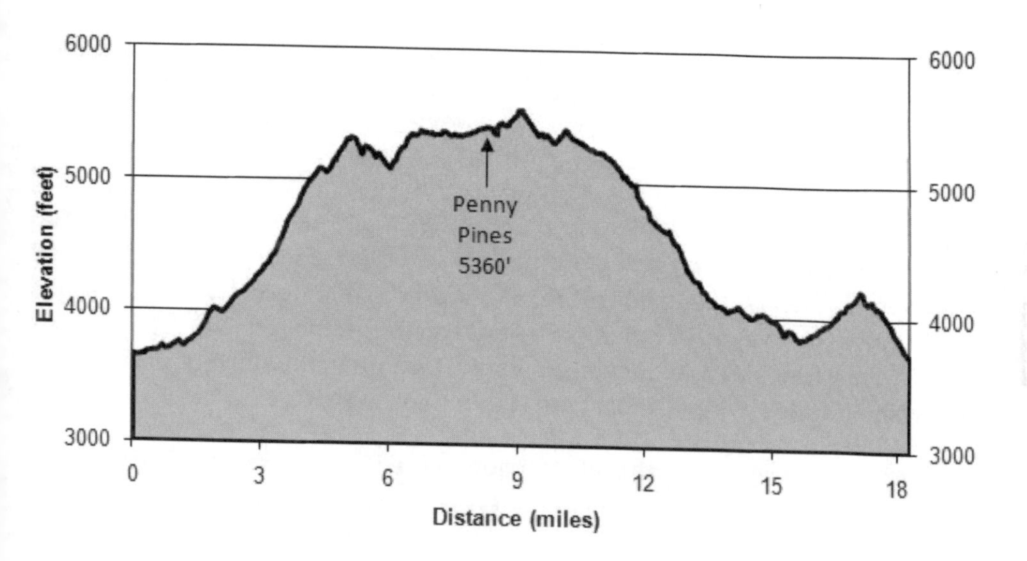

Noble Canyon, in the Laguna Mountains, is what some riders call an epic ride. It's technically very difficult with narrow single track and many rocky sections to negotiate. The ride as described starts in oaks and pines, ascends through chaparral, into Jeffrey pines and then descends through a riparian area of conifer-oaks to a dry, and exposed sage scrub and chaparral area. Spectacular views of the Cuyamaca and Laguna mountains and as far away as the San Bernardino Mountains are possible at the higher elevations. The lower sections of the trail can be extremely dry and hot in warmer months, so be sure to bring plenty of water along.

To ride the complete loop, start from the lower Noble Canyon Trailhead and follow the entrance road back to the junction of Pine Creek Road. Turn right, and cross the small bridge over Pine Valley Creek where the road quickly narrows. The area ahead is dotted with oaks, pines, and cabins on land leased from the Forest Service. The road ascends and descends easily through this section. A sign on a gate at 1.5 miles indicates the road is closed to motor vehicles during wet weather. Soon the road begins to ascend easily, and at 3.4 miles, narrows more and begins to get really steep. You may keep looking down for that extra gear.

Thankfully, the road levels out when you reach another gate at 3.8 miles, marked by a large oak tree. The three Cuyamaca Peaks are visible over the ridge to the west. The dirt Deer Park Road continues straight, our route continues right on paved Pine Creek Road (14S05). (This road is called Laguna Meadow Road on some maps.) The road ascends steeply again, and sweeps left soon passing a small spur road on the right that leads to a nice viewpoint, a good place for a snack. As if it couldn't get any steeper, the road does at 5 miles, but finally reaches a ridge with great views in all directions. You can now enjoy several wonderful descents and ascents as the road begins to reach the Jeffrey pines.

At 6.5 miles, the signed Noble Canyon Trail (5E04) crosses the road. You will be passing here on your way down. Continue ascending through the pines, many that were burned by the Laguna Fire, and soon the road levels out and reaches the Sunrise Highway at 7.8 miles. Turn right and follow the highway 0.6 mile east to the Penny Pines/Noble Canyon Trailhead. Be sure to top off your water bottle at the small water pump just past the Noble Canyon kiosk.

Follow the trail south, past the left junction to the Big Laguna Trail. Some of this area was burned by the Laguna Fire, but is recovering nicely. The trail winds its way through Jeffrey pines, and ascends moderately along the north side of a large hill. San Jacinto and San Gorgonio Mountains are visible in the distance to the north. The trail levels out for a short distance and then quickly descends and crosses Pine Creek Road twice (the trail jogs right then quickly left across an old cattle guard on the second crossing). The trail then begins ascending circling around a large hill passing the Indian Creek Trail on the right at 10.5 miles.

You cross Pine Creek (Laguna Meadow) Road one more time, and begin your descent into the upper end of Noble Canyon. The trail descends easily in places along meadows and more moderately through some rough, rocky sections all the while passing through beautiful oaks and Jeffrey pines. Wildflowers line the trail in places. At 13 miles, you'll cross a creek and follow it for a short distance through a riparian area and cross it again in about 1 mile. A trail joins from the right, you continue left.

The trail leaves the oaks and pines and enters a drier area, dominated by sagescrub and chaparral. At 14.6 miles the trail becomes very rocky for a short distance. Carefully negotiate this area, and soon you'll enjoy a nice smooth descending section of trail—a nice reprieve from the rocky trails behind you. The trail makes a sharp left hand turn, passing a connector trail that leads to Pine Creek (Deer Park) Road. Stay left following the Noble Canyon Trail sign as the trail reaches the dry creek bed below. The trail easily ascends a tributary canyon, sometimes sandy, for about 1.4 miles to a small saddle. From here, the trail swings right and it's all downhill, through a few rocky sections to the lower trailhead. Congratulations, you've just completed one of the best rides in San Diego County.

GETTING THERE

The starting point for the Noble Canyon Loop is in Pine Valley, north of Interstate 8 about 40 miles east of San Diego. Take I-8 east, exit at Pine Valley and turn left. Drive a short distance to Old Highway 80 and turn left. Follow Highway 80 northwest to the concrete bridge over Pine Valley Creek. After crossing the bridge, make a sharp right onto Pine Creek Road and follow it a short distance to the trailhead for the Noble Canyon Trail and a picnic ground on the right.

You can also do a car shuttle or get dropped off from the top of the Noble Canyon Trail at Penny Pines. For the shuttle, leave the first car at the bottom trailhead described above and drive back to Old Highway 80 and follow it east through Pine Valley to Sunrise Highway. Turn left and drive 14 miles through the Laguna Recreation Area of the Cleveland National Forest and park at the Noble Canyon/Penny Pines parking area just past mile marker 27.0. Display your Forest Adventure Pass here (you can also follow the ride description above to the upper trailhead since it's all paved to Sunrise Highway, but quite steep).

OPTIONS

There are several ways to do the Noble Canyon ride. As described here, you'll start at the lower trailhead, ascend the steep, paved Deer Park and Pine Creek Roads to Sunrise Highway, ride to the Penny Pines Trailhead, and then descend on the dirt Noble Canyon Trail. A car shuttle or getting dropped off at the top is also possible, and a lot less work.

AMENITIES

Restrooms are available at the lower Noble Canyon Trailhead parking area. Water is available at the Penny Pines Trailhead just past the kiosk describing the trail, but no other facilities. A few restaurants and stores are located in Pine Valley, as well as public restrooms and water.

There are many opportunities for camping in the Laguna Recreation Area. Laguna/El Prado Campground is the closest. Burnt Rancheria Campground is about 4.5 miles south on Sunrise Highway. The Laguna Mountain Lodge is a service partner with the Cleveland National Forest and provides cabins and motel rooms. Several locations for dispersed camping are also found in the area and require a Forest Adventure Pass.

Trip M11 – Sheephead Mountain Road

Starting Point	Buckman Springs Road, I-8
Distance	5.3 miles out and back
Elevation Gain/Loss	1300'/1300', 9.3% average grade
Riding Time	3 hours
Difficulty	Difficult, technical in spots
Road Conditions	Rough, rutted dirt roads
Season	Spring, Summer, and Fall
Equipment	Mountain bike
Optional Topo Map	Mount Laguna, CA

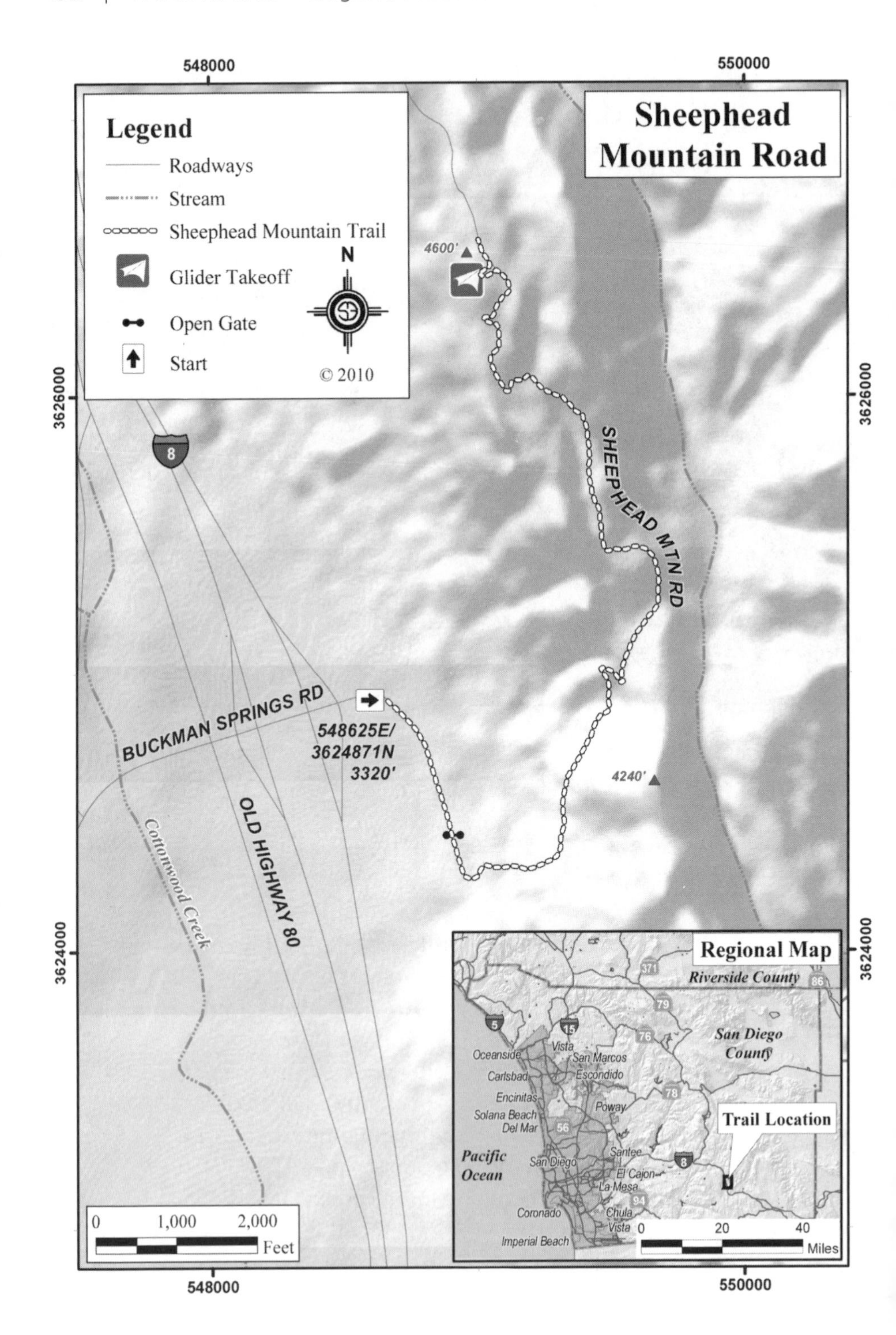
Sheephead Mountain Road
Legend
Roadways
Stream
Sheephead Mountain Trail
Glider Takeoff
Open Gate
Start
N
© 2010
548000
550000
3626000
3624000
4600'
4240'
SHEEPHEAD MTN RD
BUCKMAN SPRINGS RD
548625E/
3624871N
3320'
OLD HIGHWAY 80
Cottonwood Creek
8
0
1,000
2,000
Feet
Regional Map
Riverside County
San Diego County
Oceanside
Vista
San Marcos
Carlsbad
Escondido
Encinitas
Solana Beach
Del Mar
Poway
Pacific Ocean
San Diego
Santee
El Cajon
La Mesa
Coronado
Chula Vista
Imperial Beach
Trail Location
0
20
40
Miles

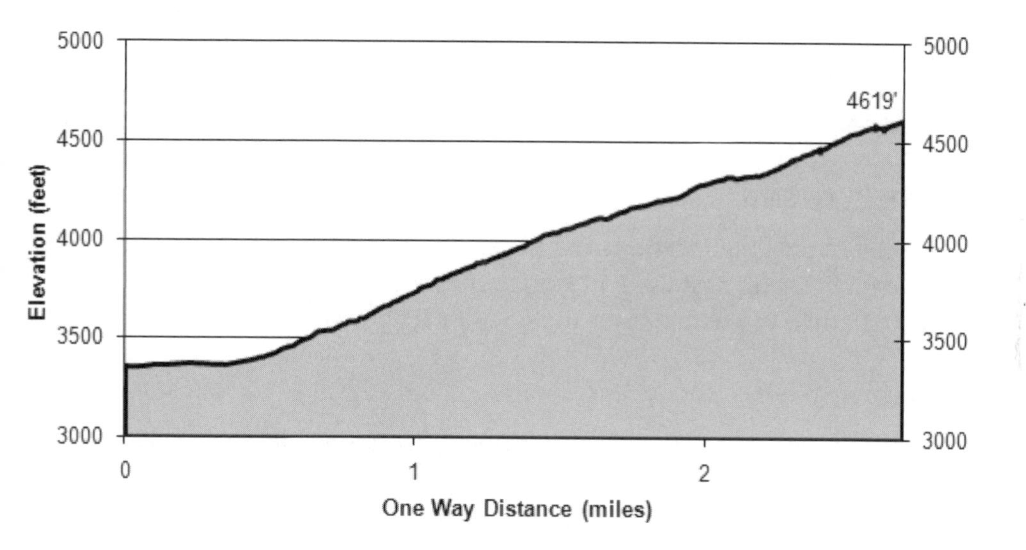

If you've ever driven along I-8 near Buckman Springs Road and noticed hang gliders and paragliders floating in the updrafts above you, and wondered where they take off, this is your chance to find out. No doubt you've seen the road carving its way up the steep ridge to the east of I-8. This is Sheephead Mountain Road that provides access to the takeoff point and at one time connected with Kitchen Creek Road and Sunrise Highway. Now private inholdings, about 6 miles in prevent you from making the complete connection. But you can still ride part of it and on a nice day and watch the fearless people jump off the cliff.

Start the ride by heading south through an open white gate. The road then curves east and starts ascending with a few rough and rocky sections now and then to make it more interesting. At 1.2 miles, the road switchbacks sharply right and then left, heading inland away from the nice valley view below and into a small, secluded valley to the east.

Soon the road veers west again and at 2.3 miles there are several small turnouts with spectacular views south and west of the Cottonwood Valley below and the ridge across the valley.

At 2.6 miles, a short steep road ascends the hill on your left to the glider takeoff point. Climb the hill and enjoy the view, you've earned it. Carpet sections on the ground here make it easier for the pilots to get a running start down the sloping hill.

You can turn around here and enjoy a fast descent back to your car, or continue on a few more miles. The road gets much worse past this point and is not described here.

GETTING THERE

Take I-8 east past Pine Valley to the Buckman Springs Road exit. Turn left (east), cross under I-8 and past the entrance to the rest area. Follow Buckman Springs Road 0.25 mile to where it turns to dirt and park anywhere.

AMENITIES

There are no amenities along I-8 and Buckman Springs Road near the start of the ride. The Buckman Springs rest area has restrooms and water. Pine Valley has several restaurants and public restrooms.

There are numerous opportunities for camping in the area. Nearby Lake Morena/Corral Canyon has a campground in the middle of an OHV area. Cibbets Flat Campground is on Kitchen Creek Road one exit farther on I-8. Burnt Rancheria Campground and Laguna/El Prado Campground are located on Sunrise Highway in the Laguna Recreation Area.

Trip M12 – Kitchen Creek and Thing Valley

Starting Point	Old Highway 80 and La Posta Truck Trail
Distance	28 miles
Elevation Gain/Loss	3780'/3780', 5.5% grade
Riding Time	4–5 hours
Difficulty	Strenuous, not technical
Road Conditions	Graded rough dirt roads, 16 miles paved
Season	Spring, Summer, and Fall as snow permits
Equipment	Mountain bike
Optional Topo Maps	Cameron Corners, Mount Laguna, CA

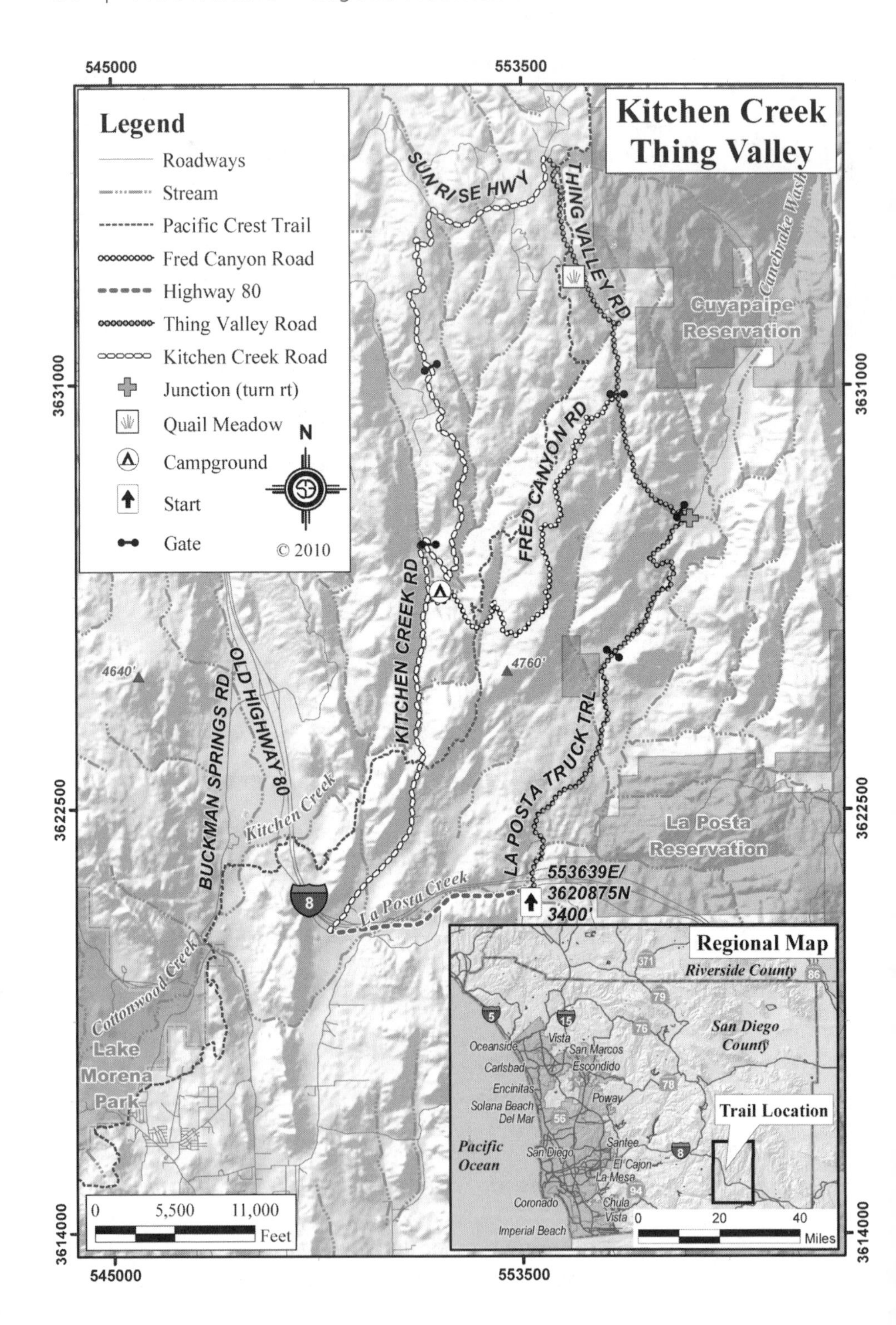
Kitchen Creek
Thing Valley
Legend
Roadways
Stream
Pacific Crest Trail
Fred Canyon Road
Highway 80
Thing Valley Road
Kitchen Creek Road
Junction (turn rt)
Quail Meadow
Campground
Start
Gate
N
© 2010
SUNRISE HWY
THING VALLEY RD
FRED CANYON RD
KITCHEN CREEK RD
BUCKMAN SPRINGS RD
OLD HIGHWAY 80
LA POSTA TRUCK TRL
Canebrake Wash
Cuyapaipe Reservation
La Posta Reservation
Kitchen Creek
La Posta Creek
Cottonwood Creek
Lake Morena Park
4640'
4760'
8
553639E/
3620875N
3400'
0 5,500 11,000 Feet
545000
553500
3631000
3622500
3614000
Regional Map
Riverside County
San Diego County
Oceanside
Vista
San Marcos
Carlsbad
Escondido
Encinitas
Poway
Solana Beach
Del Mar
Pacific Ocean
San Diego
Santee
El Cajon
La Mesa
Coronado
Chula Vista
Imperial Beach
Trail Location
0 20 40 Miles

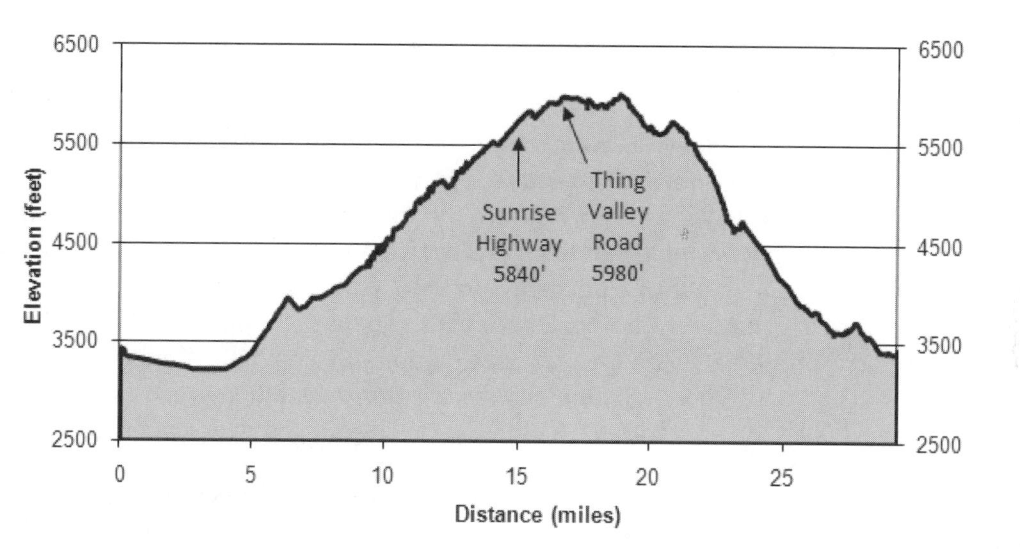

Are you ready for some serious climbing? This ride is for you, with over 3500 feet of elevation gain from dry Cameron Valley to the pines in the Laguna Mountains. The recommended route is to climb up paved Kitchen Creek Road and down the rough dirt Thing Valley Road. If you really want some punishment you could ride up and down the dirt road but riding companions might be hard to find.

From the starting point turn right (west) on Old Highway 80 and cruise easily down to Kitchen Creek Road. Turn right and follow Kitchen Creek Road as it gradually ascends north. At 4.3 miles the road begins to climb sharply and in another mile crests at a saddle where the Pacific Crest Trail (PCT) crosses the road (no bikes allowed). A series of ascents and descents along Kitchen Creek through a narrow valley, lead to Cibbets Flat Campground on the right at 7.5 miles. Restrooms and water are available here as well as the start of Fred Valley Road on the right as you enter the campground (see Options).

Continuing on Kitchen Creek Road you'll make a sharp right turn and quickly reach the lower locked gate. Pass by the gate and continue your climb traffic free. The road ascends for awhile and then contours above scenic Long Canyon and Troy Canyons to the east.

At 12 miles you'll pass the upper Kitchen Creek gate and continue the ascent on the west side of the ridge into the pines above Kitchen Valley and Kitchen Creek. Soon you'll enter the Laguna Mountain Recreational Area where the road crests slightly, and then easily descends to Sunrise Highway at 14.6 miles.

Turn right and follow Sunrise Highway past Morris Ranch Road to Thing Valley Road at 16.5 miles.

Turn right on Thing Valley Road and begin the rolling descent through the pines. Small rises and quick downhill speeds make for some fun jumps. At 17.75 miles, you'll pass a parking area on the right for the Pacific Crest Trail (PCT) trail, and then begin a great downhill run to an area with a few houses. Continue straight on a modest ascend out of a peaceful meadow. At 20 miles, the upper locked gate blocks the road from traffic. Once past the gate the junction to Fred Canyon Road is immediately on the right (see Options). Thing Valley Road changes names to La Posta Truck Trail here and starts a fast downhill descent on a loose dirt road. It's all too easy to catch a little too much air if you're not careful.

After a white-knuckle descent, the lower locked gate appears at 22 miles from the start and the major downhill is over. Just past the gate, turn right at the T intersection and begin an easy climb. It's then a fun descent around the head of a canyon with great views south to I-8 where you'll be in a few minutes. The road hugs a small seasonal creek as the downhill fun continues. The road ascends and descends several more times until you reach La Posta Creek Road, a ranch, and the I-8 overpass looming ahead. When you arrive at the pavement, your car is now a short distance away.

GETTING THERE

Take I-8 east past Pine Valley to the Kitchen Creek Road exit. Follow Old Highway 80 2.8 miles east to La Posta Truck Trail, turn left and park near the I-8 overpass.

OPTIONS

The ride can be done as a car shuttle or you can be dropped off at the top if you just want to blast down Thing Valley Road. The ride can be modified by taking 6.3-mile Fred Canyon Road either on the way up or down which bisects the loop. But the section of Thing Valley Road above Fred Canyon is very fun and should not be missed. Actually all of Thing Valley Road is a fun descent.

AMENITIES

There are no amenities along I-8 and Old Highway 80 near the start of the ride. The general store at Laguna Mountain Lodge is sometimes open but a mile or so past Thing Valley Road. There is a public restroom and water at the Laguna

Mountain Visitor Center next door that is open Friday, Saturday, and Sunday weather permitting. Water and restrooms are available in the nearby Burnt Rancheria Campground just past Thing Valley Road. Restaurants and stores can be found in Pine Valley.

There are many opportunities for camping in the Laguna Recreation Area. Cibbets Flat Campground is on Kitchen Creek Road before the bottom gate. Water and restrooms are available here. Burnt Rancheria Campground and Laguna/El Prado Campground are located on Sunrise Highway.

The Laguna Mountain Lodge is a service partner with the Cleveland National Forest and provides cabins and motel rooms. Several locations for dispersed camping are also found in the area and require a Forest Adventure Pass.

Trip D1 – McCain Valley

Starting Point	Old Highway 80, Boulevard
Distance	29 miles out and back
Elevation Gain/Loss	1785'/624' one-way
Riding Time	3–4 hours
Difficulty	Moderate (due to length), not technical
Road Conditions	Graded dirt road, 4.8 miles paved
Season	Fall, Winter, and Spring
Equipment	Mountain bike
Optional Topo Maps	Jacumba, Live Oak Springs, Sombrero Peak, CA

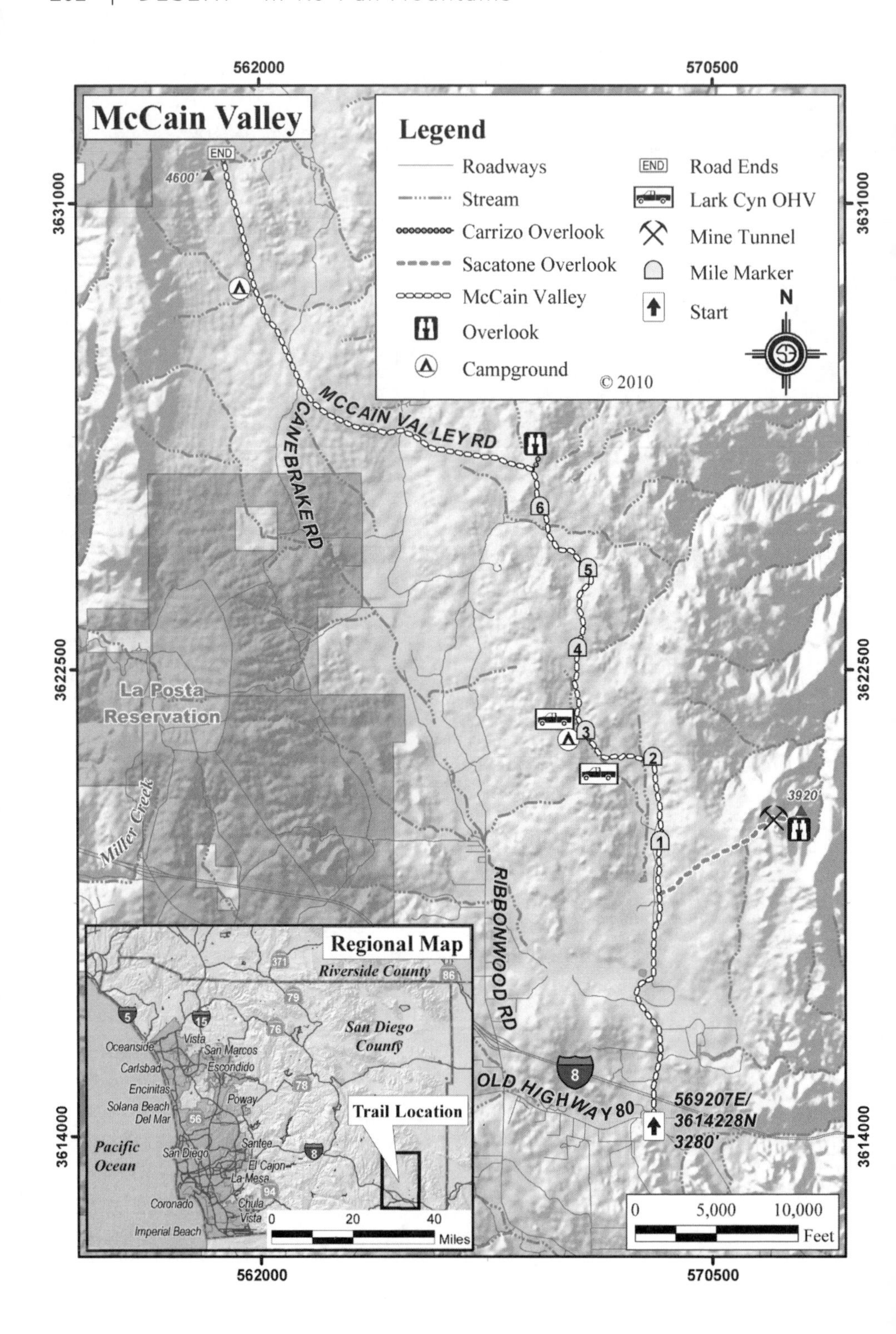

McCain Valley
Legend
Roadways
Stream
Carrizo Overlook
Sacatone Overlook
McCain Valley
Overlook
Campground
Road Ends
Lark Cyn OHV
Mine Tunnel
Mile Marker
Start
N
© 2010
562000
570500
3631000
3622500
3614000
END
4600'
MCCAIN VALLEY RD
CANEBRAKE RD
RIBBONWOOD RD
OLD HIGHWAY 80
La Posta Reservation
Miller Creek
3920'
569207E/
3614228N
3280'
0
5,000
10,000
Feet
Regional Map
Riverside County
San Diego County
Pacific Ocean
Oceanside
Carlsbad
Encinitas
Solana Beach
Del Mar
Vista
San Marcos
Escondido
Poway
Santee
San Diego
El Cajon
La Mesa
Coronado
Chula Vista
Imperial Beach
Trail Location
0
20
40
Miles

The McCain Valley Resource Conservation Area, about 65 miles east of San Diego, is a fairly remote, sparsely vegetated area separated from the hot desert below by the In-Ko-Pah Mountains to the east. McCain Valley Road, a well-graded dirt road, cuts through the valley providing the only access to the BLM-managed area. The Lark Canyon OHV (Off-Highway Vehicle) area and campground is a popular destination for off-roaders.

Start off by riding north on McCain Valley Road from Old Highway 80. At 2.4 miles the pavement ends and the graded road begins. The Sacatone Overlook road joins from the right at 2.8 miles. This slightly rougher road heads 2 miles east to a nice view of Carrizo Gorge and the railway below where a couple of tunnels are visible. A small mine is fun to poke your head into just before the overlook.

Continuing on undulating McCain Valley Road, you'll reach the Lark Canyon OHV staging and day use area at 5 miles followed by the Lark Canyon Campground a short 0.3 mile past that. Toilets are available here. At 8.7 miles, turn right for a quick 0.3 mile ride to the Carrizo Overlook with a nice view into Carrizo Wash. Toro Peak and the Santa Rosa Mountains rise in the distance to the north. Several picnic tables make this a good place to have a snack and enjoy the view.

Once back on the main road, keep going and at 14.5 miles the road ends. Turn around here and retrace your route to return to the car and go get that hand-dipped chocolate you've been thinking about.

GETTING THERE

Take I-8 east past Pine Valley to the Highway 94/Campo/Boulevard exit in Boulevard. Turn right on Ribbonwood Road and then left on Old Highway 80 and continue about 1.8 miles to McCain Valley Road. Turn left and park by the side of the road.

AMENITIES

A Mexican restaurant and the recently reopened Wisteria Candy Cottage, providing hand-dipped chocolate and old fashioned candy since 1921, can be found on Old Highway 80 in Boulevard near the start of the ride. The town of Jacumba, about 6 miles east on Old Highway 80, has a restaurant and a market. Camping is available at the Lark Canyon Campground on McCain Valley Road.

Trip D2 – Table Mountain

Starting Point	In-Ko-Pah Park Road, Jacumba
Distance	13.5 miles out and back, lollipop
Elevation Gain/Loss	615'/615'
Riding Time	3 hours
Difficulty	Moderate, slightly technical in spots
Road Conditions	Rough graded dirt road, some rocky sections
Season	Fall, Winter, and Spring
Equipment	Mountain bike
Optional Topo Maps	In-Ko-Pah Gorge, Jacumba, CA

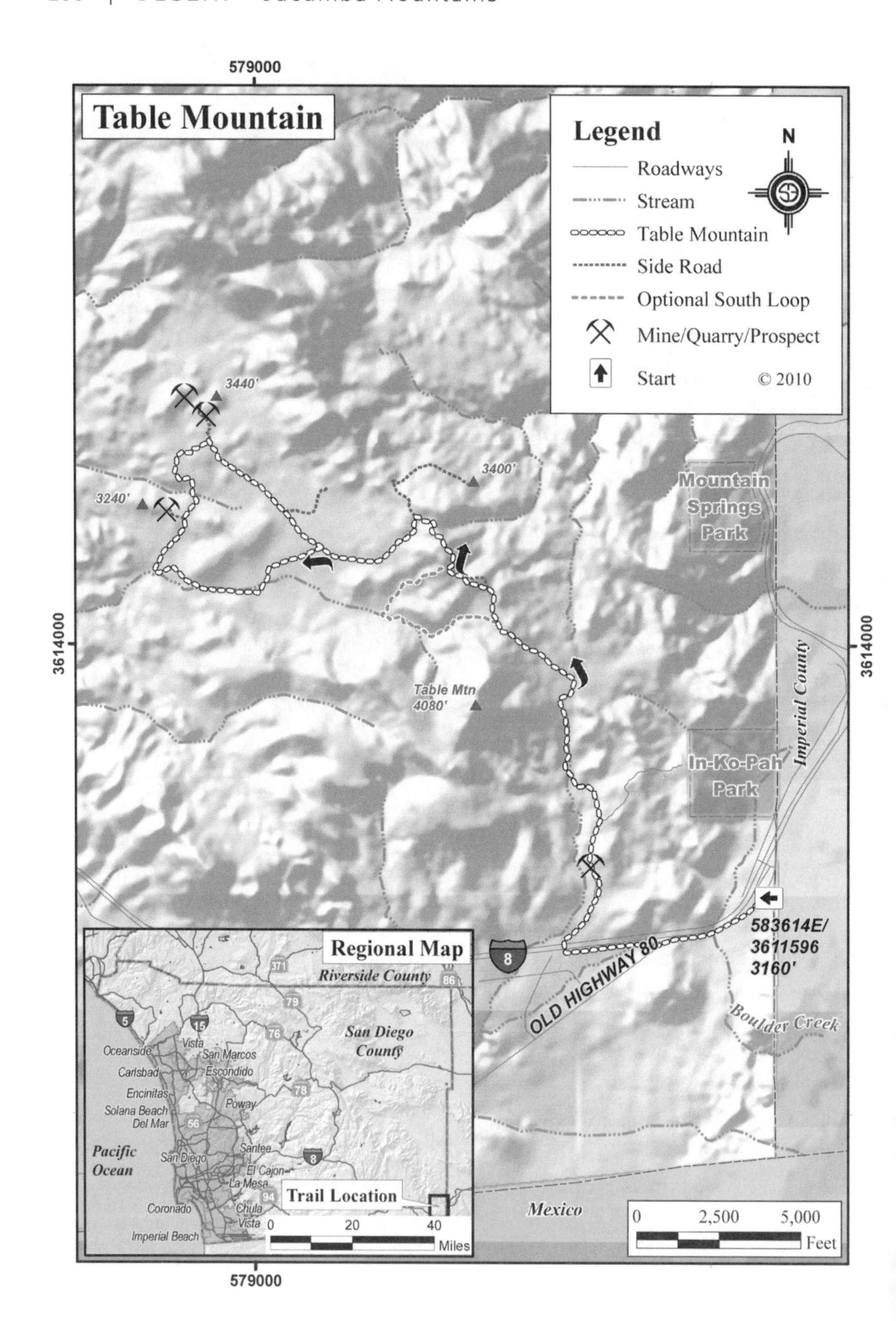

Table Mountain
579000
3614000
Legend
Roadways
Stream
Table Mountain
Side Road
Optional South Loop
Mine/Quarry/Prospect
Start
© 2010
N
3440'
3400'
3240'
Table Mtn
4080'
Mountain Springs Park
In-Ko-Pah Park
Imperial County
583614E/
3611596
3160'
8
OLD HIGHWAY 80
Boulder Creek
Mexico
0
2,500
5,000
Feet
Regional Map
Riverside County
San Diego County
Oceanside
Vista
San Marcos
Carlsbad
Escondido
Encinitas
Solana Beach
Del Mar
Poway
Pacific Ocean
San Diego
Santee
El Cajon
La Mesa
Coronado
Chula Vista
Imperial Beach
Trail Location
20
40
Miles

Table Mountain and the surrounding mountains is a beautiful area with jumbles of granitic boulders reminiscent of the Wonderland of Rocks in Joshua Tree. This is a transitional zone between mountain chaparral and low desert chaparral with many interesting plants and animals. When the desert is too warm to ride you can still enjoy this ride. This area was inhabited by the Kumeyaay where they lived and gathered yucca, jojoba, chia, and scrub oak acorns. It is still considered a sacred area by descendents of the Kumeyaay. This ride will take you around Table Mountain where you can enjoy the beautiful vistas and transitional zone vegetation.

Start by heading west (left) along the shoulder of Old Highway 80 and turn right onto a dirt road at 0.6 mile just above the border checkpoint. Follow the road as it parallels I-8 and at 1.2 miles turn right and follow it under I-8. Head north passing several old mining roads on your left that climb onto Table Mountain providing spectacular views. You can extend your ride or save them for another day. At 1.8 miles you'll pass the remnants of the Mica Gem mine mill on the right. Muscovite mica was once mined near here. As you continue on, ignore the private road to the right and then stay left at the triple junction at 3.0 miles.

Soon the road crests a small hill and the rocky Jacumba hills, Table Mountain, and Tule Mountain loom into view. At 3.8 miles you reach a junction near a summit with a small tower. You have a choice of staying straight on the road, or heading right up a short, steep road with a great view and then down a fun single-track that rejoins the road a short distance ahead.

At the next small hill with a tower, stay right (the left road here drops down a steep, rocky slope that is not recommended) and circle around the north side of the hill. Just before the road drops out from under you, pause for a moment to enjoy the beautiful vista of the rocky, granitic hills before you. Silent I-8, with ant-like cars making slow progress, is visible in the distance. Now the road descends quickly to a junction where you'll turn left (right heads north, then east and dead ends in 0.8 mile).

At 4.5 miles note the junction from the right, this is where you will return after circling the lollipop portion of the ride. Turn left and follow the road past several campsites and a prospect covered with quartz. The road disappears into a sandy wash that may require you to walk a bit it if hasn't rained recently. Soon the road picks up again to the right. Once on the road again, turn right at the next opportunity. A cement catch basin nearby captures rain water for small animals. The road then heads north past an open area that once was an Indian village (no bikes allowed). At about 6.0 miles, a road to the left leads to a collapsed old mine. Continue north down a rocky section, through a wash and eventually to an area with roads leading to several prospects and quarries. Turn right and follow the road past the foundation and trash from an old miners dwelling on the right, back to the junction you encountered earlier. Turn left and head back up the steep hill, past the two hills with the towers and back to your car.

GETTING THERE

Take I-8 east to Jacumba and exit at In-Ko-Pah Park Road. Turn right and drive a short distance on Old Highway 80 to an open dirt area on your left. Turn in there and park anywhere. To shave 2.4 miles off of the ride, drive the initial part of the ride along the dirt road next to I-8 and park just beyond the I-8 underpass.

AMENITIES

A Mexican restaurant and the recently reopened Wisteria Candy Cottage, providing hand-dipped chocolate and old fashioned candy since 1921, can be found on Old Highway 80 in Boulevard. The town of Jacumba, about 5 miles west on Old Highway 80, has a restaurant and a small market. Camping is available at the Lark Canyon Campground on McCain Valley Road.

Trip D3 – Valley of the Moon

Starting Point	In-Ko-Pah Park Road, Jacumba
Distance	6 miles out and back
Elevation Gain/Loss	1000'/1000', 10.6% uphill grade
Riding Time	2–2 1/2 hours
Difficulty	Difficult, technical
Road Conditions	Rough, rutted dirt road, some rocky sections
Season	Fall, Winter, and Spring
Equipment	Mountain bike
Optional Topo Map	In-Ko-Pah Gorge, CA

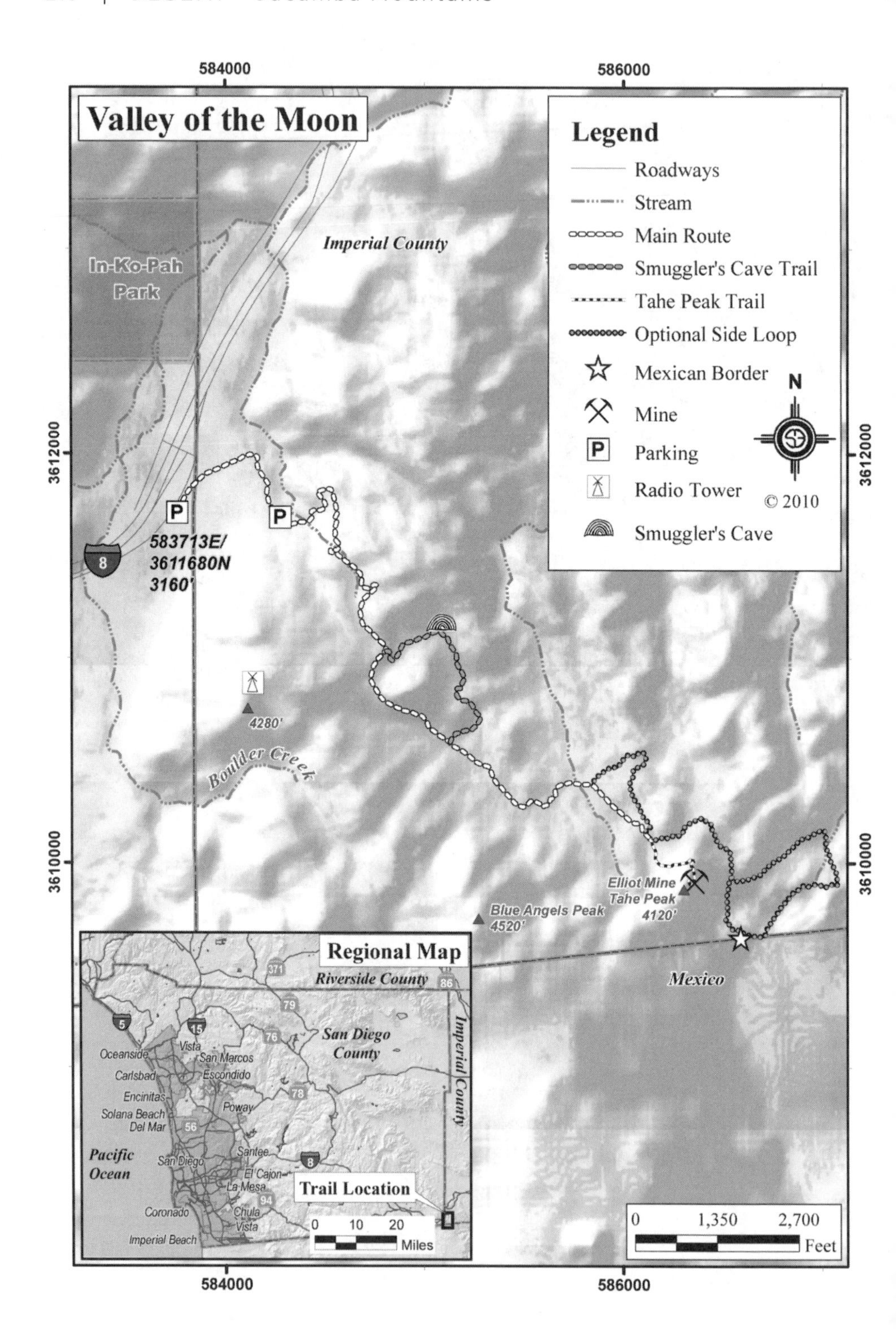
584000
586000
Valley of the Moon
Legend
Roadways
Stream
Main Route
Smuggler's Cave Trail
Tahe Peak Trail
Optional Side Loop
Mexican Border
Mine
Parking
Radio Tower
Smuggler's Cave
N
© 2010
Imperial County
In-Ko-Pah Park
3612000
3610000
8
583713E/
3611680N
3160'
4280'
Boulder Creek
Elliot Mine
Tahe Peak
4120'
Blue Angels Peak
4520'
Mexico
Regional Map
Riverside County
San Diego County
Imperial County
Oceanside
Vista
San Marcos
Carlsbad
Escondido
Encinitas
Poway
Solana Beach
Del Mar
Pacific Ocean
San Diego
Santee
El Cajon
La Mesa
Coronado
Chula Vista
Imperial Beach
Trail Location
0 10 20
Miles
0 1,350 2,700
Feet

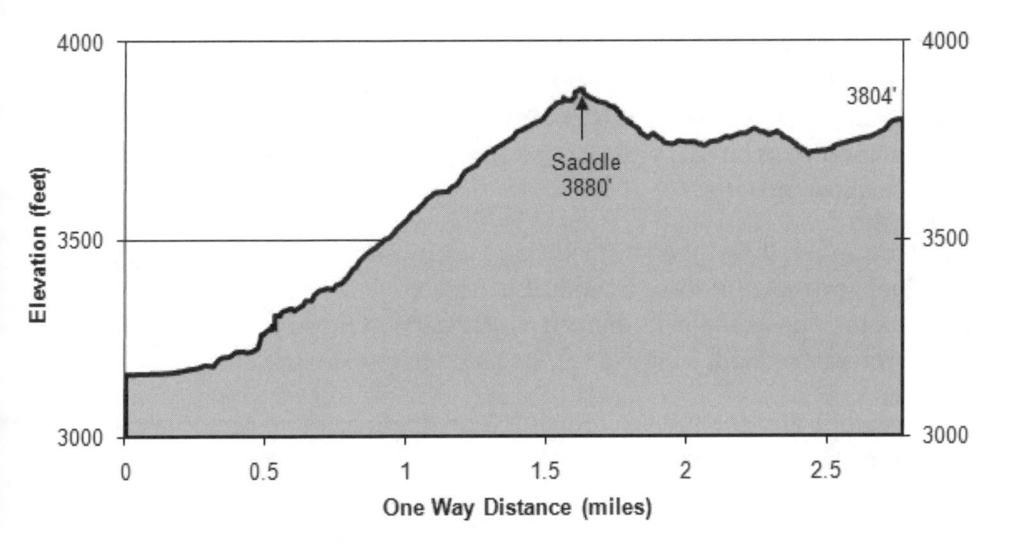

Like nearby Jacumba, Valley of the Moon is a spectacular area with jumbles of granitic boulders and peaks reminiscent of the Wonderland of Rocks in Joshua Tree. There are numerous 4WD roads you can follow winding around the piles of rocks and outcroppings as well as climb to the abandoned Elliot amethyst mine and enjoy a short hike to Smuggler's Cave.

The road begins climbing slowly past the ramshackle house at 0.3 mile with numerous No Trespassing and No Parking signs. Once pass the mess, the rutted road flattens for a moment at the parking turnout and then starts to climb again. At 0.7 mile you'll encounter a remarkably steep section covered with rough concrete, no doubt to prevent further erosion. Luckily it helps keep your tires from spinning. Another similar section farther up the road is even steeper. Rains keep the road in a constant state of flux, sometimes reasonably passable, other times rutted and more difficult.

The panoramic view of the In-Ko-Pah and Jacumba mountains below improves as you climb, assuming you can take your eyes off the road for a moment or two. In-Ko-Pah means "place of mountain people" and you can assume you are one of them if you can make it up this road.

Once you see a couple of wilderness boundary signs on the left you know the pain is almost over. At this saddle a 4WD road heads left (northeast) toward Smuggler's Cave where bikes are not allowed (see Options).

Continuing on, bear left at the next junction and climb the last small hill to the brown EC 155 marker. Follow the road southeast down a rough, rocky section of road into the valley. After a dip and a small rise, EC 157 heads left but dead-ends at the wilderness boundary in 0.2 mile. This is another way to hike to Smuggler's Cave (not covered here).

Continue generally southeast staying on EC 155 aiming for Tahe Peak, ignoring a right junction that quickly dead ends (but has a cool balanced rock nearby). Once you near the peak, several unmarked roads head left (north) winding through the rocks. You can pick any of these to meander and explore the area.

To climb Tahe and see the abandoned Elliot amethyst mine, stay straight on EC 155. At the base of the peak stay to the left up the steep rocky road which swings around the east side of the peak. Soon you'll pass the mine on the right and enjoy great views of the official Valley of the Moon below. A final steep climb takes you to the top, and a spectacular 360 degree view of the whole area. You can circle around the south side of the peak and back down to the valley below.

If you follow the numerous trails in many directions you can add several miles to the overall ride. Once you've had your fill, follow the main road back up the rocky slope and blast your way down to your car, being careful not to go too fast.

OPTIONS

The text above mentions two places you can leave the road and hike to Smuggler's Cave. It's located in a wilderness area so you must stash your bike and hike. It's a short distance on either trail to the old smuggler hideout, now a graffiti-covered bunch of granitic boulders.

GETTING THERE

Take I-8 east to Jacumba and exit at In-Ko-Pah Park Road. Turn right and drive a short distance on Old Highway 80 to an open dirt area on your left. Turn in there and stay to the left and park anywhere. To shave a little off the ride you can follow the road past the house with all the no parking signs and park in a large turnout a short distance farther. Note that the road is fairly rough and rutted getting to this parking spot and is not for low-clearance vehicles.

AMENITIES

The town of Jacumba, about 5 miles west on Old Highway 80 has a restaurant and a small market. About 6 miles past Jacumba in Boulevard, is a Mexican restaurant and the recently reopened Wisteria Candy Cottage, providing hand-dipped chocolate and old fashioned candy since 1921. Camping is available at the Lark Canyon Campground on McCain Valley Road near Boulevard.

Trip D4 – Chariot/Oriflamme/ Rodriguez Canyons

Starting Point	Highway 78, Banner Grade
Distance	16.3 miles
Elevation Gain/Loss	3050'/3050', 5% grade
Riding Time	5 hours
Difficulty	Difficult, not technical
Road Conditions	Rough graded dirt roads, jeep trails, some sand
Season	Fall, Winter, and Spring
Equipment	Mountain bike
Optional Topo Maps	Earthquake Valley, Julian, CA

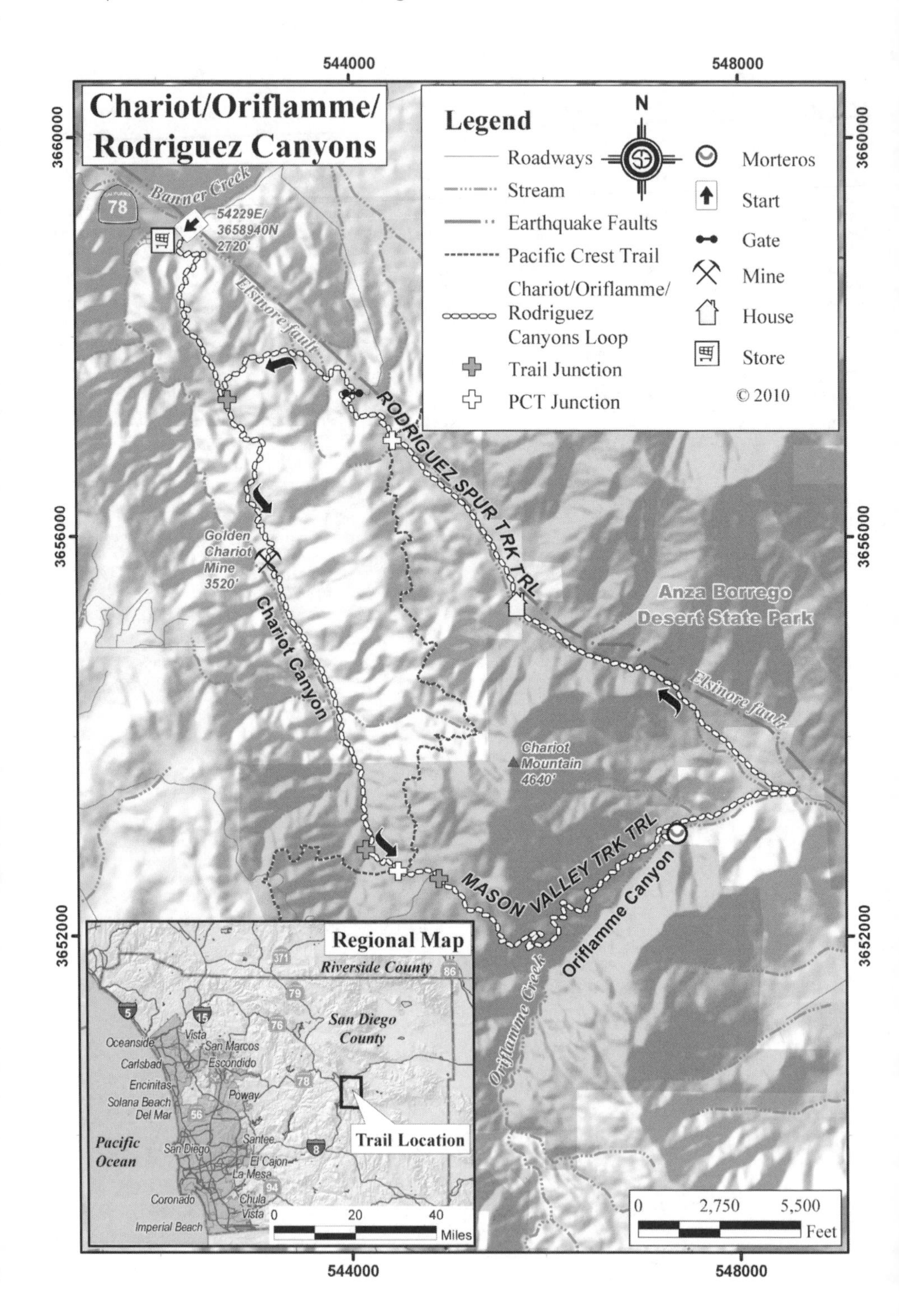
Chariot/Oriflamme/
Rodriguez Canyons
Legend
N
Roadways
Stream
Earthquake Faults
Pacific Crest Trail
Chariot/Oriflamme/
Rodriguez
Canyons Loop
Trail Junction
PCT Junction
Morteros
Start
Gate
Mine
House
Store
© 2010
544000
548000
3660000
3656000
3652000
Banner Creek
78
54229E/
3658940N
2720'
Elsinore fault
RODRIGUEZ SPUR TRK TRL
Golden
Chariot
Mine
3520'
Chariot Canyon
Anza Borrego
Desert State Park
Chariot
Mountain
4640'
MASON VALLEY TRK TRL
Oriflamme Canyon
Oriflamme Creek
Regional Map
Riverside County
San Diego
County
Oceanside
Vista
San Marcos
Carlsbad
Escondido
Encinitas
Solana Beach
Del Mar
Poway
Pacific
Ocean
San Diego
Santee
El Cajon
La Mesa
Coronado
Chula
Vista
Imperial Beach
Trail Location
0
20
40
Miles
0
2,750
5,500
Feet

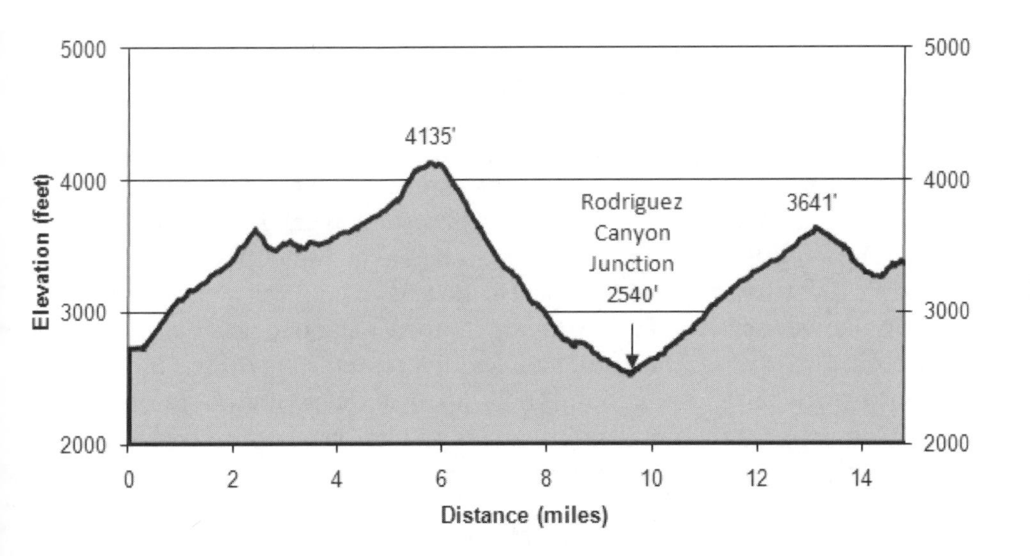

The green Laguna Mountains provide a barrier to moisture, preventing most of it from reaching the dry, desert floor to the north. The local Indians traveled back and forth through Oriflamme Canyon to escape hot summers and cold winters. As noted on the monument on Sunrise Highway, the Spanish commander Pedro Fages also traveled this route, as well as many others. Chariot Canyon is well known for the large number of mines in the area. Around 1870, gold was found mixed with quartz, seven miles down canyon from Julian. Banner City was born, and soon had seven saloons, a hotel, and several stamp mills. The Redman, later named Chariot, Ready Relief, and Golden Chariot mines were opened and soon working overtime. The Banner toll road was built to provide faster access to the area. This ride travels through part of Oriflamme Canyon as well as Chariot and Rodriguez Canyons where you can still see some of the remains of the old mines.

Start by riding uphill past the Banner Store, and turn left immediately on the dirt Chariot Canyon Road. Pass through the gate and make sure it's closed behind you. The road ascends moderately to the east, and then curves south offering increasingly better views of Banner Canyon and the old mining roads on the upper slopes. The well-graded Rodriguez Canyon Road intersects from the left at 1.4 miles. This is where you will exit and blast back to the car in a few hours.

Continuing straight, at 2.2 miles you reach a saddle. There is a great view behind you and in the valley ahead—the dilapidated buildings of an old gold mine. Enjoy the nice downhill grade, and pause for a closer view of the Golden Chariot

Mine ruins at 2.9 miles: old buildings, a toppled windmill, and scattered mining equipment. You'll see many no trespassing signs along the way, but traveling the road is legal.

Glancing ahead, you can see the road ascending out of the scenic valley, but not before you cross a seasonal creek with oaks providing some nice shade at 4.2 miles. The remnants of an old building are visible on the right. When you spot the Pacific Crest Trail (PCT) California Hiking and Riding Trail sign on the right, the cruise is over, as the road then heads southeast and begins steeply ascending a ridge. The road reaches a plateau and the Mason Valley Truck Trail, at 5.6 miles. The truck trail ascends about 3 miles to the Sunrise Highway (at the Pedro Fages Monument at mile marker 36) and is an alternate way for hikers and bicycle riders to gain access to this area through a locked gate.

Continue straight, on what is now the Mason Valley Truck Trail, another 0.6 mile across rolling terrain to the steep, rocky descent that zigzags its way down the north side of Oriflamme Canyon. As you descend, the view into Oriflamme Canyon and the lower reaches of Rodriguez Canyon is quite beautiful. At the bottom of the grade, turn right on a small unmarked road at 8.3 miles, and take a break in the shade by Oriflamme Creek. If you explore the nearby rocks, you can find Indian morteros, and across the creek are remnants of some rock foundations.

Back on Mason Valley Truck Trail, follow it another mile to the Rodriguez Canyon junction at 9.5 miles, which is easy to miss. Turn sharply left, and follow the four-wheel-drive road northwest, as it ascends moderately through sometimes sandy and sometimes rocky stretches as the canyon begins to narrow. When the road splits, stay left to see a small concrete building at 11.8 miles. The removal of invasive trees is in progress, with many littering the landscape.

At 10.6 miles you leave the state park and keep following the long string of telephone poles. Ignore the road heading left at 12.5 miles, and continue on the unrelenting slow, sometimes sandy, ascent. Finally, you reach a saddle where the PCT crosses the road one final time and you can see the Valle de San Felipe in the distance. Enjoy the fast descent, but stop for the barbed wire gate partway down the slope. The road swings west and enters a peaceful valley, passing the Right Fender Ranch, complete with a right truck fender marking the entrance, and then begins ascending the south side of the valley. A short 0.4 mile later, the climbing is finally over, and you can enjoy the quick descent to the junction of Chariot Canyon Road. Turn right to head back to the start.

GETTING THERE

To reach the starting point, take Highway 78 from Julian down the Banner Grade to the Banner Store and park just beyond it, in a turnout on the same side of the road. On the way down the grade, watch for signs of the Elsinore Fault etched low on the canyon wall to your left. The Elsinore, Earthquake Valley, and Chariot Canyon faults all run through this area.

AMENITIES

The Banner Store is by the start of the ride and a small country store is located at mile marker 21 on Highway S2. Primitive camping and pit toilets are available in Blair Valley (no water).

Trip D5 – Blair/Little Blair Valley

Starting Point	Highway S2 Blair Valley, Anza-Borrego Desert State Park
Distance	8.7 miles
Elevation Gain/Loss	590'/590'
Riding Time	2–2 1/2 hours
Difficulty	Easy, not technical
Road Conditions	Dirt roads, some sand, 0.7 mile paved along Highway S2
Season	Fall, Winter, and Spring
Equipment	Mountain bike
Optional Topo Map	Earthquake Valley, CA

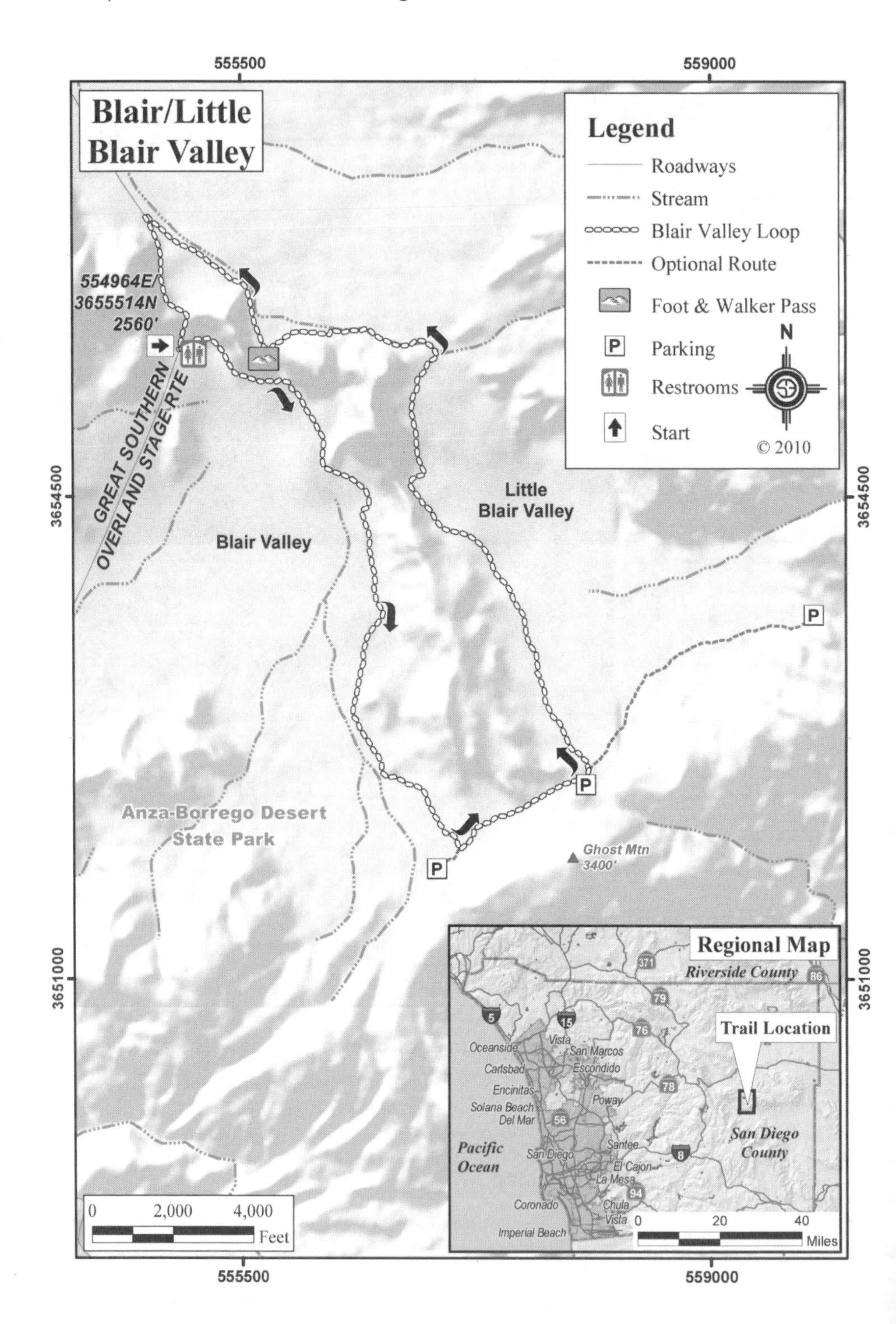
Blair/Little Blair Valley
Legend
Roadways
Stream
Blair Valley Loop
Optional Route
Foot & Walker Pass
Parking
Restrooms
Start
N
© 2010
555500
559000
3654500
3651000
554964E/ 3655514N 2560'
GREAT SOUTHERN OVERLAND STAGE RTE
Blair Valley
Little Blair Valley
Anza-Borrego Desert State Park
Ghost Mtn 3400'
0 2,000 4,000 Feet
Regional Map
Riverside County
Trail Location
Oceanside
Vista
San Marcos
Carlsbad
Escondido
Encinitas
Solana Beach
Del Mar
Poway
Pacific Ocean
San Diego
Santee
El Cajon
La Mesa
San Diego County
Coronado
Chula Vista
Imperial Beach
0 20 40 Miles

This ride takes you through scenic Blair Valley and Little Blair Valley. Today campers relish the nice sheltered spots nestled against the low hills with beautiful views of the surrounding mountains, just as the Kumeyaay people did for many years before the Spanish and other European settlers arrived in California. You will have the opportunity to visit the location of a Kumeyaay village and take optional hikes to a Native American rock art site and to the top of Ghost Mountain to see the Marshal South homesite.

Begin by cycling southeast on the road through Blair Valley as it hugs the edge of the small hills on your left and skirts the meadow to your right. Sometimes after rains the roads can be muddy and the meadow filled with water. The large mountain to your right is Granite Mountain.

The historic Southern Emigrant Trail and the Butterfield Overland Stage passed through this area. The small gap in the hills on your left is Foot and Walker Pass, where passengers on the Butterfield Overland Stage in the 1850s often had to get out and help the driver push their wagon over the pass. The scattered vegetation in the area is characteristic of the high desert: creosote bush, ocotillo, cholla cactus, yucca and especially agave—the latter in spectacular bloom in springtime if there has been enough rain.

At 3.2 miles you'll reach the junction to the parking area for Ghost Mountain, an optional side trip (see Options). Stay left to continue the loop. At 3.9 miles the turnout for the Morteros Native American village site is on your right, a short hike away. See Options for more details. Continuing on a short distance, the road to the Native American rock art site joins from the right. See Options for more details about this side trip.

Stay left to continue the main loop, passing several nice camp sites along the way. You are now entering Little Blair Valley with small rock hills surrounding the normally dry lake bed. In the spring after abundant rain, small flowers cover the lake bed in a sea of color. At the end of the lake bed stay straight as the road begins to climb a bit. Turn left at the S2 sign and follow the sandy road as it begins to descend and swing west around the rocky ridge.

At 7.4 miles the uphill side of Foot and Walker Pass is on your left and the California Riding and Hiking Trail crosses the road here as well. It's easy to visualize the plumes of dust kicked up by horses and wagons making their way across the pass over a century ago. At about 8 miles you'll reach Highway S2. Turn left and exert the last bit of work to traverse the little pass separating Earthquake Valley from Blair Valley as you return to the starting point.

GETTING THERE

To reach the starting point take Highway 78 from Julian down the Banner Grade and follow it east into the desert. (On the way down the grade, watch for signs of the Elsinore Fault etched low on the canyon wall to your left.) The Elsinore, Earthquake Valley, and Chariot Canyon faults all run through this area. At the Scissors Crossing junction, bear right on Highway S2 (The Great Southern Overland Stage Route of 1849), and continue about 6 miles to the entrance to Blair Valley on your left. It is just after the small pass separating Earthquake Valley from Blair Valley.

OPTIONS

There are a few interesting side trips you can take on this ride. At the southern end of Blair Valley a junction heads right a short distance to the base of Ghost Mountain. If you have a way to secure your bike this is an interesting semi-rough hiking trail that provides a great view of the area. Marshal South was a writer that moved to Ghost Mountain with his wife in 1932 and for 15 years built a house, raised 3 children, and lived close to nature. The ruins of their home, "Yaquitepec," or "Hill of the Yaqui" are visible on the hike.

About 0.7 mile farther is a parking area on the right signed Morteros that was a seasonal Native American village site for the Kumeyaay people. It is a short walk to the village site (no bikes) where Kumeyaay women pounded large rock pestles into rock grinding holes (morteros), turning mesquite pods, pine nuts, and chia seeds into flour.

Immediately after that is a 1.4 mile road on the right to another parking area and a trail to a Native American rock art site. It is about a 15-20 min walk (1 mile) to a large boulder on the right with the pictographs. Bikes are not allowed on the trail, so you will need a way to secure your bike or stash it in the nearby rocks.

AMENITIES

A small country store is located at mile marker 21 on Highway S2. Primitive camping is available in Blair and Little Blair Valley. There are pit toilets near the ride start but no water.

Trip D6 – Grapevine Canyon/ Jasper Trail

Starting Point	Yaqui Well, Anza-Borrego Desert
Distance	23.5 miles, lollipop route
Elevation Gain/Loss	3500'/3500'
Riding Time	5–6 hours
Difficulty	Difficult (due to length), not technical
Road Conditions	Dirt roads, 4.3 miles paved
Season	Fall, Winter, and Spring
Equipment	Mountain bike
Optional Topo Maps	Ranchita, Tubb Canyon, CA

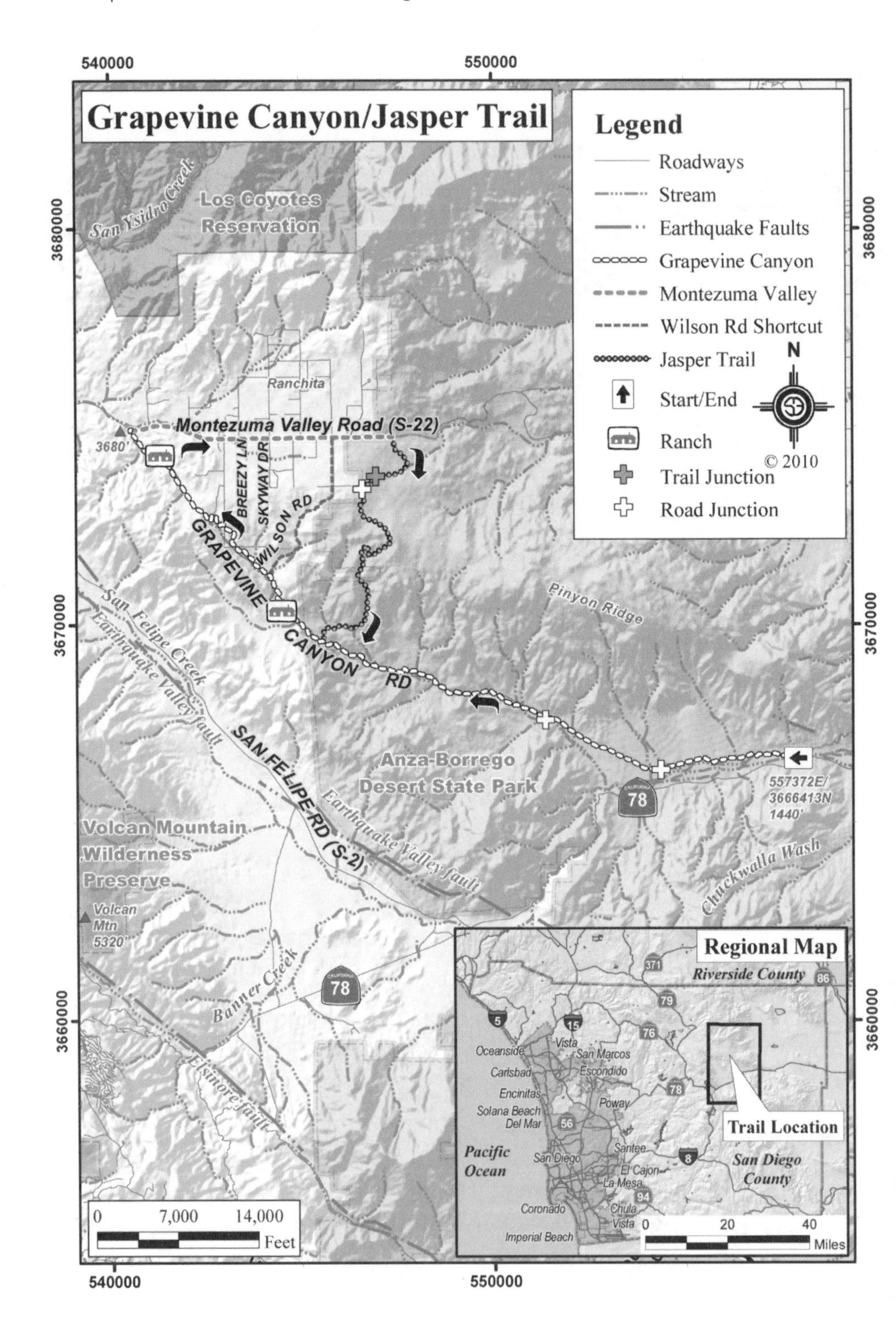

Grapevine Canyon/Jasper Trail
Legend
Roadways
Stream
Earthquake Faults
Grapevine Canyon
Montezuma Valley
Wilson Rd Shortcut
Jasper Trail
Start/End
Ranch
Trail Junction
Road Junction
N
© 2010
540000
550000
3680000
3670000
3660000
San Ysidro Creek
Los Coyotes Reservation
Ranchita
Montezuma Valley Road (S-22)
3680'
BREEZY LN
SKYWAY DR
WILSON RD
GRAPEVINE CANYON RD
Pinyon Ridge
San Felipe Creek
Earthquake Valley fault
SAN FELIPE RD (S-2)
Anza-Borrego Desert State Park
78
557372E/ 3666413N 1440'
Chuckwalla Wash
Volcan Mountain Wilderness Preserve
Volcan Mtn 5320'
Banner Creek
Elsinore fault
0 7,000 14,000 Feet
Regional Map
Riverside County
371
86
79
5
15
76
78
56
8
94
Oceanside
Vista
San Marcos
Carlsbad
Escondido
Encinitas
Poway
Solana Beach
Del Mar
Pacific Ocean
San Diego
Santee
El Cajon
La Mesa
Coronado
Chula Vista
Imperial Beach
Trail Location
San Diego County
0 20 40 Miles

This ride takes you through scenic Grapevine Canyon, along Highway S22 in Ranchita, and then down the fun Jasper Trail. Originally, Grapevine Canyon was a main travel route east before Highway 78 was constructed through Sentenac Canyon. Now these trails are used by everyone from four-wheel-drive groups and motorcyclists to mountain bikers and equestrians. The ride described here, starts at Yaqui Well and climbs to Highway S22 and then back down Jasper Trail to the starting point but it can also be done as an all-downhill run with a car shuttle.

Start off by following Grapevine Canyon Road west as it works its way along the base of the rugged Grapevine Hills. At 2.2 miles continue past a left junction that heads across San Felipe Creek to Highway 78. The rocky road begins to head northwest and at 4.3 miles you'll pass a second junction heading to Highway 78.

Soon the road veers into the sandy wash that can be easy to ride after recent rains, or a little difficult if not. The drainages from small canyons feed in from the right as the canyon begins to narrow. At 6.3 miles the road veers right out of the wash, and begins to climb through a moderately rocky area. Keep your eyes open for the willows and trees in the wash on your left, where Angelina Spring feeds the area. A few flat boulders near the south side of the road have morteros, indicating this was a popular area for the native people living here many years ago. You might be able to imagine Indian women pounding large rock pestles into the rock grinding holes turning mesquite pods, pine nuts, and chia seeds into flour.

The road makes a sharp left turn, almost coming back on itself, drops into the wash again and quickly passes a left junction that goes a short distance to Angelina Spring. Stay right and continue up the wash as it winds in and out around the vegetation. About 1.2 miles farther Stuart Spring is nearby and sometimes visible.

At 8.5 miles note the Jasper Trail (marked California Riding and Hiking Trail) joining from the right where you will exit in a couple of hours. Continuing straight, the canyon widens and you exit the Anza-Borrego Desert State Park at 9 miles. The road leaves the wash again and passes the W Bar W Ranch and makes an interesting jog right and then left around the head of a small canyon.

The road continues climbing and at 10 miles you'll reach the junction of Wilson Road. Right on Wilson Road takes you 2.75 miles on a fairly steep ascent over several hills joining Highway S22, cutting about 7 miles from the ride (see Options).

To continue, bear left staying on Grapevine Canyon Road and ignore a road heading right at 11.5 miles. The road swings left, and then climbs northwest a short distance farther and at 12 miles you'll reach a small summit and then it's mostly downhill to Highway S22 along a sandy road past several ranches.

Turn right onto the pavement at mile 13.8 and follow it east past several roads, including Wilson Road where the short cut you passed earlier meets the highway. S22 gradually ascends, passing a small store on the way, and soon after the Anza-Borrego Desert State Park sign begins to descend sharply. Watch carefully for the signed Jasper Trail on your right between mile markers 6 and 7.

The Jasper trail heads south through dense chaparral past a small spur road on your left at 18.5 miles. You'll pass the California Riding and Hiking Trail at 19 miles and the Old Culp Valley Road at 19.3 miles. The trail begins ascending a steep hill and then you'll reach a high point at 20.4 miles. This is a good spot to check out the view and grab a snack before the fast descent to Grapevine Canyon.

The road descends quickly, and then up and down several times and soon makes a northward, then southward jog to avoid a steep ravine. From here the road heads mostly south, still descending rather quickly. The canyon then begins to widen and the roads swings west and then south to join Grapevine Canyon Road at 23.3 miles. Turn left and enjoy the nice downhill run back to Yaqui Pass Campground and your waiting car.

GETTING THERE

To reach the starting point, take Highway 78 from Julian down the Banner Grade and follow it east into the desert. On the way down the grade, watch for signs of the Elsinore Fault etched low on the canyon wall to your left. The Elsinore, Earthquake Valley, and Chariot Canyon faults all run through this area. At Scissors Crossing junction stay straight and follow San Felipe Creek down through Sentenac Canyon. At Highway S3 at Yaqui Pass, turn left and then quickly left into the primitive Yaqui Pass Campground. Park near the road.

Some people prefer to start on S22, Montezuma Valley Road, at the top of Jasper Trail, but you then have to climb back up to end the ride when you're tired. Another option is to get dropped off at the top of Jasper Trail or Grapevine Canyon and be picked up at Yaqui Pass Campground.

OPTIONS

The ride can be shortened by heading up Wilson Road instead of following Grapevine Canyon Road all the way to S22. It's steep in a few places but cuts about 7 miles from the trip.

AMENITIES

A small country store is located at mile marker 21 on Highway S22. Primitive camping is available at the start of the ride at Yaqui Pass campground. Tamarisk Grove campground is across the street from the starting point and charges to camp. There are many other locations to primitive camp including Blair and Little Blair Valley. There are pit toilets near the start of the ride.

Trip D7 – Dos Cabezas Road

Starting Point	Highway S2, near Ocotillo
Distance	6-14 miles depending on route
Elevation Gain/Loss	450'/450', depending on route
Riding Time	1–3 hours
Difficulty	Easy (sandy in spots), not technical
Road Conditions	Dirt roads, some sand, 0.8 mile paved
Season	Fall, Winter, and Spring
Equipment	Mountain bike
Optional Topo Maps	Carrizo Mtn, In-Ko-Pah Gorge, Jacumba, Sweeny Pass, CA

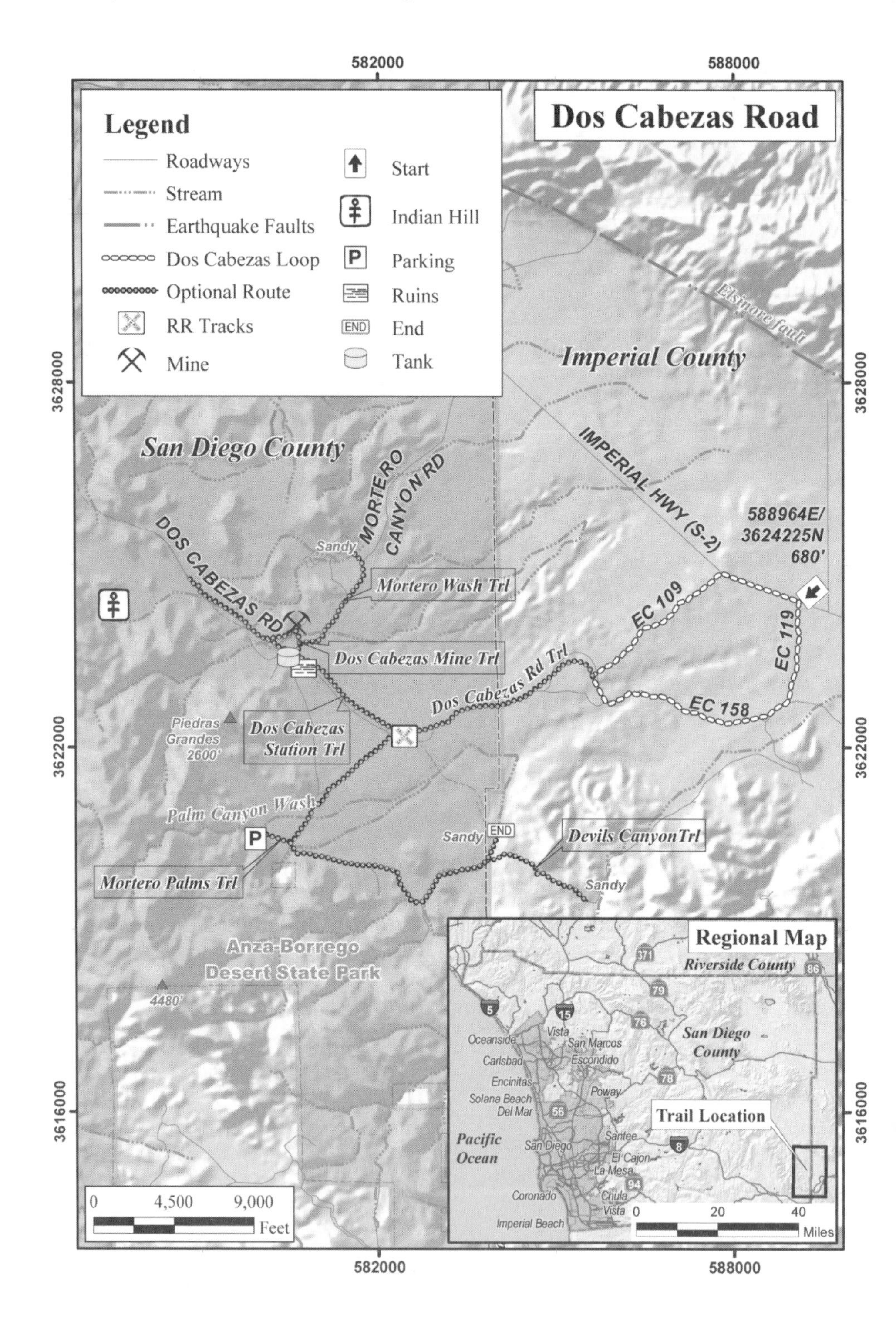

Dos Cabezas Road
Legend
Roadways
Stream
Earthquake Faults
Dos Cabezas Loop
Optional Route
RR Tracks
Mine
Start
Indian Hill
Parking
Ruins
End
Tank
582000
588000
3628000
3622000
3616000
Elsinore fault
Imperial County
San Diego County
IMPERIAL HWY (S-2)
MORTERO CANYON RD
DOS CABEZAS RD
588964E/
3624225N
680'
Sandy
Mortero Wash Trl
EC 109
EC 119
EC 158
Dos Cabezas Mine Trl
Dos Cabezas Rd Trl
Piedras Grandes 2600'
Dos Cabezas Station Trl
Palm Canyon Wash
Sandy
END
Devils Canyon Trl
Mortero Palms Trl
Sandy
Anza-Borrego Desert State Park
4480'
0 4,500 9,000
Feet
Regional Map
Riverside County
San Diego County
Oceanside
Vista
San Marcos
Carlsbad
Escondido
Encinitas
Solana Beach
Del Mar
Poway
Pacific Ocean
San Diego
Santee
El Cajon
La Mesa
Coronado
Chula Vista
Imperial Beach
Trail Location
0 20 40
Miles

This ride takes you alongside the San Diego and Arizona Railway, dubbed the "Impossible Railroad." The dream was for a direct rail line from San Diego to the east and construction started in 1908. A number of calamities, including tunnel cave-ins, fires, and Mother Nature slowed progress. The rail line eventually opened on November 15, 1919, and John D. Spreckels drove the final $286 gold spike. The railroad crosses 14 trestles and goes through 21 tunnels in Carrizo Gorge and across the famous wooden Goat Canyon Trestle. The trestle is 200 feet high and 750 feet long, the tallest curved wooden trestle in the world. The line closed several more times and eventually reopened to freight traffic in 2004. You won't get close to the Goat Canyon Trestle on this ride, but you can easily ride to the historic remnants of the Dos Cabezas station and water tower.

Start riding south on Dos Cabezas Road as it slowly ascends through the scattered vegetation. At 1 mile you'll reach the intersection of EC 158, turn right and follow it west as it works its way closer to the railroad tracks. Ignore several roads to the left and at 2.8 miles follow the road as it drops into a big sandy wash and swings south up the small ridge on the other side.

At this point the road is paralleling the tracks as they begin to make a large curve called "Big Bend," first heading north and then southwest. Near the top of the bend, at 3.4 miles is the junction of EC 109. You can turn right here and ride 1.8 miles back to Highway S2, turn right and then 0.8 mile on the pavement to the starting point for a total distance of 6 miles.

If you're up for more adventure, note this spot for your return, and keep going straight. Follow EC 158 as it swings wide around "Big Bend." Ignore several more roads heading left and right and soon you reach the railroad tracks at 5.7 miles. You have several choices here. Straight across the tracks takes you to Piedras Grandes, Mortero Palms, and Devils Canyon (see Options). To visit the historic Dos Cabezas station and the Dos Cabezas Mine, turn right and follow the tracks west.

Sometimes freight trains are parked on this double section of track. Soon the large water tank looms in the distance marking the remnants of the Dos Cabezas station. When you reach the tank, the foundations of the station are across the tracks and beyond the tank a short distance. The loading ramp is just up the tracks from the tank. It is said that the ghosts of trains from the past still linger in the area.

The Dos Cabezas Mine, an area dug into the hillside with tailings all around, is visible about 0.3 miles to the northwest. You can follow the road north from this spot, descend into the wash and ascend the other side to the mine. A small concrete marker can be seen on the road near the mine.

To finish the ride, head back the way you came, east along the tracks staying on EC 158. Follow it back around "Big Bend" and then turn left at EC 109 and enjoy the gentle descent 1.8 miles to Highway S2. Turn right and then ride 0.8 mile on the pavement back to the starting point. If you rode all the way to the Dos Cabezas area your total distance is about 14 miles.

GETTING THERE

Take I-8 east about 85 miles to the small desert town of Ocotillo. Turn left under I-8 and follow Highway S2 4 miles to Dos Cabezas Road on your left marked EC 119, shortly after the power lines. Park alongside the dirt road.

Note: The railroad does not permit any hiking or biking along the tracks or right-of-way, but you may cross the tracks perpendicularly. The tracks are regularly patrolled.

OPTIONS

There are many roads in the Dos Cabezas area and some of them are shown on the map. You can explore the remnants of the historic Dos Cabezas Station as described above. To explore Mortero Palms or the Devils Canyon area, follow the ride above to where the road crosses the tracks at 5.7 miles. Ride across the tracks and turn right. At the next junction turn left and follow the road through a wash and by a small pile of rocks on your left.

At the next junction, right takes you to the Mortero Palms Trailhead where a hiking-only trail leads 0.5 mile to a large grove of palms. Straight leads quickly to a road going left toward Devils Canyon or straight a short distance to Dos Cabezas Spring. Feel free to explore the road toward Devils Canyon. There are a number of places to camp near large piles of granitic boulders but note that it can get very sandy past the boulders.

AMENITIES

There are very few facilities in Ocotillo. A small store is just north of I-8. A gas station with snacks, cold drinks, and a restroom is just south of I-8. The town of Jacumba, before you drop down into the desert, has one small store and a couple of gas stations.

There is plenty of primitive camping in the Anza-Borrego Desert area. Remember to stay on the designated roads (both bikes and cars) and if in your vehicle, you must not park more than a car length from any road.

Trip D8 – Fossil Canyon

Starting Point	Shell Canyon Road, near Ocotillo
Distance	8.4 miles out and back
Elevation Gain/Loss	320'/320', round trip
Riding Time	2 hours
Difficulty	Easy, not technical
Road Conditions	Dirt road, 5.3 miles paved
Season	Fall, Winter, and Spring
Equipment	Mountain bike
Optional Topo Map	Carrizo Mtn., CA

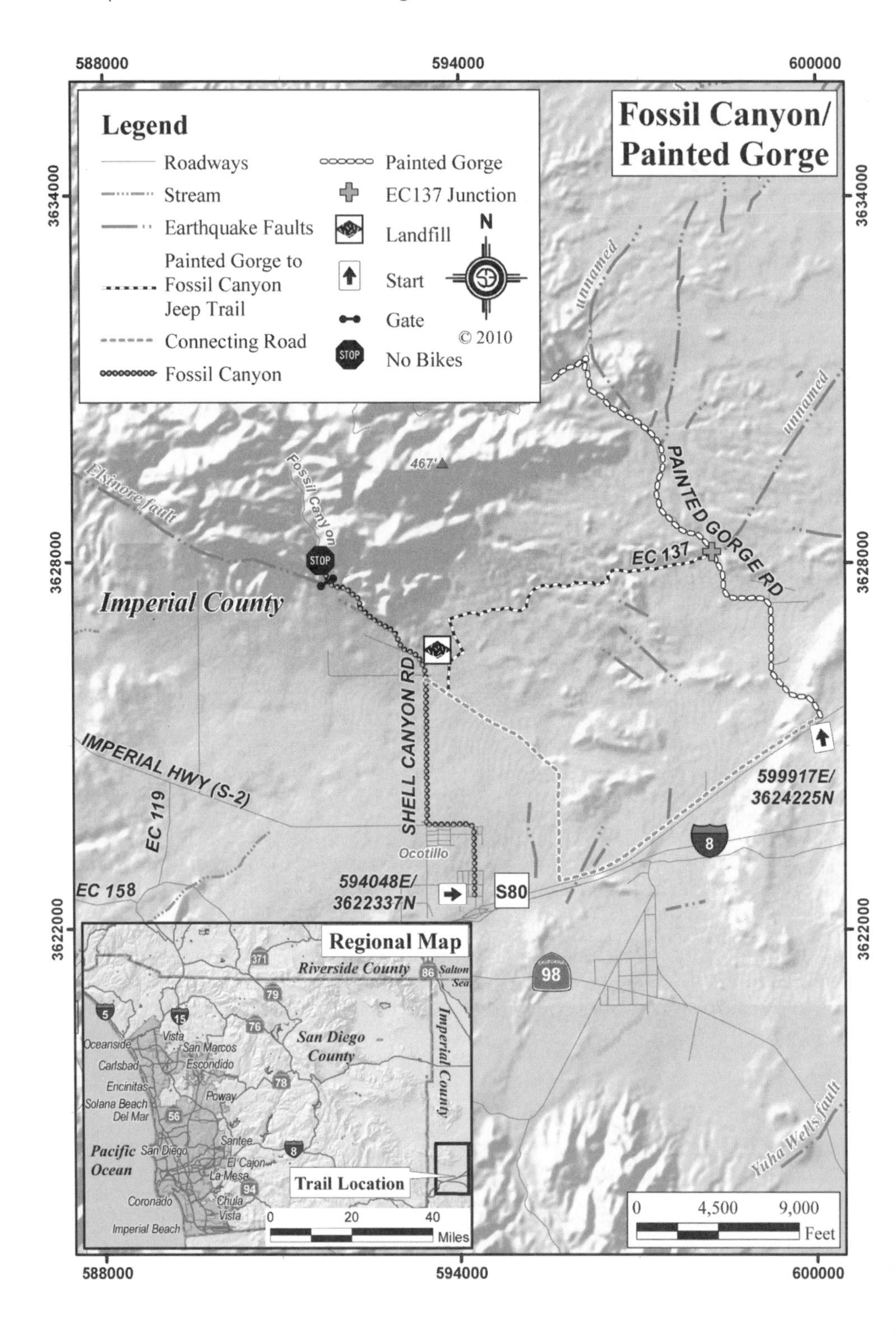

Fossil Canyon/
Painted Gorge
Legend
Roadways
Stream
Earthquake Faults
Painted Gorge to Fossil Canyon Jeep Trail
Connecting Road
Fossil Canyon
Painted Gorge
EC137 Junction
Landfill
Start
Gate
No Bikes
N
© 2010
588000
594000
600000
3634000
3628000
3622000
unnamed
Elsinore fault
Fossil Canyon
467'
STOP
Imperial County
PAINTED GORGE RD
EC 137
SHELL CANYON RD
IMPERIAL HWY (S-2)
EC 119
EC 158
Ocotillo
594048E/
3622337N
S80
599917E/
3624225N
8
98
Yuha Wells fault
0
4,500
9,000
Feet
Regional Map
Riverside County
Salton Sea
San Diego County
Imperial County
Pacific Ocean
Oceanside
Vista
San Marcos
Escondido
Carlsbad
Encinitas
Solana Beach
Del Mar
Poway
Santee
San Diego
El Cajon
La Mesa
Coronado
Chula Vista
Imperial Beach
Trail Location
0
20
40
Miles

Fossil Canyon, also known as Shell Canyon or Alverson Canyon, is located near the small desert town of Ocotillo. The sandstone and mudstone canyon walls contain white shell fossils and coral pieces representing 5 million years of geologic history. Thomas Wayland Vaughn did a study of the reef-coral fauna of Carrizo Creek in 1916 based on fossils found by Dr. Stephen Bowers. They indicated the reef-coral fauna in this area is Atlantic and Pacific indicating that the Atlantic and Pacific were connected somewhere in Central America. The Panama Isthmus connection eventually closed and the coral became almost extinct on the Pacific side.

This ride is relatively short but if you have a way to secure your bike you can venture past the foot-traffic-only gate and examine the 5-million year history revealed in the canyon. Start by riding north on Imperial Highway (S2) and follow the road as it bends west. At 1.2 miles turn right at the stop sign onto Shell Canyon Road and follow it straight until it turns to dirt around 3.4 miles. The road heads through yellow mud hills marked with numerous motorcycle tracks. You can have fun winding around the small hills before continuing on. This is also an area where some people camp. The Elsinore Fault runs northwest from here along the base of the Coyote Mountains.

The walls of the canyon begin to narrow and at 4.2 miles you'll reach the gate. No riding is allowed beyond this point. Stash your bike nearby and walk up canyon a bit and look for the fossils embedded in the low hills. It's also a great place to have a snack amongst the colorful hillsides. You might encounter a geology group on a field trip examining the fossils and interesting strata. Retrace your route to return to the starting point.

GETTING THERE

Take I-8 east about 85 miles to the small desert town of Ocotillo. Turn left under I-8 and park off the road near here. To shorten the ride, follow Highway S2 1.3 miles to the stop sign at Shell Canyon Road. Turn right and drive a short distance and park off the road.

OPTIONS

If you have a way to secure your bike the hike up the canyon is worth seeing, especially if you like geology. Another fun option is to take the jeep trail that follows the power lines and connects to the Painted Gorge ride. Before Shell Canyon Road turns to dirt take the paved road heading southeast for 0.25 mile and turn left onto a jeep trail. It skirts the southeast corner of the dump and in about 1 mile joins EC 137. Turn right and follow the power line road as it winds through colorful mud hills, passes an old lava flow, climbs in and out of washes, and in 3 miles joins Painted Gorge Road. You can return the way you came or turn right and follow the gravel road 2.3 miles to the pavement. Turn right on S80 and ride 4.1 miles to return to your car at Ocotillo.

AMENITIES

There are very few facilities in Ocotillo. A small store is just north of I-8. A gas station with snacks, cold drinks, and a restroom is south of I-8. The town of Jacumba, before you descend to the desert has a small store and a couple of gas stations.

There is plenty of primitive camping in the Anza-Borrego Desert area. Remember to stay on the designated roads (both bikes and cars) and if in your vehicle, you must not park more than a car length from any road.

Trip D9 – Painted Gorge

Starting Point	Painted Gorge Road, near Ocotillo
Distance	11 miles out and back
Elevation Gain/Loss	370'/370' round trip
Riding Time	3 hours
Difficulty	Easy, not technical
Road Conditions	Dirt and well graded roads
Season	Fall, Winter, and Spring
Equipment	Mountain bike
Optional Topo Map	Painted Gorge, CA

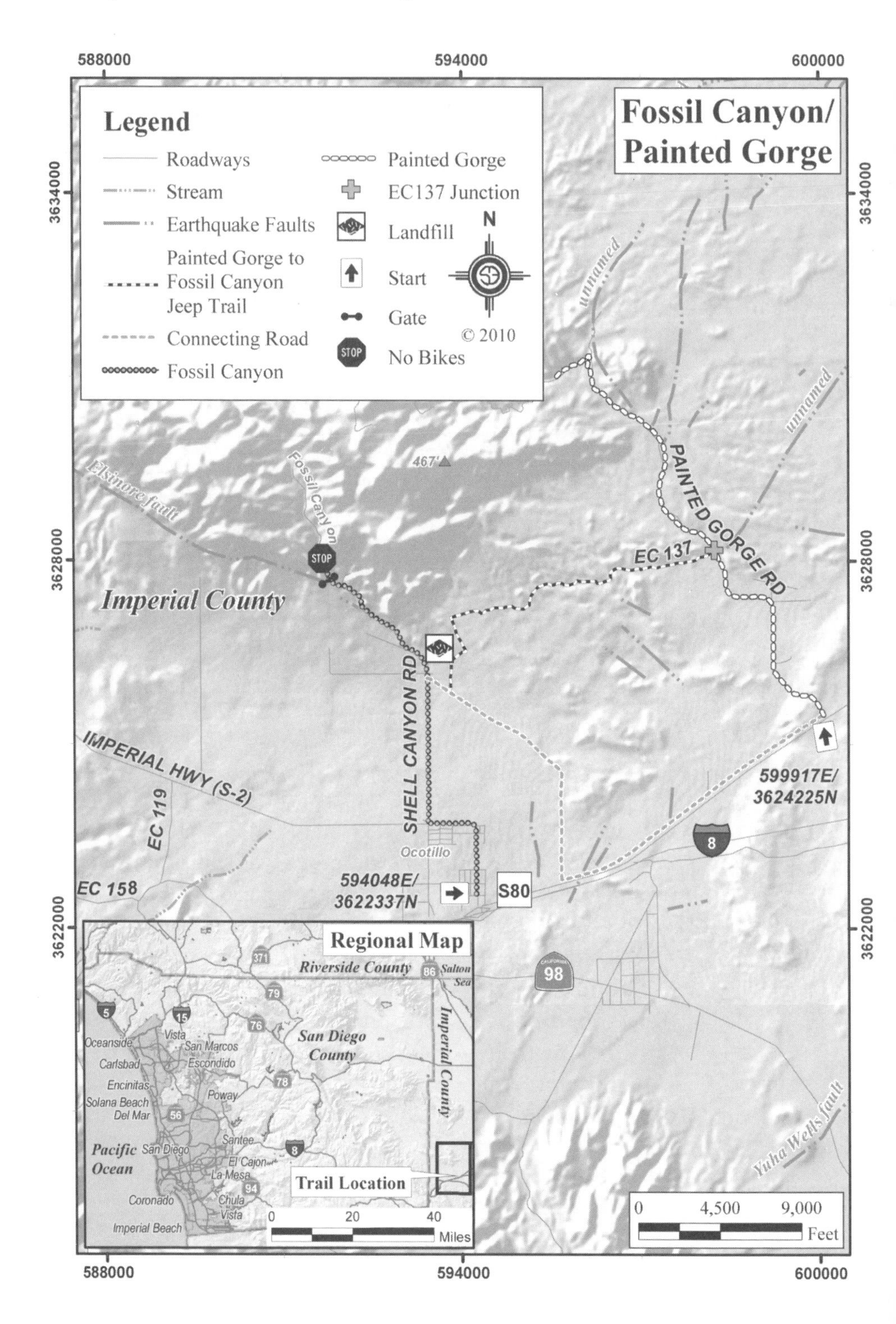
Fossil Canyon/
Painted Gorge
Legend
Roadways
Stream
Earthquake Faults
Painted Gorge to
Fossil Canyon
Jeep Trail
Connecting Road
Fossil Canyon
Painted Gorge
EC137 Junction
Landfill
Start
Gate
No Bikes
N
© 2010
588000
594000
600000
3634000
3628000
3622000
Elsinore fault
Fossil Canyon
467'
Imperial County
PAINTED GORGE RD
EC 137
unnamed
SHELL CANYON RD
IMPERIAL HWY (S-2)
EC 119
EC 158
Ocotillo
594048E/
3622337N
S80
599917E/
3624225N
8
98
Yuha Wells fault
0
4,500
9,000
Feet
Regional Map
Riverside County
Salton Sea
San Diego County
Imperial County
Pacific Ocean
Oceanside
Vista
San Marcos
Carlsbad
Escondido
Encinitas
Solana Beach
Del Mar
Poway
Santee
San Diego
El Cajon
La Mesa
Coronado
Chula Vista
Imperial Beach
Trail Location
0
20
40
Miles

About 85 miles east of San Diego near the small, sleepy town of Ocotillo is a canyon of sedimentary, metamorphic, and igneous rocks that reminds one of an artist's palette of pastel oranges, reds, purples, browns, and blacks. The nearby hills change colors depending on the angle of the sun. This ride will take you into the gorge where you can experience the beautiful colors first hand.

From the starting point, follow the gravel road through an ORV area and scattered ramshackle buildings, trailers, and shipping containers. At 1.4 miles stay left at the Painted Gorge sign and avoid the dogs at play as the sign indicates. At 2.3 miles pass under the power lines and by the EC 137 sign on your left that connects to the Fossil Canyon ride (see Options).

Soon, light colored hills topped with dark soil begin to surround the road evoking the feeling of riding through a chocolate dessert. The road begins to ascend slightly as you pass through an off road vehicle playground where you might decide to play as well.

If you've had your fill of dessert, continue on and at 4.5 miles the road crests a small hill and drops into Painted Gorge Bowl. The surrounding multi-hued hills are quite impressive. A kiosk with a map describes the area. You can head straight past the kiosk and curve left into Painted Gorge. At one time vehicles could continue on, but these days the road and your ride, ends 0.5 mile up the gorge to protect the lambing area of Peninsular bighorn sheep. But all is not lost, as you return to the bowl, the colors in the return direction are even better. Reverse your direction and enjoy the change of colors as you head back to your car.

GETTING THERE

Take I-8 east about 85 miles to the small desert town of Ocotillo. Turn left under I-8 and immediately turn right on S80 or Evan Hewes Highway. Drive 4 miles to Painted Gorge Road on your left marked by a BLM sign. Park anywhere off the road here.

OPTIONS

An optional ride follows the jeep trail along the power lines and connects to the Fossil Canyon ride. At 2.3 miles from the pavement on Painted Gorge Road, the power lines cross the road and an EC 137 sign marks the jeep trail to the left. Follow this road 3 miles west as it climbs in and out of washes, passes an old lava flow, and winds through colorful mud hills. Turn left when you near the dump and follow the road 1 mile south as it passes by the southeast corner of the dump. At the pavement turn right, and follow the Fossil Canyon ride directions. You can also turn left and follow the pavement 2.75 miles to S80, turn left and ride another 3.25 miles back to your car.

AMENITIES

There are very few facilities in Ocotillo. A small store is just north of I-8. A gas station with snacks, cold drinks, and a restroom is south of I-8. The town of Jacumba, before you descend to the desert, has a small store and a couple of gas stations.

There is plenty of primitive camping in the Anza-Borrego Desert area. Remember to stay on the designated roads (both bikes and cars) and if in your vehicle, you must not park more than a car length from any road.

Trip B1 – Santa Ana River Trail

Starting Point	Highway 38, San Bernardino Mountains
Distance	10.7 miles one-way
Elevation Gain/Loss	1050'/2300' one-way, 3.7% grade
Riding Time	2 1/2–3 hours
Difficulty	Difficult, technical, steep exposure
Road Conditions	Dirt trail
Season	Late Spring, Summer, Fall
Equipment	Mountain bike
Optional Topo Maps	Big Bear Lake, Moonridge, CA

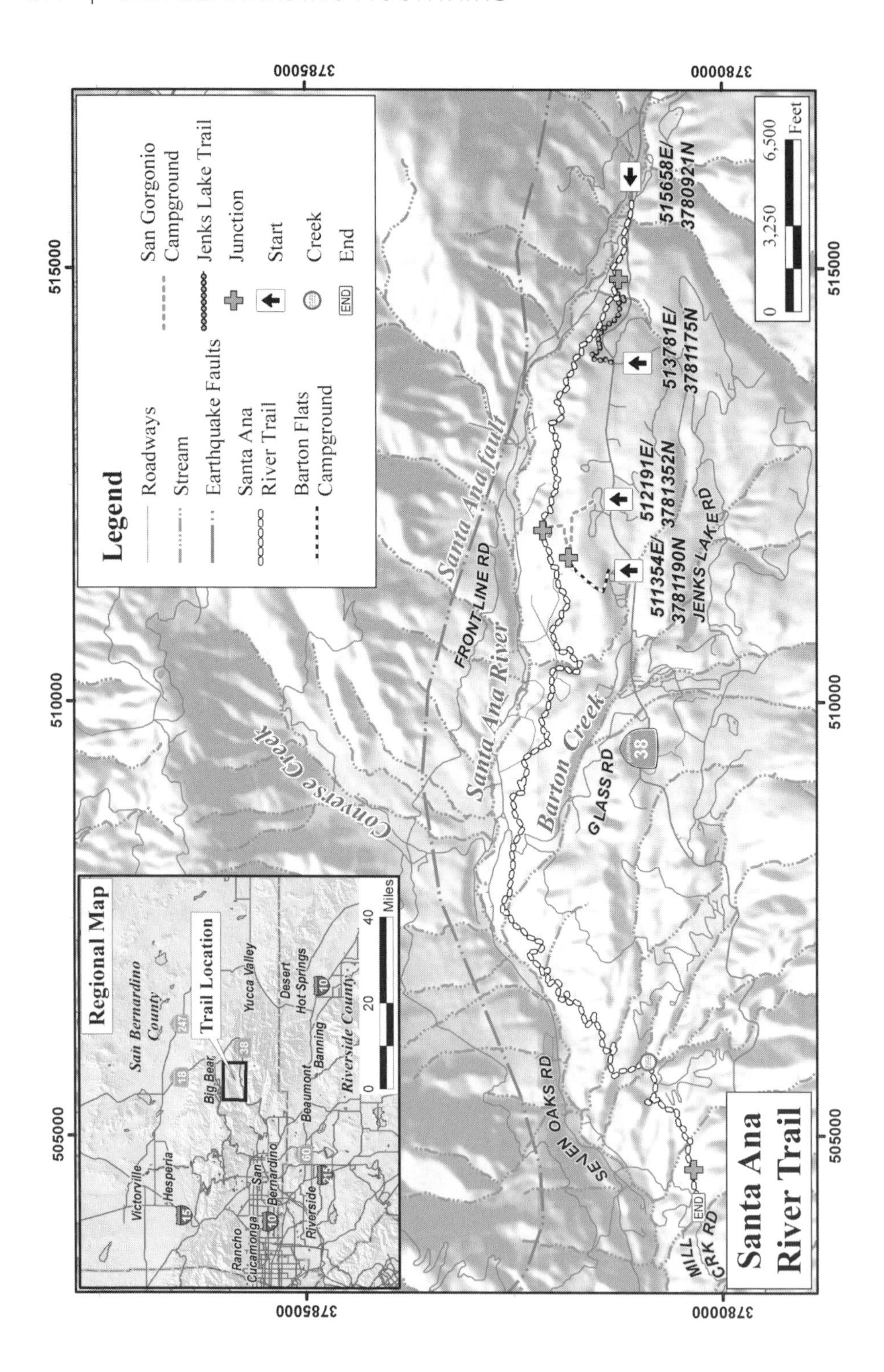
Santa Ana River Trail
Legend
Roadways
Stream
Earthquake Faults
Santa Ana River Trail
Barton Flats Campground
San Gorgonio Campground
Jenks Lake Trail
Junction
Start
Creek
End
Regional Map
Trail Location
San Bernardino County
Riverside County
Victorville
Hesperia
Rancho Cucamonga
San Bernardino
Riverside
Big Bear
Yucca Valley
Beaumont
Banning
Desert Hot Springs
Miles
0
20
40
Feet
0
3,250
6,500
3785000
3780000
505000
510000
515000
Converse Creek
Santa Ana fault
FRONT LINE RD
Santa Ana River
Barton Creek
GLASS RD
38
SEVEN OAKS RD
MILL CRK RD
JENKS LAKE RD
END
511354E/ 3781190N
512191E/ 3781352N
513781E/ 3781175N
515658E/ 3780921N

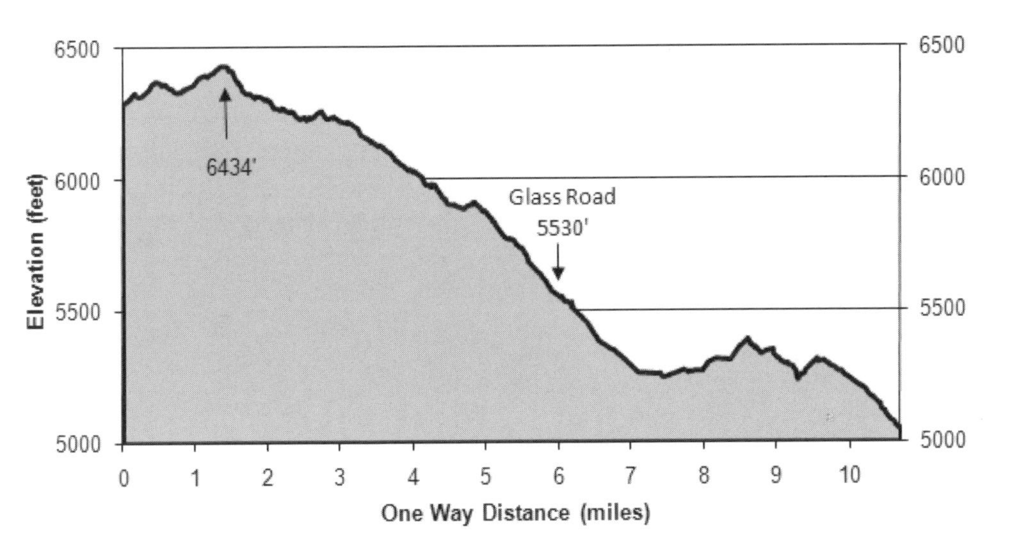

The Santa Ana River is the largest river in southern California. It starts in the San Bernardino Mountains and passes through San Bernardino, Riverside, and Orange Counties, eventually emptying into the Pacific Ocean, although much of the river is perennial past Riverside. Dollar Lake and Dry Lake, both a little over 9000 feet on the north side of San Gorgonio, are its highest sources of water. It passes through a beautiful canyon along Highway 38 in the San Bernardino Mountains paralleling the Santa Ana Fault. This ride will take you on a fun 10-mile, zigzagging single track trail on the slope above the canyon. The trail is exciting, and sometimes called epic, but not for beginners or anyone uncomfortable riding narrow trails with plenty of exposure on steep slopes.

Start by riding west on the small road that parallels Highway 38 past a few cabins. In a short distance, take the trail junction on the left labeled 2E03. It ascends easily above the cabins. At 0.5 mile is a trail heading 1 mile up to Highway 38 and Jenks Lake Road East. Continue straight, as the trail winds this way and that, ascending and descending with plenty of exposure to keep you on your toes. The Barton Flats Trail turnoff is on the left at 2.9 miles and the junction of the rough, 1N45 trail descending right to the river. Stay straight, and enjoy the mostly downhill ride through shady, oak-conifer forest and occasional sections of manzanita, to Glass Road at 6.1 miles. The views along the trail into the canyon below are wonderful.

To continue, jog left across the pavement and right onto the continuation of the trail. At 9.2 miles you'll encounter Stetson Creek. You can stay straight, and sharply descend to a shallow creek crossing, or turn right and carry your bike across a few rocks and logs. This is a great place to have a snack and enjoy the shady, bubbling creek.

Ascend from the creek crossing, and soon you will encounter a trail descending from the left, stay right and continue downhill. At 10.3 miles the trail splits, with the left branch—a more rugged alternative, ascending sharply. Continue straight to reach Middle Control Road at 10.7 miles, and the end of the ride.

GETTING THERE

This bonus ride gives you a chance to explore beyond the boundaries of San Diego County and ride through a scenic valley in the beautiful San Bernardino Mountain Range that was designated a National Forest more than a hundred years ago.

The ride described here is a car shuttle, or you can be dropped off at the start and picked up on Glass Road for a distance of 6 miles or on Middle Control Road/Mill Creek Fire Road for 10.5 miles (recommended).

Take I-15 north to I-215 north, and then I-10 east to Redlands. Exit at Orange Street and turn left (north) and drive a short distance to Highway 38 (E Lugonia Avenue). Take Highway 38 east about 20 miles to Angeles Oaks. Continue east on Highway 38 another 11 miles to a small parking area on the left opposite the South Fork Campground. (After Jenks Lake Road East, Highway 38 descends quickly to this spot near the junction of the Santa Ana River.) Display your Forest Adventure pass when parking here.

OPTIONS

This ride can be done as an out and back, in either direction which would double the mileage, but it's better as a car shuttle enjoying the mainly downhill trend. Another option is to exit at Middle Control Road and descend to the Santa Ana River, and follow River Road, which changes to 7 Oaks Road (1N45) back to the starting point. The paved 7 Oaks Road/River Road is on a south-facing, exposed slope the entire way and can be hot, so this route is not recommended.

AMENITIES

A restaurant is located in Angeles Oaks. Water and restrooms are available in the South Fork Campground near the start of the ride or at any campground on Highway 38.

Appendix 1

Rides According To Difficulty

EASY RIDES

Number	Name	Distance (miles)	Time (hours)	Elevation Gain/ Loss	Technical Difficulty
S1	Lagoon Trail	2.7	30 min	10'/10'	
C1	Guajome Park	2.7	0.5–1	15'/15'	
C3	Rancho Carrillo	3	30 min	180'/180'	
S5	Piedras Pintadas	2.3 – 5.3	1	120'/120'	
C6	Darkwood Canyon	3	30 min	150'/150'	
S2	Santa Fe Valley	3.6	1	200'/110' ow	
S3	Del Dios Gorge	6.3	1.5	410'/150' ow	
M9	Big Laguna Trail	6	1-2	300'/300'	
C10	Marian Bear Park	6.5	1.5	150'/150'	
D8	Fossil Canyon	8.4	2	320'/320'	
D5	Blair/Little Blair Valley	8.7	2–2.5	590'/590'	
S4	North Shore Lake Hodges	11.5	2–2.5	180'/180'	
D7	Dos Cabezas Road	6–14	1–3	450'/450'	
D9	Painted Gorge	11	3	370'/370'	

EASY TO MODERATE

Number	Name	Distance (miles)	Time	Elevation Gain/ Loss	Technical Difficulty
C12	Balboa Park-Florida Canyon	3–5	1–2	50'/50'	Slightly
C9	Rose Canyon	7.6	1–2	250'/250'	
C11	Tecolote Canyon Natural Park	6.2	1.5	300'/300'	
S6	Mule Hill & San Pasqual Valley	10.3	2–2.5	560'/465' ow	
C5	Los Peñasquitos Canyon Preserve	12	2–3	325'/325'	Some north side

MODERATE RIDES

Number	Name	Distance (miles)	Time	Elevation Gain/ Loss	Technical Difficulty
F6	Suycott Wash	5.5	2	1020'/1020'	Slightly
M5	Sloan Canyon	6.3	1.5–2	400'/825' ow	
C7	Lusardi Creek Loop	9.5	2	1030'/1030'	
M8	Oakzanita Peak	8.6	2	1060'/1060'	Slightly
F4	Lake Poway and Twin Peaks	11	3	550'/550'	Some Del Poniente
D2	Table Mountain	13.5	3	615'/615'	Slightly
C13	Sweetwater Reservoir	14.5	3–4	800'/750' ow	Slightly
D1	McCain Valley	29	3–4	1785'/624' ow	

EASY TO DIFFICULT

Number	Name	Distance (miles)	Time	Elevation Gain/ Loss	Technical Difficulty
C2	Calavera Lake	1.6–4	1–2	50' to 350'	Some
F3	Sycamore Canyon and Goodan Ranch	4–6	1–2	400' to 600'	Martha's Grove Technical

MODERATE TO DIFFICULT RIDES

Number	Name	Distance (miles)	Time	Elevation Gain/ Loss	Technical Difficulty
F1	Daley Ranch	3–9	1.5–3	200' to 600'	Some
F2	Elfin Forest	3–10	2–4	715'/715'	Some
C8	Black Mountain	2–10	1–3	475'/475'	Some
S7	Santa Ysabel Preserve	7 & 15	2–3	925' & 2300'	
M7	Cuyamaca Grand Tour	18	5–6	1925'/1925'	
M3	Indian Flats	24	4	2220'/2220'	

DIFFICULT RIDES

Number	Name	Distance (miles)	Time	Elevation Gain/ Loss	Technical Difficulty
C4	Rancho La Costa	4–6	2–3	550'/550'	Some
M11	Sheephead Mountain Road	5.3	3	1300'/1300'	Some
D3	Valley of the Moon	6	2–2.5	1000'/1000'	Technical
S8	Volcan Mountain Preserve	5	2–3	1200'/1200'	
F7	Cowles Mountain	5.5	2	1190'/1190'	Some
M4	Anderson Truck Trail	8 & 13	2–3 & 3–5	1000' & 1800'	Some
B1	Santa Ana River Trail	10.7	2.5–3	1050'/2300' ow	Technical
D4	Chariot/Oriflamme/Rodriguez	16.3	5	3050'/3050'	
D6	Grapevine Canyon/Jasper Trail	23.5	5–6	3500'/3500'	

STRENUOUS RIDES

Number	Name	Distance (miles)	Time	Elevation Gain/ Loss	Technical Difficulty
F5	North Fortuna Peak	8.5	2.5–3	1530'/1530'	Technical
M9	Noble Canyon	18.3	5	2825'/2825'	Technical
M12	Kitchen Creek & Thing Valley	28	4–5	3780'/3780'	
M1	Nate Harrison Grade	29	5	5625'/5625'	
M2	East Palomar Mountain	35	6	4650'/4650'	
M6	Boulder Creek	39	6	4760'/4760'	

NOTES:

In Elevation Gain/Loss “ow” means one way measurement. Reverse these numbers for the return route.

Appendix 2

References and Suggested Reading

Copp, Nelson, and Jerry Schad, *Cycling San Diego*, 3rd Ed. San Diego: Sunbelt Publications, 2008.

Fragnoli, Delaine, and Don Douglass, *Mountain Biking Southern California's Best 100 Trails*, 2nd Ed. Anacortes, WA: Mountain Biking Press, 1998.

Fetzer, Leland, *San Diego County Places Names A to A*, San Diego: Sunbelt Publications, 2005.

Greenstadt, Daniel, *San Diego Mountain Bike Guide*, 1st Ed. San Diego: Sunbelt Publications: 1998.

Huegel, Tony, *California Desert Byways*, 2nd Ed. Berkeley: Wilderness Press, 2003.

Lindsay, Diana, and Lowell Lindsay, *The Anza-Borrego Desert Region*, 5th ed. Berkeley: Wilderness Press, 2006.

Schad, Jerry, *Afoot and Afield in San Diego County*, 4th ed. Berkeley: Wilderness Press, 2007.

Appendix 3

San Diego Cyclist's Directory

GROUPS, CLUBS, AND RIDES

Bicycling the Roads and Trails of San Diego Meetup group
www.meetup.com/sandiegocyclists/

California Bicycle Coalition
http://www.calbike.org/

International Mountain Biking Association
http://www.imba.com/

Knickerbikers
http://www.knickerbikers.com/

Rock MTB
http://www.rockmtb.com/

San Diego County Bicycle Coalition
http://www.sdcbc.org/

San Diego County Trails Council
http://www.sdctc.com/

San Diego Mountain Biking Association
http://www.sdmba.com/

San Diego Multiuse Trails Coalition
http://groups.yahoo.com/group/MultiUseTrails

Sierra Club, San Diego Chapter
http://sandiego.sierraclub.org/home/index.asp

Sierra Club Bicycle Section
http://sandiego.sierraclub.org/bicycle/

GEOLOGY, CONSERVATION, AND HISTORY

The Journal of San Diego History
https://www.sandiegohistory.org/index.html

The Kumeyaay History
http://www.kumeyaay.info/kumeyaay_indians.html

Native American Research California Indians Portal
http://www.kumeyaay.info/california_native_research.html

San Andreas Fault
http://geology.com/articles/san-andreas-fault.shtml

San Diego Association of Geologists
http://www.sandiegogeologists.org/

San Diego History Center
https://www.sandiegohistory.org/

REFERENCES BY REGION

Coastal

City of San Diego Black Mountain Open Space Preserve
http://www.sandiego.gov/park-and-recreation/parks/blackmtn/index.shtml

Preserve Calavera
http://www.preservecalavera.org/calavera.html

City of Carlsbad Trails
http://www.carlsbadca.gov/services/departments/parksandrec/trails/Pages/default.aspx

Friends of Carrillo Ranch
http://www.carrillo-ranch.org/Carrillo.html

City of Encinitas Parks, Trails, and Beaches
http://ci.encinitas.ca.us/Government/CityD/ParksAndRecreation/Parks+and+Beaches/ParksB.htm

Encinitas Trails Coalition
http://www.trails4encinitas.org/

Guajome Park
http://www.sdcounty.ca.gov/parks/Camping/guajome.html

City of San Diego Los Peñasquitos Canyon Preserve
http://www.sandiego.gov/park-and-recreation/parks/penasq.shtml

Friends of Los Peñasquitos Canyon
http://www.penasquitos.org/

City of San Diego Rose Canyon Open Space Park
http://www.sandiego.gov/park-and-recreation/parks/rosecan1.shtml

Friends of Rose Canyon
http://www.rosecanyon.org/

City of San Diego Parks and Recreation
http://www.co.san-diego.ca.us/parks/index.html

County of San Diego Parks and Recreation
http://www.sdcounty.ca.gov/parks/index.html

Sweetwater Reservoir Riding and Hiking Trail
http://www.sweetwater.org/our_water/swr_randh.html

Tecolote Canyon
http://www.sandiego.gov/park-and-recreation/parks/teclte.shtml

Foothills

City of Escondido Daley Ranch
http://www.ci.escondido.ca.us/glance/uniquely/daley/index.html

Elfin Forest/Harmony Grove: Elfin Forest Recreational Reserve
http://www.olivenhain.com/index.php/about-us/elfin-forest-recreational-reserve

Escondido Creek Conservancy
http://www.escondidocreek.org/

Goodan Ranch/Sycamore Canyon Preserve
http://www.sdcounty.ca.gov/parks/openspace/Sycamore_Goodan.html

Friends of Goodan Ranch and Sycamore Canyon Open Space
http://goodanranch.org/

Mission Trails Regional Park
http://www.sandiego.gov/park-and-recreation/parks/mtrails.shtml

City of Poway Lake Poway
http://www.poway.org/index.aspx?page=671

San Dieguito River Park, Trans-County Trails

San Dieguito River Park (includes all the trails)
http://www.sdrp.org/

San Diego Journal of History Mule Hill
https://www.sandiegohistory.org/journal/75spring/mulehill.htm

City of Escondido San Pasqual Battlefield
http://www.ci.escondido.ca.us/glance/uniquely/battlefield/index.html

Trans-County Trail
http://www.sdnhm.org/fieldguide/places/index.html

Volcan Mountain Preserve Foundation
http://www.volcanmt.org/

County of San Diego Santa Ysabel Preserve
http://www.sdcounty.ca.gov/parks/openspace/Santa_Ysabel.html

Mountains

Cleveland National Forest
http://www.fs.fed.us/r5/cleveland/

Cleveland National Forest Camping Information Descanso (Laguna) and Palomar Ranger Districts
http://www.fs.fed.us/r5/cleveland/recreation/camping/index.shtml

Cleveland National Forest Mountain Bicycle Guide
http://www.fs.fed.us/r5/cleveland/recreation/mtbike/index.shtml

Cuyamaca Rancho State Park
http://www.parks.ca.gov/?page_ID=667

Forest Adventure Pass needed for parking in certain recreation sites
http://www.fs.fed.us/r5/sanbernardino/ap/welcome.shtml

Laguna Mountain Camping
http://www.lmva.org/camping/camping.htm

Palomar Mountain
http://www.parks.ca.gov/?page_id=637

Palomar After 50 Years
https://www.sandiegohistory.org/journal/98fall/palomar.htm

Caltech Astronomy and Palomar Observatory History
http://www.astro.caltech.edu/palomar/history.html

Desert

Anza-Borrego Desert State Park
http://www.parks.ca.gov/?page_id=638

DesertUSA
http://www.desertusa.com/

Fossil Canyon and Painted Gorge
http://www.desertusa.com/magoct97/oct_painted.html

Fossil Canyon, A Journey Back In Time
http://www.geoepicenter.com/Fossil%20Canyon.pdf

Bureau of Land Management – Desert Access Guide Points of Interest
http://www.blm.gov/ca/st/en/fo/elcentro/recreation/poi/el_cajon.html

Bureau of Land Management McCain Valley
http://www.blm.gov/ca/st/en/fo/elcentro/recreation/mccain.html

Anza-Borrego Desert Natural History Association
http://www.abdnha.org/06exploring.htm

Journal of San Diego History Creation of the Anza-Borrego Desert State Park
https://www.sandiegohistory.org/journal/73fall/anza.htm

San Bernardino Mountains

San Bernardino National Forest
http://www.fs.fed.us/r5/sanbernardino/

Santa Ana River Trail Community Website
http://www.trailsafetypatrol.com/

Santa Ana River Trail
http://www.santaanarivertrail.com

BIKE SHOPS

Adam's Avenue Bikes
2606 Adams Avenue
San Diego, CA 92116
(619)295-8500
http://www.aabikes.net

Alan's Bike Shop
805 South Coast Highway
Oceanside, CA 92054
(760)722-3377
http://alansbikeshop.com

BikeBling.com
413 West 5th Avenue
Escondido, CA 92025
(760)317-5450
http://www.bikebling.com

Bike Empire
13355 Midland Rd.
Poway, CA 92064
(858)679-0306
http://bikeempire.com

Black Mountain Bicycles
9158 Mira Mesa Blvd
San Diego, CA 92126
Phone: (858)566-0712
http://blackmountainbicycles.com

BRC Bike Shop
8691 La Mesa Blvd.
La Mesa, CA 91942
(619)463-2453
http://www.brcbikeshop.com

El Camino Bike Shop
121 N. El Camino Real, Suite A
Encinitas, CA 92024
(760)436-2340
http://elcaminobikeshop.biz

Hidden Valley Bicycle
1040 E Valley Parkway, Suite B
Escondido, CA 92025-4606
(760)746-1509
http://www.hiddenvalleybicycle.com

Hi-TechBikes
7638 Clairemont Mesa Blvd.
San Diego, CA 92111
(858)-715-1517
http://hi-techbikes.com

Holy Rollers
2206 Alpine Blvd.
Alpine, CA 91901
(619)722-6402
http://holyrollersbikes.com

Inky's Bicycles
1018 Broadway
El Cajon, CA 92021
(619)442-0564
http://www.inkysbikes.com

San Diego Bike Shop (near Horton Plaza)
619 C ST
San Diego, CA 92101
Phone: (619) 237-1245
http://sdbikeshop.com/

Valley Bicycle
851 Jamacha Rd.
El Cajon, CA 92019-3206
(619)588-6222

Wheels N' Things
2910 Navajo Rd.
El Cajon, CA 92020-2118
(619)465-3976

Zumwalt's Bicycles
6425 El Cajon Blvd.
San Diego, CA 92115
(619)-582-6440
http://zcbikes.com

BICYCLE STORES WITH MULTIPLE LOCATIONS:

Bicycle Warehouse
http://bicyclewarehouse.com/

Encinitas
328 North El Camino Real
Encinitas, CA 92024
Ph: 760-635-4500

Chula Vista
680 L Street
Chula Vista, CA 91911
Phone:619-498-4900

Kearny Mesa
5710 Kearny Villa Road
San Diego, CA 92123
Phone: 858-292-8449

San Diego (Pacific Beach)
4650 Santa Fe St
San Diego, CA 92109
Phone: 858-273-7300

Vista
1964 Hacienda Drive
Vista, CA 92083
Phone: 760-639-5200

Performance Bicycle
http://www.performancebike.com

Bonita
3901 Bonita Rd
Just south of Willow Street
Bonita, CA 91902
619-422-3098

Kearny Mesa
7730 Ronson Rd.
Ronson Road at Convoy Street
San Diego, CA 92111
858-560-8666

La Mesa
8706 La Mesa Blvd.
La Mesa Blvd. at Glen St.
La Mesa, CA 91941
619-461-9680

Oceanside
3833 Plaza Drive
Tri-City Plaza
Oceanside, CA 92056
760-726-5559

San Diego
3619 Midway Dr.
Point Loma Plaza
San Diego, CA 92110
619-223-5415

Sorrento Valley
11675 Sorrento Valley Rd.
1/4 Mile South of Carmel Mountain Road
Suite A
Sorrento, CA 92121
858-792-2453

Trek Bicycle Superstore
http://treksandiego.com/

La Mesa
8495 Fletcher Parkway
La Mesa, CA 91942
(619) 668-8787
Fax: (619) 668-8799

North County
2123 Industrial Court
Vista, CA 92081
(760) 599-9735

San Diego
4240 Kearny Mesa Road
Suite 108
San Diego, CA 92111
(858) 974-8735

South County
901 Lane Avenue
(Corner of Lane & Fenton)
Chula Vista, CA 91914
(619) 216-9123

Index

The main pages for each of the rides are shown in **bold**.

C

D

E

F

G

H

I

J

K

L

T

U

W